to Stormy
From Bonnie
12/2001

The Master, Christ Jesus

Four Transcriptions of Biblical Talks

by

B. Cobbey Crisler

The Walk to Emmaus
Song of the Lamb
The Gethsemane Decision
How Christ Jesus Saw Himself

Produced by
Janet V. Crisler & Logos Productions

First Printing

Published in Carmel, California by Logos Productions.

Scripture quotations from King James version.

Library of Congress Cataloging-in-Publications Data
Crisler, Janet V.

ISBN: 0-9677581-0-6

A Tribute

To my Beloved Husband, Cobbey Crisler
who shared these talks
with audiences around the world.
He gave the spoken word, and
now I will share it as the written word.

His devoted wife,
Janet V. Crisler

*In grateful recognition to
Professor John Hawley
for three years of dedicated, diligent
transcribing of all 27 talks.*

*Special thanks to Sue Dunlap and Hallie Keel
for their meticulous proof reading.*

Foreword

Cobbey Crisler's path to his ultimate calling as Bible scholar, like many others, was not a direct one. An International Government major at Harvard College, Cobbey served after college as a lieutenant in the Air Force. He then worked in the advertising department at Mutual of New York, while also serving on the Board of his alma mater, the Daycroft School in Greenwich, Connecticut. Seeking leadership in the face of financial difficulties, the School asked him to take over as President.

In addition to his other duties, Cobbey appointed himself to the tasks of biblical scholarship and teaching a course in the Scriptures, because he thought too many youngsters were growing up without knowing the Bible, its stories and its characters. When parents learned of the course, they asked him to teach one for them and the wider community as well. Before long he was delivering lectures on the Bible throughout the United States.

Seeking to deepen the biblical experience for those enrolled in the courses, Cobbey and I took Daycroft students to Caesarea Maritima, to participate in an archaeological dig under the direction of the Biblical Archeologist, Professor Robert J. Bull. Very shortly we began leading tours to the Holy Land for trustees and friends of the School.

Cobbey had done what he wanted to do at Daycroft, and that was getting the school on a firm financial footing. Then we both were free to concentrate on lecturing and tours. After twelve years, Cobbey gave up his presidency at Daycroft, and we began focusing our lives on his Bible talks, traveling literally throughout the United States, Australia and New Zealand.

Cobbey loved the sharing and giving. If one man's life exemplified the Harvard motto, *Veritas,* his did. His main interest was in having people discover their own truth through the Scriptures. He asked his students to be aware of Jesus' recommendation to "Search the Scriptures..." He always believed the real meaning of Scripture was just beneath the surface, and that what we needed to do was, he said, "Put on our scuba tanks and plunge beneath to the depths of their meaning." His research of the original texts in ancient Greek and Hebrew led to producing an audio-tape series based on twenty-seven talks including such titles as *The Walk to Emmaus, The Case of Job,* and *Heal the Sick: A Scriptural Record.* His lecture on *Jesus and Equality of Woman,* first delivered in the 1970's, attracted considerable favorable attention during the early stages of the contemporary women's movement.

One Christmas, while we were visiting the site of ancient Shiloh, Cobbey tested an idea about how Jesus and the disciples could be heard by "the multitude." He told me where to stand and then paced off a number of steps. I listened as he spoke. Later he persuaded the Cambridge, Massachusetts, acoustics firm of Bolt, Beranek and Newman, Inc. to send engineer Mark Myles with him to Israel. There they developed and tested the idea and later Cobbey recorded their findings, which were published in 1976 in the very prestigious archaeology magazine, *Biblical Archeologist*, under the title of "The Acoustics and Crowd Capacity of Natural Theaters in Palestine." Cobbey also co-authored two books with Professor Robert J. Bull: *Come See the Place: The Holy Land Jesus Knew,* and *Fishers of Men: the Way of the Apostles.*

In 1986 a biography of Cobbey Crisler was presented in the book, *Who's Who in Biblical Archaeology,* "a compilation of men and women of superior achievement and status who are devoting their professional lives to helping the world better understand the Bible."

Although he did not have formal training in biblical scholarship, Cobbey's tireless devotion and standards of research earned him the respect of Bible scholars. Stimulated by his discussions with them, his principal attention was directed toward communicating his enthusiasm for the Bible to the laity and the public.

The decision to memorialize my husband's endeavors through a scholarship fund at Harvard Divinity School, enables graduate scholars of high caliber to matriculate in their chosen field of New Testament studies. With the founding of The Crisler Biblical Institute, I am now assured the continuity of his excellent standard for Biblical scholarship will be conveyed to future generations, as he would have envisioned.

Transcription Notes

The purpose of these transcriptions is to preserve the speaker's words. They were prepared from tape-recordings authorized by Logos Productions in 1997 of unscripted lectures delivered extemporaneously from notes in the wide margins of Cobbey Crisler's Cambridge King James translation of the Bible. Earlier versions of the talks may differ.

The Citation Index contains the full text of all King James Bible citations under tape and side designations in which they occur. Biblical quotations and Hebrew, Greek and Latin words in the commentary are italicized. Brackets enclose additions: by the original translators, by the speaker in some Bible citations, and by the transcriber (of names of biblical books, chapter and verse numbers which the speaker mentions but does not cite, of some audience comments or questions, and of an occasional word of footnote). Some spoken words which appeared to be unnecessary for the reader, such as "and, but so, turn to, well" etc., were deleted.

The transcription, Citation and Word Indices including bracket additions were prepared by Professor John Hawley, tranScriptures of Columbia, S.C.

Table Of Contents

First Century Roman Road at Emmaus Photograph by Gordon N. Converse

THE WALK TO EMMAUS
Volume 1

by B. Cobbey Crisler

CONTENTS

Notes: The transcript was produced from a tape of an unscripted lecture delivered extempore. Earlier tape versions may differ. Biblical quotations and Hebrew, Greek, Latin, French and German words in the commentary are italicized. Brackets enclose additions by the original Bible translators and the transcriber: such as book names, chapter and verse numbers which the speaker mentioned, but did not cite, some audience comments or questions, and an occasional word or footnote. Some spoken words which appeared to be unnecessary for the reader, such as "and, but, so, turn to, well," etc, were deleted. The Citation Index contains the full text of all *King James Bible* citations which the speaker cited or mentioned. The purpose of the transcript is to preserve the speaker's words verbatim.

***

by B. Cobbey Crisler

BEGIN TAPE 1, SIDE A

Thank you, Mr. Dale. How is the mike? OK? We have to live with these things, you know. There's even one in heaven, according to the *Book of Revelation*.[12:7] Work on that. It's called an angel and its full name is Michael. [To his friends he's known as "Mike." [Chuckles] I knew you wanted to get it. So, I wanted to give it to you. [Laughter]

We should be equipped for a journey tonight. [**The Walk to Emmaus**]. It's a very special journey, not requiring alpine equipment, sneakers, or anything else that's physical, because our journey is a mental one. It's a very special one. We can repeat one that's mentioned in the Bible. Tonight, together, we can embark on it. I hope you all have your Bibles with you in your laps, open to Luke 24. That was a big hope, wasn't it, with all those specifics?

Why is it important to have your own Bible? Because I want you to be sure I am not making it up as I go along. [Chuckle] Everyone should come to his or her own conclusions as we go through here. We're dealing with discovery which is the only real method of education. Religion for so many years forgot there was such a thing as discovery and dealt in dogma.

I think that some of you have heard me remark before the little word that I work the hardest to hear is not even in the Oxford English Dictionary. That word is "Wow!" Why do I work so hard to hear that one do you think? What does "Wow!" signify? [Voice: "Life goes on."] Something's happening where? [Voice: "Inside."] Has it been implanted? Has it come from here to there? Or is it just something that's already within that's awakened? It's discovery, isn't it? Dogma never gives you discovery. Therefore, dogma never gives you "Wow!" It gives you "Bow Wow." [Laughter]

Luke 24 [:13-31] gives us the only account of the walk to Emmaus in the Bible with the exception of one small verse in the last chapter of Mark [16:12]. That doesn't mention Emmaus. It only mentions two disciples in a walk in the country. We can be very grateful for Luke. If you read the invitation to tonight's session, you will recognize that I am placing a major importance on this event. It is not I that is placing that. I feel it is the text itself giving major importance to this walk to Emmaus. The theory I will present tonight is one none of you have to buy, because that would be dogma, unless you discover it yourself as we go through. The theory is, that the spark that eventually caught fire in Christianity spreading throughout the known-globe, started on that walk to Emmaus. Let's see if we can prove that.

Luke 24:13. The narrative begins. If we can do this tonight, all together ,go back these many centuries, and begin to think like first-century Jews. In other words, let's get back to those times and see if we can actually feel the tenseness, the excitement, the adventure, the expectations of that particular period. That may seem hard to do, but the Bible provides much of the environment if we dig enough to find it.

Where does this occur? It starts from what city? [Voice: "Jerusalem."] Jerusalem. What has occurred there just this weekend? Remember, we're back to that period. [Voices: "The crucifixion."] The crucifixion. Of whom? [Voice: "Jesus."] And who is he? [Voice: "The Christ."] All of you say he's "the Christ." But being first-century Jews, would all of you agree? [Voices: "No."] Do you think that the city of Jerusalem was well aware of this event? Maybe even turned on its ear?

There is an indication from the text that everyone should know about it. Because, the two disciples even turned and rebuked Jesus who they don't know is Jesus, and say, "What are you a stranger?" So, the news is out. What are these two disciples doing? They're leaving Jerusalem. Where's the action, as we know it? In Jerusalem. What does that tell you about the two disciples? It's either something they know or they don't know. What do you think it might be? They're heading in the opposite direction. [Voice: "It might be safer."] It might be safer. How much do they know at this point in the narrative? We've said the crucifixion has occurred. Has anything else occurred? [Voices: "Resurrection."] We know that. Do they? [Voice: "No."] Are you sure? It's important now to get the exact moment in history that this whole thing is occurring.

Luke 24:10 tells us that the women had seen what? They'd seen the empty tomb and they reported it to the disciples. The news is out that there's an empty tomb. Does human nature say immediately, "Ah, hah! Jesus was raised from the dead!"? [Voices: "No."] In fact, the easiest conclusion is what? [Voice: "Somebody stole the body."] Somebody stole the body, and you remember that was actually mentioned at the end of one of the other gospels [Mathew 28:12,13] where the Jews were reported as paying the guards who had fallen asleep to spread the news that his disciples had stolen the body.

Let's look at the text very carefully to see exactly whether they really know the resurrection or not. We can all become Bible scholars by sticking very close to the text. At least, we can, with some validity, indicate what the Bible account is saying, regardless of human opinions about the Bible accounts, who wrote it, or anything else. At least we can become so familiar with the account itself that we'll know some of these shades of differences that may make a major difference before we are through.

Luke 24:11 tells how they responded. Idle tales they didn't believe. Didn't believe the women. Isn't that a funny reaction! [Laughter] Do you think, though, in using common sense in regarding the text, do you think those two disciples, if they had been fully aware that Jesus had been raised from the dead and was in Jerusalem, that they would be heading in the opposite direction? It doesn't seem to make sense, does it? Regardless of what they were told, how much weight did they put behind the news? It sounds like it was nothing at all. Certainly that verse backs it up. *"Their words seemed to them as idle tales."*

Who were these two disciples anyway? Only one is named who is Cleopas and the other is not. There's a tradition around, and every time I give this, a lot of people say it's Peter or it's Simon. It can't be Peter because later on we're told that the two disciples return to Jerusalem, and guess who's behind closed doors? The eleven disciples; that would include Peter.

There is an early tradition. I think Eusebius [Bishop of Caesarea, c. 313-339] records that an early tradition said that the other disciple's name was Simon, and both Cleopas and Simon were among the seventy. That's as good a theory as any. Yet, it's still several hundred years from the event. The text, if we're going to stick to it, only gives one, Cleopas. And we know one thing, they are obscure disciples. That is a point to consider. Because if we were Jesus, would we waste our time with obscure disciples heading in the opposite direction?

What does one of Jesus' parables recommend to his followers? Go after the one that was wandering and bring it back [Luke 15:3-7]. That shepherd motive behind what Jesus did is basic, perhaps to our understanding of this story. It also shows something about his character. Compared with ours, we look kind of sad probably, and wouldn't have done the same thing. But there's a divine purpose behind all of this or Jesus would not have done it. He certainly told us he was dedicated to doing God's will and not his own. So, God's will is obviously being fulfilled in this event.

These two disciples are so engrossed in talking, and talking about what? Everything that had happened. Do you think that it had made a deep impression on them? I would imagine so. They may be going off into the country just to get into the "cool" of the countryside away from the white hot heat of what had just happened. An innocent man accused and criminally executed by the two finest forms of human law known to the ancient world, the Roman and the Jewish.

They're so deeply engrossed in this. What do you think their mood must have been like? Luke 24:17 says, "Sad," the last word in it. But it's more serious than that. From what standpoint do you think they were discussing all of this? From Jesus' standpoint? [Voice: "No."] Probably their own. When you're kind of wrapped up in self like that, it's very difficult to notice what's going on around you. And guess who joins them? And they don't recognize him. Don't you think that's a little odd? Three years with their Master, or at least a portion of it, and they don't recognize him. [Voice: "He was dead. How could he be there?"] O.K., he was dead, how could he be there? Where were their expectations? Where were they looking for him if they were looking for him at all? [Voice: "In the grave."] In the tomb.

That reminds me of some of the objectives of archeology. Archeologically speaking, history is only confirmed if you can find something in the earth. A coin with maybe the profile of the Herod or Caesar. That's great. Everybody gets extremely excited because it does date pretty well the level at which it's discovered. Inscriptions are wonderful. At Caesarea, which is the dig we participated in, the Italian archeologist found the first epigraphic evidence that Pilate was in Palestine. Outside the Bible's record and Josephus [Jewish priest and scholar, historian of the Jews, A.D. 37/38 to after 93], here was an inscription on stone. It was a reused stone found in the theater at Caesarea. You've seen that theater on television if you've seen Leonard Bernstein conduct several performances there. In excavating that theater they found the stone which had Tiberius' name [Roman emperor 42 B.C.- 37 A.D]. on it who was the Caesar of the time and Pontius Pilate. Archeologists can now say, "Pilate was there. We found the stone that said it."

If we had to rely on that exclusively for evidence, how would we do as far as Jesus is concerned? Anybody found any coins for him? Any inscriptions? No architectural monuments? No books have been dug up contemporaneously? We haven't found his name have we in that early first century? Archeologically, Jesus then may be a nonentity by definition. You know that many religionists had almost come to that conclusion not too many years ago. In fact, even the idea introduced that Jesus was an invention. Fortunately, one major scholar made the remark something similar to this that "It would be impossible to invent Jesus. He's too unique."

Despite the fact that none of this evidence remains, and perhaps never did exist, what does that do for you [with regard to] Jesus? Are any doubts remaining about the possibility that he existed? How do you think Jesus would rather be remembered? Would he have told us? Were his disciples looking for him precisely in the place where archeologists would be looking for him? Could Christ Jesus found a church on that average view? In fact, as I thought about it I realized we can find Herod in the earth and we can find Caesar in the earth, but we cannot find Jesus there. Nor did he intend for anyone apparently to find him there. That's a whole new breakthrough for humanity: not to be found in the earth, not needing even earthly evidence.

If his disciples were looking for him there, maybe that's one of the major points they needed straightening out on. Otherwise, how could Jesus have founded a church on an average point of view? While they were still looking for him that way, he joins them and he asks what they're talking about. Do you think he knew? [Voice: "Yes."] So, why is he asking? Is he playing a game? No. How long a time does he have with his disciples between the resurrection and the ascension. [Voice: "Forty days."] Forty days. That isn't very long. Where had all his disciples gone after three years of a pretty heavy ministry with Jesus day after day? He was crucified and what happened? [Voice: "They went fishing."] They went fishing. They scattered.

Where had Jesus found most of them? Fishing. Christianity was about to end where it began, in a fishing boat. But here we all are tonight. It did not end there. But that's what was happening, despite the three years of active ministry of Jesus with the disciples. Which leads one to surmise that something radical must have occured in the forty-day period and was of extreme, vital, importance to Jesus and to his church. If so, we should be able to find where it is because the text should tell us.

In Luke 24:18 Cleopas' remark here is somewhat amusing, tragically so, because he turns to Jesus. Can you imagine how they must have bit their tongues over several of the things that were said here? *"Are you just a stranger in Jerusalem?"* "Haven't you been watching 'Eyewitness News,' "we'd say in the twentieth century?" "Don't you know what's going on? Everybody knows what's going on."

Luke 24:19. But Jesus persists in inquiring, *"What things?"* Again, is it a game? What does he need to know? What is he after? He may know, but what is he really after? Exactly what is surfacing in their thought about this crucifixion? Where were their priorities? What lasted with them? What impressed them the most? Where were they mentally about it? Because Jesus apparently had to build there.

They go through the details about Jesus and how he was condemned and crucified.

If we really want an insight into where they were mentally, [see] Luke 24:21 up to the colon. What kind of attitude is that? Disappointment? Disillusionment? It's even stronger than that, maybe. Hoplessness. Discouragement. But even stronger. Maybe condemnation, of whom? Remember whom they're talking to, and let the possible indication of where they are mentally seep in. They say, "We trusted..." Already the implication is what? We were let down. *"We trusted that it had been..."* All hope is gone. *"It had been..."* Closed, past. *"It had been he which should have redeemed Israel."* That is a pretty hopeless thing. It looks like it may be blaming Jesus directly. We trusted, but we were let down. We were betrayed, maybe.

Let's get back to assuming the role of the first-century Jew. Exactly what are we expecting as first-century Jews? What are we expecting as far as the Messiah is concerned? What are you and I looking forward to? What have we been taught in Sabbath school all our lives? What're we looking forward to? [Voice: "A Messiah."] A Messiah who will be a king. What do you mean by king? A ruler. A warrior. A political leader to free them from the yoke of any oppressor. And primarily, since the current one was the Roman, to relieve them from that.

Was that the disciples' view of the Messiah? It's very important. Do you think that either disciple or average first-century Jew embraced within their expectation of the Messiah the fact that the Messiah would suffer and would end on a criminal's cross? Are you sure? Did he tell the disciples that? [Voice: "They read it in the newspaper."] Yet, you're saying that the disciples didn't know it. They didn't believe it, or they didn't know it? [Voice: "They heard what they wanted to hear."] O.K. They heard what they wanted to hear. Of course, that never happens in the twentieth century, does it? [Loud laughter] Isn't that terrible of those disciples? We listen to everything anyone tells us. And everybody listens to us, right?

We're going to prove this step by step as we go along to see if Jesus told the disciples. And also to see if the disciples had any idea that the Messiah would suffer, any expectation of that. Does it sound like they did if the two disciples were so enrapt in the tragedy of the event that they were heading in another direction? Does that sound like they comprehended their Master was to go through some of this and emerge victorious? It doesn't look like the comprehension was there whatever Jesus had said to them earlier.

They do announce that a rumor is around and who's spreading it? [Voice: "The women." Loud laughter] I heard a man very hesitatingly say that. That's right, but it does bring to light one of the social customs of that age. Women were simply not permitted to bear witness in a court of law. Their word was not believed unless they were backed up by the "good, old, reliable male." This shows something that's very important.

I've just developed a course that's called "Jesus and the Equality of Woman" which from the text itself shows how Jesus totally ignored the customs of his day and simply regarded womanhood as God regarded it. It's interesting, that even though women were not allowed to bear witness unless backed up by the man, that Jesus chose a woman to bear witness to his resurrection and she carried the news to the disciples despite the social custom of those days.

[Luke 24:22,23] You can see here there's a sort of an apologetic tone, "*Certain women made us astonished, and they came saying that they'd seen a vision of angels, which said that he was alive.*" There's a lot of conviction behind all of that.

Luke 24:24 rushes in to back some of it up in case the stanger thinks that they had been listening to these women. *"Certain of the them which were with us* [those are the men] *went to the sepulchre, and found [it] even so as the women had said: but him they saw not."* That tells exactly the state of the news. It says that the angels had said he was alive, that's all.

[Do] you know why manhood is in such confusion at this hour? Because they ran and womanhood stayed to find out. If you read John's [20:1-8] account, guess what happens? Mary [Magdalene] goes and tells Peter and John. And John takes great pains to tell us in his gospel that he outran Peter to the tomb. It's great! You can tell he's got to be the author of that passage. [Loud laughter] He beats Peter to the tomb. They look in. They don't see a body and guess where they go? Home! [John 20:10] They go home but Mary stays and Mary gets rewarded for staying because she sees Jesus and is the first one who does. [John 20:11-18]. So his disciples miss that point of being there first hand, and they hear it from a woman.

Luke 24:25 At this point, with all of this social custom coming in, Jesus abruptly ends this whole line of attack, starting a new one, he says, *"O fools, and slow of heart to believe all that the prophets have spoken."* You've got to decide who's more way out because the disciples have just been talking about current events and Jesus is saying instead that they were slow because they didn't believe the prophets. The prophets wrote hundreds of years before.

END TAPE 1 SIDE A

BEGIN TAPE 1, SIDE B

Who goes back that far for an explanation of current events? The human mind just doesn't quite buy that, even in the twentieth century. We don't even believe our weather man, and that's only twenty-four hours [Laughter]. In fact, the human mind is simply not constituted to comprehend prophecy.

The more I've thought of that, the more I've found two major themes in the Bible that the human mind simply doesn't comprehend: one is prophecy and the other is healing. The more I worked on that, the more it became clear that that's quite obvious why the human mind doesn't comprehend either prophecy or healing because the human mind cannot do either one. What the human mind cannot do, it generally dismisses as incomprehensible, and therefore may be even impossible. Yet here we find the entire book, known as the Bible, composed of so many individual books [written by many different hands in many different places at many different times], based squarely on prophecy and healing. Here Jesus goes back in an apparent explanation of current events, things that happened just this weekend. He is going back to documents already hundreds of years old. What is he assuming are in these documents that is so important?

[In Luke 24:26] he tells us some of it. Notice that point. He says what? Why is it the first point? *"That Christ should suffer."* He is apparently finding this where? He says it's in the prophets. Isn't that generally known? Why is it so novel? We have to examine that. Is it generally known?

Remember up there [in Verse 21] the two disciples said, *"We trusted that it had been he which should have redeemed Israel."* That view is the general view we've already seen that the first-century Jew had, political leader, king. Now Jesus is saying that they were slow not to see in the prophets that the Christ was to suffer *"and enter into his glory."*

The problem and the solution, the cross and the crown in prophecy. If the disciples had only seen the crown, then they needed a Bible lesson apparently.

In Luke 24:27 look at what Jesus does. He starts where? At Moses and goes how far? All the prophets. Then what does he do, give them a general Bible lesson that it all started in seven days, and then the water just poured in, and Noah built an ark, and it landed on Mount Ararat? What kind of Bible lesson was he giving them? Very specific, isn't it? Concerning himself. Remember, forty days he had with his disciples.

His disciples had missed something essential or they would not have scattered. Is Jesus concentrating on what had been missed in this period, so that he could leave and Christianity was in good hands? Prepared thought. It's pretty clear what, according to Luke's account, Jesus did. He went through the Scriptures on this walk to Emmaus. Did the two, walking with him, know it was Jesus while they were getting this Bible lesson? [Voices: "No."] They did not.

Before we go any further, I think we have to understand the Bible context of prophecy, because I mentioned a weather report just before. Turn to Amos, which you will have no difficulty locating. It will help to know, it's between Joel and Obadiah. [Laughter]. Amos is often credited by scholars as being the first literary prophet, that is the first one who had his words recorded in a contemporary way, right after they were uttered or very close to the time which they were uttered, so they became Scripture in that way, something written, not just oral tradition. So it would be interesting to know what this first literary prophet felt about prophecy and how he, himself, thought he got into the business.

Amos 3:7 is Amos's view of prophecy. *Surely the Lord God will do nothing,* [except but], *or* [unless], *he revealeth his secret unto his servants the prophets.* What is that really saying? If we take that to be literally true, what is Amos saying? At least we can say [that] Amos believes with full conviction that prophecy starts where? With God and comes *via* the prophet which we could say symbolizes those that are listening, the receptive thought of humanity, and apparently for whom? For humanity.

Will God leave anything out? Not according to this. [It] says, *Surely the Lord God will do nothing, but he reveals it to the prophet.* If that is honestly, literally, true, that means it would be like what to an engineer who is building a building? [Voice: "A blueprint."] A blueprint which he could constantly consult to even understand the fulfillment. Therefore, studying prophecy would apparently tell us when to expect fulfillment, or what fulfillment would look like, and studying fulfillment would help to also locate and enrich prophecy, like a hand-in-glove promise-and-fulfillment, all from the one Source. That's a pretty radical point of view. Do you and I regard prophecy that way? Do we really have that kind of conviction in prophecy?

In Amos 7 we find another view of this prophet about how he got into the business. I love this because when we're looking for a new job we fill out a resumé and do it on an IBM Executive Typewriter [or today a Microsoft Word 98 computer program], and we write it like we love to read it. We want our prospective boss to know exactly our best qualities, so our best foot is forward in every paragraph. Amos doesn't write his resumé that way. Maybe that's why none of us are prophets. But maybe we could be as we understand what it takes to be a prophet.

Amaziah was the priest at Bethel. He wanted to get rid of Amos like [it] was his first concern. Amos was stirring up everybody and saying things that he [Amaziah] didn't want anybody to hear. He wanted just a nice, soothing, calm, relationship with the people. And besides, Amos came from the southern kingdom of Judah, and now he's up in Israel at Bethel stirring things up. Amaziah politely, but firmly, suggests that Amos go home.

Amos 7:14 hands Amaziah his resumé. He says, *"I [was] no prophet."* We'd never say that, would we? "Neither [was] I a prophet's son;" I don't even have that by the right of heredity."*But I [was] an herdman, and a gatherer of sycomore fruit."* Guess what everybody else was at that period, practically the same, especially around Tekoa [in the foothills on the western side of the Dead Sea] even today the town of Tekoa is just simply an agricultural society. He was an herdsman a gatherer of sycamore [fig] fruit. Whose idea [was this]? How did Amos get in the prophecy business? The Lord took him. Did you see that? It sounds almost like it was by the scruff of his neck in Verse 15, *"The Lord took me."* Was it Amos' idea? It was God's idea. That's how he got into business.

It's God's idea, *"as I followed the flock."* Just think of that shepherd-motive. Of course, that left us all out. We could never be prophets because there's simply no room to keep sheep any more. [Laughter] Or is it what is necessary mentally in keeping sheep that is a prerequisite of being a prophet in thought? All you have to do [is express] humility. All you have to do is make a list of the qualities that it requires to stay up twenty-four hours with sheep. [Laughter] You'll see how far we're away from being maybe prepared to be a prophet. But it does something to thought. It introduces clarity and things apparently become visible and appreciable to us right here that we didn't see before because of dull ears, or blind eyes, which Isaiah [42:7] talked so much about. Following the flock, the shepherd-motive.

Remember how often Jesus drew a contrast between the hirelings and the shepherd. He made the distinction very clear. We can apply that disctinction right to our own profession. I hope we aren't in a profession. We're rather in something we can call practice rather than profession. Because Jesus said, "The hireling..." An hireling is someone who works for his paycheck. You know how bright our eyes become when that Friday approaches bi-monthly, or whenever we may get it. But Jesus said [John 10:13] *"The hireling fleeth, because he is an hireling,"* and here's your distinction, *"and careth not for the sheep."* The shepherd-motive then is what? [Voice: "One who cares."] One who really cares.

I think this is partly what a lot of young people were feeling, and maybe not expressing correctly, in the last decade or so. This element of caring is so needed in our profession. Just bringing that to our job. Really caring is the shepherd-motive. What was Jesus doing out on that road to Emmaus with these two disciples if he didn't care? He was not a hireling. [Amos 7:15] says, *"The Lord took me as I followed the flock, and the Lord said unto me, Go, prophesy."* What's he doing in the very next line. [Amos 7:16] *"Now therefore hear thou the word of the Lord."* He dropped everything and went. You remember when Jesus appointed his disciples they dropped their nets and went [Matthew 4:20; Mark 1:18]. There's another quality in being a prophet or a disciple. Are we ready for that one?

Let's turn to II Peter in the New Testament to get a much later view of prophecy. Let's see if it coincides with what we have just seen in Amos. Many scholars think that II Peter is the last book to enter the canon [the books of the Bible recognized as geniune and inspired] of our Scripture. In a way, we may be looking at bookends here with a lot in between *Amos* [and] *II Peter.*

In II Peter 1:16 we have the author saying, *"We haven't followed fables, as a matter of fact, we were eyewitnesses."* That's a real favorite word right now, isn't it? Because what is considered the best evidence in a court room? Eyewitness evidence, and yet, would you like your life to depend on somebody else's eyewitness evidence? We say in one breath how great it is. And in the next breath, if our lives depended on it, we're not so sure of it. Suppose we had to rely on eyewitness evidence for the validity of Jesus existence, would it grow stronger or weaker as the years went on? And it has [gotten weaker], hasn't it? Those who rely on eyewitness evidence for Jesus finally got to the point of even challenging his historicity [historical authenticity]. Peter says, *"Not fables; we're eyewitnesses,"* but he doesn't rely on that.

II Peter 1:19 says, *"Something is much higher and more sure,"* or reliable, than eyewitness evidence, and he calls it what? He calls it *"prophecy."* Would Amos have agreed with that? Would Jesus have agreed with that in going back in that walk to Emmaus in going through all these prophets? There's a high regard for prophecy from three rather important individuals in history, who were able to do things with their lives that the average human being, even in the twentieth century, hasn't been able to do. Maybe it's the result of their outlook. Maybe it's some understanding of what prophecy is all about that may have permitted these things to occur.

II Peter 1:20, another view of prophecy, the prophecy of the Scripture is not what? [Voice: *"of any private interpretation."*] Isn't that a relief? Isn't that a great relief that no matter what my opinion is about the Scriptures, it doesn't matter? Or yours. Because it's not opinion and it's not private.

II Peter 1:21 tells us what it is. We have to understand that here is prophecy being defined by the Bible itself. If we go into the Bible to criticize prophecy, we have to at least take it on its own terms. Both Amos and Peter are saying that *"prophecy did not come by the will of man."* It wasn't man's idea. That's [what] Amos said; he didn't get into business because it was his idea. He was picking fruit. And when; it didn't *"come by the will of man: but holy men of God spake [as they were] moved by the Holy Ghost."*

That word "ghost" is *pneuma* in Greek. It means "spirit, air, wind, ghost," all those things, pneumatic tire [comes from this]. Apparently air and wind imply what? There's action. There's where the action is. It's movement; *"holy men of God spake [as they were] moved."* The initiative never came from man. That's why we don't understand it; couldn't be good if it didn't came from man. That movement by the *Holy Pneuma* is what begins the Bible. In Genesis 1[:2] *"The Spirit* [or pneuma,] *of God* ***moved**."* Look at the action in Genesis 1!

If that's the kind of movement we want to be a part of, apparently we can't be, unless we're in touch with what's motivating prophecy. Because the holy men of God spake as they were moved. So if we get involved in prophecy, then we're going to be moved. Moved to do what? Who knows? But, it's God's will being done, according to the context of the Scripture.

We find [in Luke 24:29] they stopped to eat because they see a neon sign flashing. The Emmaus Hilton has a vacancy. They eat off a bowl somewhat similar to what you see here probably. From all indications, maybe even earlier than Jesus' period. It's a wooden bowl made out of grape wood and found near one of the Dead Sea Scroll caves. It looks like it was made in the Philippines. [Chuckle] It's the same kind, classic shape. It's a food bowl of the period. As they are eating, Jesus breaks bread. Of course, that's an immediate identity factor because they were so used to that.

[In Luke 24:31] it says, *"their eyes were opened, and they knew him;"* That means a lot. *"and he vanished out of their sight."* Isn't that peculiar? Once they know him, he vanishes. Do they need him physically any more? [Voice: "No."] Look at how that mood has been changed.
[In Luke 24:32] they compare notes about what they were feeling when

Jesus was talking. Both of them say that their hearts were burning within them. That's not the heart burning you hear on television commercials. [Laughter] This is the kind of thing, right there, that I believe is the beginning of the Christian church. The burning heart. Who needs to sell anybody else if you're sold? What happens when everyone else finds that you're sold? They come and want to know why. That spark in one heart catches in another. What happened? Their hearts were burning. Very frankly, ladies and gentlemen, if tonight in going through our walk to Emmaus, our hearts don't burn within us, we haven't been on the walk. We'll have to go on that eventually. But try hard tonight so you don't have to have it as a later effect. Because we're going to do the very same thing Jesus did with his disciples.

Isn't it marvelous we don't have to look for Jesus in the earth any more than his disciples? Isn't it almost totally, humanly unique because time is telescoped? The disciples had no advantage over you or me. We both have the same Scriptures and agelessly, we can find Jesus where? [Voice: "In the Scriptures"] That's what he said. That's where he's pointing his disciples to. Do you think he understood that his twentieth century followers could be as close to him as his immediate disciples? In that respect there's virtually no materiality or earth supression left in the view of the followers towards the Founder. It says that *"he opened the Scriptures."*

[Luke 24:33] They weren't tired any more. They headed right back where they started, to Jerusalem. Maybe that's what Jesus had wanted. Because back in Jerusalem the eleven disciples were quivering behind closed doors, and who were with them? Does it say? *"And them that were with them."* Who were they?

Luke is one of a two-volume work, the second volume being the *Book of Acts*.

[Acts 1:13,14,15] In that opening chapter of Acts, Luke tells of the very next meeting that is similar. He not only names [eleven] disciples, he says the women are there. He says Mary is there, the mother of Jesus. [Peter] adds them all up and says 120 were there.

If it's possible that there were that many there, in that one room, what did it constitute? What was all there? The whole Christian church. It was the first church meeting. The first Christian church meeting and it was being addressed by its Founder shortly but they didn't know it.

[Luke 24:33,34,35,39] Jesus went out to get those two so they could be part of it. In fact, they got there just ahead of him. He even enabled them to make the announcement, of what they'd seen on that road. But it was not their privilege to tell them what Jesus was going to tell them. After he goes through a lot of exercising in showing [them] that he's really Jesus, for instance, the hands and the feet. They were all down with microscopes and everything else to make sure that this could've been a man that went through the crucifixion, and it was Jesus himself. Still they didn't get it. We really shouldn't blame them because I'm not so sure how we would've responded.

[Luke 24: 41,42,43] Finally, he asks if they have any meat. He proceeds to eat a meal in front of them just to show that everything was working just fine, thank you. Just to get their thought focused on what he was really there for. Try that recipe, broiled fish and honeycomb. I think it's even in my wife's cookbook. At least she made me eat it. [Laughter] It's not bad. It sounds kind of, you know, but it's alright. But he isn't there to eat.

In [Luke 24:] verse 44, in the same night, Jesus is doing something that should sound very familiar. Twice in the same night he is doing the identical thing. You know he would not be going through this if it were not absolutely essential for his church to know. And he's talking to his whole church at the moment. And what is it? What's different this time though? He goes [into] the law of Moses, the prophets, **and** the Psalms. But don't we all think the Psalms a book of poetry, not prophecy? Who's ever considered that the Psalms was a book of prophecy? That's what he said.

In [Luke 24] verse 45 it says, *"He opened their understanding, that they might understand the scriptures,"* implying that until they got this, they wouldn't comprehend the Scriptures. They would lose the key.

In [Luke 24] verse 46, look, if this doesn't sound like an engineer reading his blueprint, *"It is written, and thus it behoved Christ to suffer, and to rise from the dead the third day."* "It's written" and this is what must occur. Again, the emphasis on Christ's suffering.

Just from a scholarly point of view, so that you know this, there is really no scholarly evidence that you can bank on that shows anyone writing prior to the first century A.D. about a Messiah who would suffer. Which means we may be looking at the first time the concept was ever introduced publicly; and it came through Jesus. In other words, he read in the Scripture something no one else had seen, or had known was there, or had applied to the Messiah. Is that true?

Here is what Professor Davies, one of our top New Testament scholars, says, which is rather interesting:

> "It was scandalous enough to point to the figure of Jesus of Nazareth as the Messiah, but to point to a crucified Jesus as such, was monstrous. Most Jews had certainly not anticipated a Messiah who should suffer. No Jews, we may be certain, had anticipated a Messiah who should endure the shameful death of crucifixion. Such a death, in the light of Deuteronomy, placed Jesus under the condemnation of the law. To proclaim Jesus as Messiah was to proclaim that one whom the law had condemned was upheld by God."

That was the kind of thing Jesus faced on the cross. Ending his experience criminally in the eyes of humanity, how could he ever convince anyone that he was the Messiah with that kind of view of Scripture? Maybe then, here is the density on the subject that this forty days must break. Maybe Jesus' place in prophecy is the one important fact that the disciples had failed to grasp. Maybe that was the one essential fact on which he must build his church.

[Matthew 16:16] Just test it. When Peter said to him, *"Thou art the Christ!"* what did Peter mean? Did he mean the suffering Christ? [Voice: "No."]

[Matthew 16:17] Jesus commended his answer, *"Blessed art thou, Simon Bar-jona."* Because it's the first breakthrough that his disciples had. The insane had it before his disciples [Matthew 8:29;Mark 3:15; Luke 8:28]. They called him the Son of God and the Messiah. Here suddenly his disciples break through and say, *"You are the Christ."* When you read that account in Matthew's gospel, you'll find something very interesting. After Jesus commends Peter for what he said *"flesh and blood hath not revealed it unto thee, but my Father."* Remember, we've already seen Amos [3:7], and Peter [2 Peter: 1:16,19,20,21] later, talking about what the Father reveals...

END TAPE 1, SIDE B

BEGIN TAPE 2, SIDE A

...rather than flesh and blood, and prophecy has got a lot to do with it.. Do you know what happens in the very next two verses?

[Matthew 16:18 *"And I say also unto thee, That thou art Peter, and upon this rock I will build my church; and the gates of hell shall not prevail against it."* Matthew 16:19 *And I will give unto thee the keys of the kingdom of heaven: and whatsoever thou shalt bind on earth shall be bound in heaven: and whatsoever thou shalt loose on earth shall be loosed in heaven.*]

[Consequently] Peter thought very highly apparently of himself and all of that.

And Jesus felt that now was the time he might be able to tell his disciples.

[Matthew 16:21] Then Jesus spake to them plainly about his approaching betrayal, and that he would be turned over by the Jews to the Romans, and that he would be executed, and he would rise again from the dead. We all admitted that Jesus had said these things. Where were the disciples? Weren't they hearing? Weren't they listening?

[Matthew 16:22] You know what Peter's response was? *"Be it far from thee, Lord: this shall not be unto thee."*

[Matthew 16:23] Do you know what Jesus said to him? *"Get thee behind me, Satan: thou savourest the things that be of men and not the things that be of God."* That's the exact reverse that he said in [Verse 17 above] previously. [Then] he said, *Flesh and blood hadn't revealed the point that he is the Christ, but the Father.* But now when he said that Jesus would not suffer, he said, *You're not reading God's Word correctly. You're savouring the things that be of men.* That's quite interesting because it's the reverse. It's pretty obvious that Jesus didn't found his church on a person who, as human nature does so regularly, can reverse its field without notice practically. What Jesus was commending, and what he said he would base his church on, was that vision that Peter did see that he was the Christ, because the minute you say Christ to a first-century Jew you mean the one in the Old Testament. The only difference between the disciples' view and the first-century Jew's view of Jesus is what? Apparently neither one recognized that the Messiah would suffer. But the Jews were still expecting the Messiah. And the disciples said the Messiah was Jesus.

This extra point of the suffering and a **complete** overhauling of the Scriptures in their thinking was left to the walk to Emmaus and what followed immediately afterward, when his entire church [got] together and Jesus [went] over the law of Moses, the prophets and Psalms.

This point that he is making where he opens the Scriptures to them, we want to test this out, because we have said that the disciples didn't comprehend it.

John 20 is about the same point in the narrative of Jesus as Luke 24 as far as the state of awareness of Jesus' resurrection.
John 20:9 *"As yet,"* important two words, *"they knew not the scripture,*

that he must rise again from the dead." See the next. Verse what happens to them?

John 20:10 *"Then the disciples went away again unto their own home."* That's when they went home. The implication is that if they knew the Scripture, they wouldn't have gone home. We had a question, did Jesus tell anybody? Did he really let his disciples in on this.

John 5:39 This is by way of having the text answer the questions rather than me or you. I'm sure it's familiar to everyone. He says there are two reasons for *"searching the Scriptures."*(1) *"eternal life"* (2) *"they are they which testify of me."* What he was saying at Emmaus doesn't sound totally novel, does it? So, maybe he wasn't that specific.

John 5:46 How more specific could you get except chapter and verse? *"...had ye believed Moses, ye would have believed me: for **he wrote of me.**"* If Jesus honestly believed that, he's talking about someone who lives 1200 years prior to his own existence. He is saying the highest figure in Jewish history wrote of him. If you were a first-century Jew, and you heard that, how would you feel? Would you take that lying down? In some cases they didn't. Yet the conviction behind that is decidedly there, ***"he wrote of me."*** Let's check it out.

Deuteronomy, one of the books of the Bible attributed to Moses and one of Jesus' favorite books in all the Old Testament.

Deuteronomy 18:15 quotes Moses as predicting something. In other words, Moses himself is what? [Voice: "A prophet."] A prophet. Let's separate it into its proper ingredients. It all starts with whom? He says, [Voices: *"The Lord thy God"*] *"The Lord thy God will raise up unto thee,"* will, it's future tense, *"will raise up unto thee a Prophet."*

To use a crude example, you remember in the story of Cinderella, the glass slipper only fit Cinderella. If we're going to take Amos' view about prophecy, where the Lord reveals His secret leaving nothing out to the receptive thought, the prophet. And we take that view that it's like an engineer's blueprint, and that anyone that knows it's there, can refer back to that blueprint. And, with a certain amount of spiritual illumination cast on the blueprint, should be able to see the divine hand in history. Which, of course, is the entire Bible. That's the main point, the divine hand in history, and specifically in prophecy. Therefore, prophecy and its fulfillment should dovetail. And the glass slipper should only fit the one for whom it's designed.

If we have the remotest idea of suggesting that Jesus is the fulfillment of any of the Old Testament prophecy we're about to go through, then we have to do it as objectively as possible. We have to set the prophecy here [pointing on the chalkboard] and the fulfillment here [pointing on the chalkboard] and see how they blend.

Point one says, *"the Lord thy God will raise up unto thee a prophet.* Was Jesus a prophet? Did he also predict things to come after him? That checks off.

Point two says, *"from the midst of thee, of thy brethren,"* meaning, he would be from the Jews? That checks off.

The third point says, *"like unto me,"* like unto whom? [Voice: "Moses"]. A Moses-like prophet. Let's remember the Jews did expect certain appearances that were prophesied. If they were familiar with this verse at all, they would be looking for a prophet who would be like unto Moses, who would remind them of Moses.

Here is an example of how studying the prophecy completely illuminates the fulfillment. If this is true, and you desire in a scholarly way try to relate it to the fulfillment to see if it might match up, then *"like unto me"* has to *fit.* I recommend a special study on your own. Look in a Bible concordance under the name "Moses." See how many times Jesus uses it, contrasting, or building on what Moses did. See how many times the people in the gospel also were reminded through what Jesus did of what Moses had done earlier. It's like a floodlight turned on the gospel by prophecy itself. It's a wonderful thing just to test out. Moses is like you and me. He was told by God to say something and he left something out.

Deuteronomy 18:18 That seems apparent at least, because when you read verse 18, it's now God talking. Skip down that verse until you get to the new material that Moses apparently had left out. What's new? [Voices not clear] Yes, Moses had not said that. Is that an important inclusion? God says, *"[I] will put my words in his mouth; and he shall speak unto them all that I shall command him."* Please remember those words. Put them on your mental shelf in your memory. Even the words "command," and "speak," and "words" because we're going to run into them later on, and you will have to refresh your thought about it.

Lest you think that a modest requirement, I'll wager that none of us in this room who were told to do something, or asked to do something by even someone we loved very dearly this morning, that we probably left something out, or we didn't do it completely, or exactly in the way that we we're expected, or perhaps somebody didn't fulfill what we asked. Here is a man being described that would come that would speak everything that God had commanded him throughout his entire career.

That glass slipper does not fit too many in the history of humanity.

John 6:14 the loaves and fishes incident right after all the fragments were collected in twelve baskets, one undoubtedly for each disciple. Guess what the people who had just eaten thought of in verse 14. What we've just read now should just leap out of the page in a special illumination. The people said, *"You must be"* what? [Voices: "the prophet"] *"that prophet"* What prophet? *The one.* How can we be sure that it's the one in Deuteronomy? Here is an expectation in the Jewish thought. What were they reminded of? Why would they immediately have thought of that? [Voices: "the manna"] The manna, certainly. Because they just had had loaves and fishes, thousands were fed. There wasn't anything equal to that in their memory in their entire history since Moses. They were reminded of Moses. The minute they were reminded of Moses, they remembered the prophecy that said *"a Prophet like unto me."* Isn't it wonderful that it just clicked in there? Even for the average thought of the period. Unless we think that's way off as a theory, look in John 6: 32 and you will see Jesus himself drawing attention to it.

John 7:40. Here we have what again? The people are saying it again so it's in the popular expectation. They're saying, *"this is the Prophet."* Notice the next line.

John 7:41.*"Others said,"* No, *"this is the Christ."* It's two separate expectations. The popular expectancy is for the Christ and another figure, the prophet. We'll find later that they join in the Christian view of the fulfillment of prophecy. When we ask where that Christian view came from, and find that it's the last chapter of Luke [24], where Jesus was the first to interpret the Scriptures that way, we can perhaps dare say that Jesus himself was the first to equate this passage in Deuteronomy with the Messiah, not a separate figure at all, but with the Messiah.

John 12:49. What sounds familiar? *"I have not spoken of myself; but the Father which sent me he gave me a commandment, what I should say, and what I should speak."* Do you think Jesus knew the Scriptures well enough to know that he was virtually paraphrasing a prophecy, and anyone who was intelligent enough to recognize that would know what he would mean? John 12:50, the way he ends it. He says, *"even as the Father said unto me, so I speak."*

We're going to move beyond the law of Moses into some of the other portions of the Scripture that Jesus apparently went into in the walk to Emmaus. The walk to Emmaus becomes much more than a geographic walk. It's a walk through the Bible. I use it more in that symbolic way than geography.

Matthew 27:32 We're going to see some of the details of the crucifixion. Remember Jesus kept emphasizing that the prophet had said that the Messiah would suffer.

Matthew 27:33. We know of a place of a skull or Golgatha.

Matthew 27:34 We're aware that the drink he was given has almost an exact recipe which you can be assured is not in my wife's cookbook. [Laughter] It says, *he tasted it but he would not drink.*

Matthew 27:39 Then it says, *"they that passed by"* beneath the cross *"reviled him, wagging their heads,"* Please remember that, *"wagging their heads."* Remember we're reading the fulfillment. We're going to go back to prophecy shortly to test it out.

Matthew 27:43 and Psalms 22:8 Then we find at the bottom of the cross that the chief priests and the scribes and the elders, the ones who knew the Scripture best, presumably, saying, - if we would all read together I think it will really bring it more to thought. Let's read it out loud. - *"He trusted in God; let him deliver him now, if he will have him: for he said, I am the Son of God."* How would you characterize that remark? It's rather what? Wasn't enough to nail him on the cross without that sarcasm that he said he was the Son of God. So, let God say that. It really isn't worthy of those who are holding high theological positions of that period, or any period. But that seems to be human nature.

Certainly it stirred Jesus to the very roots of his being, the real roots of his being. That, of course, would refresh him on the cross. Do you think it reminded him of anything? If it did, do you think it was partly responsible for the very next thing that is uttered audibly?

Matthew 27:46 and Psalms 22:1 The very thing that many Christians wish their Master had never uttered, *"Eli, Eli, lama sabachthani? ...My God, my God, why hast thou forsaken me?"* Just keep in thought the sequence of this.

Psalm 22:7,8. As Jesus may have done with his disciples which caused their hearts to burn within them. Perhaps ours will too. Let's read together verses 7 and 8 out loud. *"All they that see me laugh me to scorn: they shoot out the lip, they shake the head, saying, He trusted on the Lord that he would deliver him: let him deliver him, seeing he delighted in him,"* a passage maybe one thousand years earlier than the event. Do you think that if you were disciples and Jesus was reading these two passages and you had witnessed to that, that any hair on your head could be horizontal?

You saw those events, and Jesus is describing them from centuries-old documents, and that isn't all. They could have recalled the next thing Jesus said on the cross after the scribes and Pharisees had said that. They could have recalled that Jesus said something they wished he hadn't said. Yet suddenly, in the light of what they see here, and in the light of the fact that how better could Jesus, as a Scriptural student, sound a trumpet note for every Scriptural student from his time through our century, than to do what every Jewish boy did in memorizing the Psalms, because they would recognize the Psalm by the first verse.

Psalm 22:1 ["*My God, my God, why hast thou forsaken me?*"] Is that a coincidence? Was Jesus saying to every receptive thought [that] he told people to search the Scriptures to find him? No one can really comprehend what he said on the cross unless they find it here in Psalm 22. Because it's not simply a cry of agony, even though it came from the very depths of an agonizing experience. It was a quotation from the Scripture and a Scriptural student of Jesus' caliber would not quote from Scripture unless he meant it like a direction signal in the horizon down through the ages, pointing to the very same Scripture. Isn't it as if he were saying, "Read this if you want to understand why I am here." So, let's read it. I'm sure the disciples suddenly had the Bible given to them as they never had before. Suddenly the suffering aspects of the Messiah in prophecy came out through the very pioneer who had fulfilled those prophecies.

Psalm 22:13 Suddenly we find that "*They gaped upon me [with] their mouths,*"

Psalm 22:14 describes "*I am poured out like water, and all my bones are out of joint.*" Anyone remember John's [19:34] description of what happened when the spear pierced his side? It said, "*Blood and water poured out.*"

Psalm 22:15 says, "*My strength is dried up like a potsherd; and my tongue cleaveth to my jaws.*" A very vivid description of a man who is in thirst.

Do you remember one verse in the gospel of John [19:28]? I'll read it to you just while you're looking at that Psalm 22 verse. Listen to how John does this. John was one of the fellows who went fishing. But look how he is writing for the record. "*After this, Jesus knowing that all things were accomplished,*" How did he know? Did he know the blueprint? "*That the scripture might be fulfilled, saith, I thirst.*" Those disciples didn't even know that before the walk to Emmaus and before the time that Jesus talked to them in that room.

Psalm 22:16 Look at the last part, *"they pierced my hands and my feet."* Psalm 22:18 *"They part my garments, ...and cast lots upon my vesture."*

Coincidence? Or is it what Amos [3:7] said right from the beginning? *"The Lord God will do nothing, but he revealeth his secret to his servants the prophets."* Amos believed that with great conviction. Jesus told his disciples they didn't even understand the Bible if they didn't know it [Ye do err not knowing the scriptures. Matthew 22:29]. Even in our day, Professor Dodd, probably our leading New Testament scholar, said, "If we do not comprehend prophecy and its importance, we lose the substructure of New Testament theology and its ground plan."

Professor William Albright, America's greatest contribution to Bible scholarship - he just passed away about three years ago or so - has pointed out that when you see a verse in the New Testament that quotes the Old, by all means, don't just go back to that verse, study its entire context.

Psalm 31:5 Sound familiar? We find that one other of the famous last words of Jesus from the cross is what? A quotation from Scripture. *"Into thine hand I commit my spirit"* Notice that the thought is completed with the remark, *"thou hast redeemed me, O Lord God of truth."* Suppose that weren't uttered by Jesus on the cross aloud, but that he completed that thought mentally. He knew the Bible well enough to have just finished the thought. If so, look what the final thought would have been before what Luke [23:46] describes as giving up the ghost. Is it defeat? *"Thou has redeemed me."* It's already happened. *"Thou hast redeemed me, O Lord God of truth."* What a grand way of meeting the last enemy! He considered it was no contest and it had already been won. *"Thou has redeemed me, O Lord God of truth."* You know what his definition of the devil was? *"A liar and the father of it"* [John 8:44]. Just the opposite of what this would indicate, *"Lord God of truth!"*

Psalm 69:21 and Matthew 27:34 You see how we're making all these local stops. *["They gave me also gall for my meat; and in my thirst they gave me vinegar to drink."]* When they handed that mixture to Jesus on the cross do you think he knew it was coming? [Voice: "Yes."] If he knew the blueprint, he was abandoned by everyone except the women at the base of the cross and John. The only comfort he obviously had was his recognition of his mission and his assignment in the Scriptures. When something cruel and malicious happened to him, if he knew it was in the Scriptures, he knew he was on the way, and doing what he was required to do. What a comfort to know that the Father had forewarned him and that he was prepared for every step because he read the blueprint.

END OF TAPE 2, SIDE A

by B. Cobbey Crisler

BEGIN TAPE 2, SIDE B

It wasn't just Jesus who ran into incredulity among his fellow human beings, but we find the opening question in Isaiah 53 being a recognition of the very same thing.

Isaiah 53:1 "*Who hath believed our report?*" Notice the description that follows. It sounds almost biographical and yet written hundreds of years before the New Testament.

Isaiah 53:3 We're told of a man who *"is despised and rejected of men; a man of sorrows."*

Isaiah 53:5 *"He [was] wounded for our transgressions." The New English Bible*, probably the most scholarly of our recent translations, says it is a better translation to substitute "pierced" for "wounded." *"He was pierced for our transgressions."* [And] *"with his stripes we are healed."* What are stripes literally? They're the marks of lashes. Remember, the slipper has to fit? So, the slipper calls for a man of sorrows, someone who would be pierced, and someone who whould have the marks of lashes. That's pretty specific.

Isaiah 53:7 It says that, *"He was oppressed, and he was afflicted, yet he opened not his mouth."* If we had time, we could go into the New Testament and find examples for almost every line of Isaiah 53. We wouldn't be the first ones who did it. It's the most popular chapter in the entire Old Testament for New Testament authors. Every verse except one is either quoted directly or alluded to in the New Testment. So, they found this pretty exciting. It says, *"He opened not his mouth."* How does that fit? Remember anything like that? [Voices inaudible.] That's right.

Isaiah 53:8 *"He was taken from prison, and from judgment."* Pilate even sat on the judgment seat.

Isaiah 53:9 It says, "he *made his grave with the wicked."* Two thieves, on either side. And then the next line. I'll use the *Revised Standard Version* translation. The next line says, *"with a rich man in his death."* Matthew [27:57] tells us that Joseph of Arimathea was a rich man, and you know what has an authentic ring about that? Matthew was a disciple. Therefore, if his gospel is really based on his recollection, and interestingly enough, it's Matthew and John who are more excited over prophecy than any of the others, and they are the only two [gospels] named for disciples. They were the only two in that room listening to Jesus. We may suddenly find that the exciting news that Jesus fulfilled

God's revelation of him to the prophets, the entire incentive for the gospels themselves. The excitement to pick up that good news or gospel. At least it's worth considering.

Matthew who has the characteristic that we recognize him by, because he always says, "that it might be fulfilled" [9 times], "that was spoken of the Lord" [4 times], "by the prophet saying" [7 times], all over his gospel. He's so thrilled to find these things. And put them in there. But he doesn't when it comes to Joseph of Arimathea, which makes it even stronger. All he says is that *"Joseph of Arimathea, a rich man"* and so on. He doesn't say "that it might be fulfilled, it was spoken of the prophet, of the Lord by the prophet Isaiah, saying," and so forth.

It continues in Isaiah 53:10 *"When thou shalt make his soul an offering for sin."* When the lamb was slain, that was the offering, he was killed. The verse should end there, but it doesn't. Isaiah says, *"When thou shalt make his soul an offering for sin"* when you've killed the lamb, *"he shall see [his] seed, he shall prolong [his] days,"* after being killed. Is it possible that Isaiah's clarity of thought also foresaw the resurrection? It says, *"He will prolong [his] days after being killed,"* it's what its saying to the first-century Jew. How long were his days prolonged? [Voices: "Forty."] Forty. It was during those forty days that probably Jesus went right back to that verse. And the centuries joined united by God's Word, promise and fulfillment.

Isaiah 53:7 describes Jesus or the Messiah, actually neither one is correct from a scholarly point of view. So, let me go back on that. I'm jumping to conclusions there. In fact, many scholars today call this the "suffering- servant" passage and don't equate it with the Messiah. It was the Messiah, but we'll see how the New Testament is definitely equated with the Messiah. *"He is brought as a lamb to the slaughter,"* and we know how important the symbol of lamb becomes later in the *book of Revelation.*

Let me tell you what a sophomore in my class said that absolutely electrified me. In an answer to a question I wrote in a final exam at Daycroft. It was on the Bible and on this particular gospel. I said, "Why do you think the Jews did not even remotely consider Jesus a possibile fulfillment of their own Scriptures as the Messiah?" Here was his answer, absolutely beautiful, showing that the direct access for inspiration has no regard for age group. He said, "Because the Jews were expecting a lion and God sent them a lamb." That's not only inspired, it's accurate. Even what Professor Davies said, the Jews were simply expecting a sacrificial animal, one who would suffer. If you were looking for a lion, you'd let the lamb walk right on by, wouldn't you?

Remember, it was the Passover season; and if John's chronology is correct in his gospel, as Jesus was being nailed to the cross, the lambs were being slaughtered in the Temple. Maybe as many as 250,000 of them as **Josephus** [Jewish priest and historian, A.D. 37/38 to after 93] records at one point. The drains of the Temple running with the blood of slaughtered animals, and on that hill, the real Lamb, the lamb pointed to in prophecy. Remember, it was John the Baptist who first maybe hinted at that when he said, *"Behold the lamb of God"* [John 1:29].

Isaiah 61 has some importance to us too because the question should be raised, and may have been already by you in thought. Did Jesus ever try to get up in public and say, "Look, I'm the Messiah?"

While it is recorded that when he went to his hometown and visited the synagogue, that as was the custom often to those who they knew, or who were visiting, and they wished to honor, they handed him a scroll. It was the scroll of Isaiah. He opened it by accident? By coincidence? By design? By revelation? Anyway, it opened to Isaiah 61. You could imagine what Jesus must have sounded like reading, and especially when he was reading something that he was convinced his whole mission was to fulfill. If you've ever heard authority behind reading, that would have been it. It really shook the synagogue because they knew these verses quite well. They knew these voices point to the Messiah. This was part of the Messianic expectation, because Messiah in Hebrew means "anointed one." The very root of that word is used in verse 1.

Isaiah 61:1,2,3. *"The Spirit of the Lord God [is] upon me; because the Lord hath* ***anointed*** *me"* What has God anointed the Messiah to do? *To preach, to bind up, to proclaim liberty, to comfort, to appoint, to give unto them beauty.* All of those things are part of the standard, accepted role of the Messiah. He read that with authority that must have rooted everyone to their chairs. Because when he went back to the platform to his own seat, the service simply stopped. Nothing went on. They were all looking at him. He got up, and he looked at them and he said [Luke 4:21], *"This day is this scripture fulfilled in your ears."* Do you know what they did to him for that? They tried to throw him off the cliff [Luke 4:29]. That was what they did to the "scapegoat." The effort almost symbolically was to turn the Messiah into a scapegoat instead of a lamb, even to pervert the prophecy in that way. *But he walked through the midst of them unharmed* [Luke 4:30]. From that point on we don't hear Jesus announcing his role publicly. We find him protecting it, but we do find him doing it privately. Such as to the woman of Samaria who first says to him, *"We know that the Messiah is coming. Jesus said, "I that speak unto thee am he"* [John 4:25,26].

That ends the regular course on the Walk to Emmaus. [The aftermath of the Walk to Emmaus] will take approximately twenty minutes [and is meant] to supplement. I was giving this course for years when suddenly I realized I hadn't proved it out thoroughly. I'm saying this is the important primary thing in the early church. The only way I can really prove it is to test the only document we have that tells about the primitive church. That's the *book of Acts.*

Acts 2:1. *It's the day of Pentecost,* fifty days [seven weeks] after Passover. How many days has Jesus remained with them? So, giving that weekend, we have about one week after Jesus has left them completely.

Let's see how the disciples are now responding. Are they fishing? No, they're not. Peter delivers the first free lecture sponsored by the Christian church. [Chuckles] First Church of Christ, Jerusalem, cordially invites you and your friends. [Laughter] How does Peter approach this lecture?

Acts 2:22 Peter calls *"Jesus of Nazareth, a man approved of God."* How could he prove that Jesus was approved of God? By what? [Voice: "By a miracle?"] By prophecy. God speaking to the prophet.

Acts 2:23 says Jesus was *"delivered by the determinate counsel and foreknowledge of God,"* How come Peter knows that? Did that come to him by himself? He didn't even know it. Remember, he was the fellow that rebuked Jesus [Matthew 16:22], *It's not going to happen to you.* Now suddenly he's saying, "Look what the Scriptures say."

In fact, in [Acts 2] Verse 25 and for ten verses, you can take them home with you and study them yourself, there are quotations from the Scriptures. We just simply didn't have time for it tonight.

Acts 2:25 says, *"David speaketh concerning him,"* the "him" being [Voices: "Jesus."] You remember Jesus himself said *"Moses wrote of me"* [John 5:46]. Now here Peter is saying, *"David speaketh concerning him"* Almost ten verses there.

Remember Jesus' religion is a religion of results. I don't care how perfect or beautiful a theory this walk-to-Emmaus thing may sound like, it's worthless unless it produces results. Let's see if it has any results.

Acts 2:41 tells us the first results of the first walk to Emmaus taken by anyone after Jesus is gone results in what? [Voice: "Three thousand..."] *Three thousand new members.* That's not a bad result of a lecture. [Laughter] We could ask why isn't it happening today? Is it important for hearts to burn within us first? Because that's what was going on as far as the apostles are concerned. Three thousand new members.

Acts 3:1 and 18 find Peter and John together now with lecture number two for the Christian church. Remember, Jesus had set the standard for the church meeting. The first church meeting he got up and read the Bible and then provided the key for the Bible [Luke 4:17-21]. That's exactly what these early church meetings begin to look like. In fact, Professor Davies says, "The primitive church meetings, the first church meetings, were probably nothing else as much as they are like a Bible class." In effect, what we are doing tonight may be exactly what the primitive church did.

Some scholars have even indicated that a study of the Greek words on how Paul approached his audience will show you that he didn't just preach to them. He asked them if these things were so by using the interrogative. He said whether Christ should suffer, as we'll see later on. According to these scholars, they say what that meant was, Paul was eliciting from them their own conclusions. They were examining the Scriptures together. He expected it to be a discussion. Then he let them go back and either believe or not believe, depending on what they found in the Scriptures. What we're doing to night may be about as close as we can get to the early primitive church meetings.

Acts 3:18 Peter and John are saying something that sounds like they are quoting Jesus during the walk to Emmaus, *"Those things, which God before had shewed by the mouth of all his prophets, that Christ should suffer, he hath so fulfilled."* Look at the enthusiasm behind that. Someone who fifity days before hadn't even realized the facts themselves. What are the results? Let's see some of the specifics first.

Acts 3:22 . Look at what Peter and John quote. Does that sound familiar? Where did that come from? Here we have, just a week, or a little more, after Jesus had gone, we find them quoting that verse in Deuteronomy [18:15] relating it to Jesus. Is this something they did on their own? Or could we be fairly sure that's one of the versions Jesus had landed on in discusssing with his disciples in the walk to Emmaus and immediately afterwards.

The next verses ending that chapter are all on the prophetic message. You can see what a major portion of the early preaching it was.

Acts 4:4 are the results. What happened? Five thousand new members and they're only counting the men. [Laughter] That's a geometric progression almost. If that kept happening, the known-world would be Christian very shortly. Have you ever wondered how it did spread as rapidly as it did? This is an indication, apparently, [of] how important was the walk to Emmaus then and that kind of understanding is to this.

Acts 4:30 to the semicolon. They found they were able to heal. Remember the Bible never admits there is a lesser source than God for either prophecy or healing. Understanding either one should give an insight into the other. They all come from the same source. The understanding of the Bible then enables man to heal.

Acts 7:37 Notice how we spread this around. Peter and John we've been talking about. Now it's Stephen. Stephen is defending his life before the Sanhedrin. He's about to be the first martyr in the Christian church after Jesus' own crucifixion. He tries to take his trial jurors on the walk to Emmaus. What verse does he quote? It's the Deuteronomy [Chapter 18] verse [15] again.

Acts 7:52 where Stephen says, "*Which of the prophets have not your fathers persecuted? and they have slain them which shewed before of the coming of the Just One.*" Do you know who was listening to him say that? Saul. Saul has just been taken on his first walk to Emmaus without maybe even knowing it. Remember, he was the Scriptural scholar *par excellence,* the first intellect of the Christian church, and one to whom that message would mean a great deal once he grasped it. I often wonder whether the walk to Damascus for Paul was also the walk to Emmaus. He understood who his Master was, and therefore couldn't do anything but support him from that point on.

Acts 8:26 Now we skip to Philip. We have Peter and John, and Stephen. Now we have Philip. Philip swinging in his hammock in Caesarea, looking at the Mediterranean, when an angel appears, an annoying angel. Because the idea that this angel had is for Philip to get off his hammock [Laughter] and go to Gaza. No one in his right mind would go to Gaza even today. So, you know it wasn't Philip's idea. It had to be an angel of the Lord. Remember, the movement goes on when angels and the Holy Spirit get involved in things. It's an urgent movement. He goes down there and he still doesn't know what he's doing.

Acts 8:27 Suddenly in front of him is a man of Ethiopia, a black man, probably second or third in command in the kingdom under the queen, in charge of all the treasury, quite a wealthy man apparently. He has his own chariot, the fastest known means of transportation, standing stock still in Gaza. Instead he's taking a walk to Emmaus but he doesn't know it because he's got Isaiah open. If you could own your own scroll, that shows that he certainly was wealthy. Here is a non-Jew by nation, non-Jew by race, the first one who is puzzled, comes to a halt, and suddenly Philip, who came from miles away, is there, because the Spirit moved him. Still Philip doesn't know what to do .

Acts 8:29 So, the Spirit says to him, "*Go near, and join thyself to this chariot.*"

Acts 8:30 And Philip **runs** there, showing again a quality of being a disciple and of listening. He hears him read Isaiah. The custom then was to read out loud. They thought you were weird if you read to yourself. Today it's just the opposite. [Laughter] Philip says, Do you understand what you are reading? Suddenly Philip's beginning to get an idea of what he is doing there.

Acts 8:31 He [the eunuch] said, How can I unless somebody show me. And he asks Philip to come up and sit in the chariot. Get the picture? In Gaza of all places. It's a lesson for the twentieth century. A black and white man sitting together, uniting in the Scriptures. And it was the Spirit's idea that brought them together, not Philip's.

Right at the moment when he was reading the place in Acts 8:32 which mentions the lamb, and opening not his mouth that we just read in the 53rd chapter of Isaiah. What a coincidence! Or was it the divine plan?

Acts 8:34 The eunuch says to Philip, *Who is the prophet speaking of, himself or somebody else?* Bible scholars ask the same question today.

Acts 8:35 Philip had no doubt. He just rubbed his hands together with glee and began right where that man was, *right at that scripture* and preached who? [Voice: "Jesus"] Jesus. In other words, Philip said Isaiah 53 refers to Jesus. He had absolutely no qualms, no doubts, nothing about that. It is true historically that the black race became one of the first to be Chrstian. We've had a late remnant of that when Haile Salassie [1891-1975], though deposed, and despite all his faults, called himself a Christian emperor. I think we have seen some of the spiritual quality really often in the old negro spirituals which come across with a movement of their own. We have this detailed story coming out of the ancient past about this visit of Philip with the Ethiopian.

Acts 10:43 It also proved that the walk to Emmaus could work with non-Jewish backgrounds. Peter introduces it to a full room of Gentiles, Cornelius in Caesarea, he says to [them], "*To him give all the prophets witness.*" What do the Gentiles care about the prophets? They haven't even read the Old Testament. Can you imagine the hesitation with which they even approached Gentiles with this kind of thing? But even if you were a Gentile, wouldn't you be rather impressed if someone fulfilled predictions that were written hundeds of years before?

Acts 10:44,45 Suddenly we find the Holy Ghost comes to the Gentiles, much to the disgruntlement of the Jewish Christians with Peter. But the results are clear. Christianity is meant to be a universal religion and the walk to Emmaus speaks to the world and to humanity at large, not just to the Jews.

Acts 13:27 Here is Paul. He wasn't in that room but he certainly was a Bible scholar. He's saying, *they, the rulers in Jerusalem, "knew him not, nor yet the voices of the prophets which are read every sabbath day, instead they have fulfilled [them] in condemning [him]."*

Acts 13:29 Do you think Paul knew the blueprint? *"When they had fulfilled all that was written of him,"* How did Paul know if he himself didn't realize that?

END TAPE 2, SIDE B

BEGIN TAPE 3, SIDE A

The next ten verses or so are filled again with Bible verses we haven't had time for. Mark them for your later research. It is all very overwhelming indeed as you add these all together.

Acts 13:44 Do you know what the results were of Paul's preaching this? There's no reason why this can't happen in Weston, in Wellesley, in Boston, in San Francisco, in Timbuktu if the walk to Emmaus is truly burning in the hearts of individuals. *"The next sabbath day," it says, "came almost the whole city together to hear the word of God."* That's how the excitement and enthusiasm of the Word got around.

Acts 17:1,2,3 Paul crosses into Europe for the first time. How is Europe going to take Christianity? How are they going to listen to the exciting news that the one who had been announced in Scripture had appeared?

Acts 17:1 *"Now when they had passed through Amphipolis and Apollonia, they came to Thessalonica, where was a synagogue of the Jews:"*

Acts 17:2 Paul went in unto them, and for three successive sabbath days he reasoned with his congregation out of the scriptures, Reasoning sounds like it's give-and-take, right?

Acts 17:3 *"Opening and alleging,"* Here is how he did it. (1) *"that Christ must needs have suffered,"* Sound familiar? Who was the first apparently to bring that out? Jesus himself. First he had to prove by the Bible that there were prophecies that pointed to the Messiah, whom the Jews expected to suffer, that the Messiah had to suffer. Once he'd proved that, (2) [he] was to prove that the Christ would rise from the dead, also using the Scriptures. He hasn't even mentioned Jesus so far. Get the sequence? He has to show in prophecy that there were verses pointing to the fact that the Christ would suffer first. Then the final point is what? (3) That Jesus is the Christ. That's the final great news, that it's all been wrapped up right in that generation, the fulfillment of prophecy.

Acts 17:11 shows what they [Paul and Silas] did in Berea. *"They received the word with all readiness of mind, and searched the scriptures daily, whether those things were so."* Did Paul jam it down their throats? Was it dogma, or did Paul insist that it was discovery? He went through the Scriptures with them. And they went home to find out whether it was true or not.

Acts 18:28 We have Peter, and John, and Stephen, and Philip, and Paul [in Ephesus] and now we have Apollos. What was Apollos doing? *"Mightily convinced the Jews, [and that] publickly, shewing"* How? *"by the scriptures that Jesus was Christ."* You see what the church meetings were like?

Acts 26:22 Paul speaking on trial for his life in front of two thrones. One of which is occupied by Festus, the Roman governor of Judea, successor to Pilate. The other throne being occupied by King Agrippa, Herod, King of the Jews. Paul, he doesn't care who is occupying what because he wants to take them on the walk to Emmaus. He honestly says to them that he is saying nothing new *"only what the prophets and Moses had said would come."*

Acts 26:23 He spells it out again what he thinks are in prophecy. (1) same first point, isn't it? It hammers it home that no one understood *"that Christ should suffer."* That's the first Scriptural lesson that had to come across. (2) *"That he should be the first that should rise from the dead,"* The implication then is what? There are others. (3) *That Christ "should show light unto the people"* and that's the Greek word for the Jews, *and* (4) *"to the Gentiles."*

If you want to have some fun, look up "Gentiles" in the Bible concordance and look how many references in Isaiah alone are "to the Gentiles," showing the universality breaking through even in the period of Isaiah.

Acts 26:24 Festus, who was a heathen and used to all these Roman gods, really said the equivalent of our twentieth century statement, *"Paul, you are out of your skull."*

Acts 26:27 Paul heads over to Agrippa. He says, *"Agrippa, do you believe the prophets? I know that you believe."*

Acts 26:28 Pauls' persuasiveness was such that *"Agrippa"* admits that Paul almost persuaded him to be a Christian.

That's how effective the walk to Emmaus was before those two government officials.

Acts 28:23 [tells] how Paul spends his time in Rome, *"persuading them concerning Jesus,"* How did he persuade them? *"out of the law of Moses, and [out of] the prophets,"* How long? [Voice: "*From morning till evening.*"] Aren't you lucky? [Laughter] That we're about to end. If it were Paul up here, and you know he was long winded [Laughter], but when it comes to the walk to Emmaus, you almost can't help it.

If you threw out all of this, and one way to piece it together is to go through the gospels and see how many verses are quoted, and just like we're doing here, do your own research. It is just so absolutely overwhelming, *"from morning till evening."* But Paul had problems when he talks so long. He had Eutychus and all that. I don't want a Eutychus Eutychus in the audience tonight. So, we're about to wrap it up.

Acts 28:24 says, *some believed, and others didn't believe*. Did that really bother Paul? It may have in his heart, he would have liked everyone to do that. But he preferred the freedom of discovery and the free discussion of the Scriptures.

.

Acts 28:25 Go home and study it yourself and find out if it is really true [*"When they agreed not among themselves, they departed."*]

Acts 28:31 The last view we have of Paul is the last verse which says, *He preached the kingdom of God, teaching those things which concern the Lord Jesus Christ, with all confidence, no man forbidding him.*

In case you think it's just the *book of Acts,* just to give you a little tantalizing tidbit, just slip over into *Romans* [1] and read verse 2 and see the cornerstone of so much Christian preaching, where it had all come from.

Did it start with those two disciples who didn't even recognize Jesus on the road to Emmaus? Are we on that same road to Emmaus? If we are, are our eyes still holden that we really don't recognize who he is? Are we still looking at Jesus in the old way or in the way he told his disciples they had to look at him or they couldn't even build their church correctly? If we want to build church then in our consciousness, we have to have our eyes open. We have to have our hearts burning within us. And we have to have the Scriptures as open as our hearts and understanding every aspect of it. Knowing the Master we're following, enables us to be the disciple with full comprehension, otherwise we don't know him. It's the Scriptures that apparently reveal him. He said that. It was God that revealed the prophetic Scriptures. Therefore, the impact of one of Jesus' statements earlier in one of the gospels, we hope will never fall on anyone of us here, when he turned [to] the audience and said, *"Ye do err, not knowing the scriptures"* [Matthew 22:29].

Thank you very much.

[Applause]

END TAPE 3, SIDE A

CITATION INDEX TO VOLUME 1
The Walk to Emmaus

Compiled by tranScriptures, Columbia, S.C.

(Books are listed alphabetically)

ACTS
(1:13) And when they were come in, they went up into an upper room, where abode both Peter, and James, and John, and Andrew, Philip, and Thomas, Bartholomew, and Matthew, James [the son] of Alphaeus, and Simon Zelotes, and Judas [the brother] of James. **(1:14)** These all continued with one accord in prayer and supplication, with the women, and Mary the mother of Jesus, and with his brethren. **(1:15)** And in those days Peter stood up in the midst of the disciples, and said, (the number of names together were about an hundred and twenty,)

(2:1) And when the day of Pentecost was fully come, they were all with one accord in one place. **(2:22)** Ye men of Israel, hear these words; Jesus of Nazareth, a man approved of God among you by miracles and wonders and signs, which God did by him in the midst of you, as ye yourselves also know: **(2:23)** Him, being delivered by the determinate counsel and foreknowledge of God, ye have taken, and by wicked hands have crucified and slain:**(2:25)** For David speaketh concerning him, I foresaw the Lord always before my face, for he is on my right hand, that I should not be moved:**(2:41)** Then they that gladly received his word were baptized: and the same day there were added [unto them] about three thousand souls.

(3:1) Now Peter and John went up together into the temple at the hour of prayer, [being] the ninth [hour]. **(3:18)** But those things, which God before had shewed by the mouth of all his prophets, that Christ should suffer, he hath so fulfilled. **(3:22)** For Moses truly said unto the fathers, A prophet shall the Lord your God raise up unto you of your brethren, like unto me; him shall ye hear in all things whatsoever he shall say unto you.

(4:4) Howbeit many of them which heard the word believed; and the number of the men was about five thousand. **(4:30)** By stretching forth thine hand to heal; and that signs and wonders may be done by the name of thy holy child Jesus.

(7:37) This is that Moses, which said unto the children of Israel, A prophet shall the Lord your God raise up unto you of your brethren, like unto me; him shall ye hear. **(7:52)** Which of the prophets have not your fathers persecuted? and they have slain them which shewed before of the coming of the Just One; of whom ye have been now the betrayers and murderers:

(8:26) And the angel of the Lord spake unto Philip, saying, Arise, and go toward the south unto the way that goeth down from Jerusalem unto Gaza, which is desert. **(8:27)** And he arose and went: and, behold, a man of Ethiopia, an eunuch of great authority under Candace queen of the Ethiopians, who had the charge of all her treasure, and had come to Jerusalem for to worship, **(8:29)** Then the Spirit said unto Philip, Go near, and join thyself to this chariot. **(8:30)** And Philip ran thither to [him], and heard him read the prophet Esaias, and said, Understandest thou what thou readest? **(8:31)** And he said, How can I, except some man should guide me? And he desired Philip that he would come up and sit with him. **(8:32)** The place of the scripture which he read was this, He was led as a sheep to the slaughter; and like a lamb dumb before his shearer, so opened he not his mouth: **(8:34)** And the eunuch answered Philip, and said, I pray thee, of whom speaketh the prophet this? of himself, or of some other man? **(8:35)** Then Philip opened his mouth, and began at the same scripture, and preached unto him Jesus.

(10:43) To him give all the prophets witness, that through his name whosoever believeth in him shall receive remission of sins. **(10:44)** While Peter yet spake these words, the Holy Ghost fell on all them which heard the word. **(10:45)** And they of the circumcision which believed were astonished, as many as came with Peter, because that on the Gentiles also was poured out the gift of the Holy Ghost.

(13:27) For they that dwell at Jerusalem, and their rulers, because they knew him not, nor yet the voices of the prophets which are read every sabbath day, they have fulfilled [them] in condemning [him]. **(13:29)** And when they had fulfilled all that was written of him, they took [him] down from the tree, and laid [him] in a sepulchre.

(17:1) Now when they had passed through Amphipolis and Apollonia, they came to Thessalonica, where was a synagogue of the Jews: **(17:2)** And Paul, as his manner was, went in unto them, and three sabbath days reasoned with them out of the scriptures, **(17:3)** Opening and alleging, that Christ must needs have suffered, and risen again from the dead; and that this Jesus, whom I preach unto you, is Christ.

(17:11) These were more noble than those in Thessalonica, in that they received the word with all readiness of mind, and searched the scriptures daily, whether those things were so.

(18:28) For he mightily convinced the Jews, [and that] publickly, shewing by the scriptures that Jesus was Christ.

(26:22) Having therefore obtained help of God, I continue unto this day, witnessing both to small and great, saying none other things than those which the prophets and Moses did say should come: **(26:23)** That Christ should suffer, [and] that he should be the first that should rise from the dead, and should shew light unto the people, and to the Gentiles. **(26:24)** And as he thus spake for himself, Festus said with a loud voice, Paul, thou art beside thyself; much learning doth make thee mad. **(26:27)** King Agrippa, believest thou the prophets? I know that thou believest. **(26:28)** Then Agrippa said unto Paul, Almost thou persuadest me to be a Christian.

(28:23) And when they had appointed him a day, there came many to him into [his] lodging; to whom he expounded and testified the kingdom of God, persuading them concerning Jesus, both out of the law of Moses, and [out of] the prophets, from morning till evening. **(28:24)** And some believed the things which were spoken, and some believed not. **(28:25)** And when they agreed not among themselves, they departed, after that Paul had spoken one word, Well spake the Holy Ghost by Esaias the prophet unto our fathers, **(28:31)** Preaching the kingdom of God, and teaching those things which concern the Lord Jesus Christ, with all confidence, no man forbidding him.

AMOS

(3:7) Surely the Lord GOD will do nothing, but he revealeth his secret unto his servants the prophets.

(7:14) Then answered Amos, and said to Amaziah, I [was] no prophet, neither [was] I a prophet's son; but I [was] an herdman, and a gatherer of sycomore fruit: **(7:15)** And the LORD took me as I followed the flock, and the LORD said unto me, Go, prophesy unto my people Israel. **(7:16)** Now therefore hear thou the word of the LORD: Thou sayest, Prophesy not against Israel, and drop not [thy word] against the house of Isaac.

DEUTERONOMY

(18:15) The LORD thy God will raise up unto thee a Prophet from the midst of thee, of thy brethren, like unto me; unto him ye shall hearken; **(18:18)** I will raise them up a Prophet from among their brethren, like unto thee, and will put my words in his mouth; and he shall speak unto them all that I shall command him.

GENESIS

(1:2) And the earth was without form, and void; and darkness [was] upon the face of the deep. And the Spirit of God moved upon the face of the waters.

ISAIAH

(42:7) To open the blind eyes, to bring out the prisoners from the prison, [and] them that sit in darkness out of the prison house.

(53:1) Who hath believed our report? and to whom is the arm of the LORD revealed? **(53:3)** He is despised and rejected of men; a man of sorrows, and acquainted with grief: and we hid as it were [our] faces from him; he was despised, and we esteemed him not. **(53:5)** But he [was] wounded for our transgressions, [he was] bruised for our iniquities: the chastisement of our peace [was] upon him; and with his stripes we are healed. **(53:7)** He was oppressed, and he was afflicted, yet he opened not his mouth: he is brought as a lamb to the slaughter, and as a sheep before her shearers is dumb, so he openeth not his mouth. **(53:8)** He was taken from prison and from judgment: and who shall declare his generation? for he was cut off out of the land of the living: for the transgression of my people was he stricken. **(53:9)**And he made his grave with the wicked, and with the rich in his death; because he had done no violence, neither [was any] deceit in his mouth. **(53:10)** Yet it pleased the LORD to bruise him; he hath put [him] to grief: when thou shalt make his soul an offering for sin, he shall see [his] seed, he shall prolong [his] days, and the pleasure of the LORD shall prosper in his hand.

(61:1) The Spirit of the Lord GOD [is] upon me; because the LORD hath anointed me to preach good tidings unto the meek; he hath sent me to bind up the brokenhearted, to proclaim liberty to the captives, and the opening of the prison to [them that are] bound; **(61:2)** To proclaim the acceptable year of the LORD, and the day of vengeance of our God; to comfort all that mourn;

(61:3) To appoint unto them that mourn in Zion, to give unto them beauty for ashes, the oil of joy for mourning, the garment of praise for the spirit of heaviness; that they might be called trees of righteousness, the planting of the LORD, that he might be glorified.

JOHN
(1:29) The next day John seeth Jesus coming unto him, and saith, Behold the Lamb of God, which taketh away the sin of the world.

(4:25) The woman saith unto him, I know that Messias cometh, which is called Christ: when he is come, he will tell us all things. **(4:26)** Jesus saith unto her, I that speak unto thee am [he].

(5:39) Search the scriptures; for in them ye think ye have eternal life: and they are they which testify of me. **(5:46)** For had ye believed Moses, ye would have believed me: for he wrote of me.

(6:14) Then those men, when they had seen the miracle that Jesus did, said, This is of a truth that prophet that should come into the world. **(6:32)** Then Jesus said unto them, Verily, verily, I say unto you, Moses gave you not that bread from heaven; but my Father giveth you the true bread from heaven.

(7:40) Many of the people therefore, when they heard this saying, said, Of a truth this is the Prophet. **(7:41)** Others said, This is the Christ. But some said, Shall Christ come out of Galilee?

(10:13) The hireling fleeth, because he is an hireling, and careth not for the sheep.

(12:49) For I have not spoken of myself; but the Father which sent me, he gave me a commandment, what I should say, and what I should speak. **(12:50)** And I know that his commandment is life everlasting: whatsoever I speak therefore, even as the Father said unto me, so I speak.

(19:28) After this, Jesus knowing that all things were now accomplished, that the scripture might be fulfilled, saith, I thirst.

(20:1) The first [day] of the week cometh Mary Magdalene early, when it was yet dark, unto the sepulchre, and seeth the stone taken away from the sepulchre. **(20:2)** Then she runneth, and cometh to Simon Peter, and to the other disciple, whom Jesus loved, and saith unto them, They have taken away the Lord out of the sepulchre, and we know not where they have laid him. **(20:3)** Peter therefore went forth, and that other disciple, and came to the sepulchre. **(20:4)** So they ran both together: and the other disciple did outrun Peter, and came first to the sepulchre. **(20:5)** And he stooping down, [and looking in], saw the linen clothes lying; yet went he not in. **(20:6)** Then cometh Simon Peter following him, and went into the sepulchre, and seeth the linen clothes lie, **(20:7)** And the napkin, that was about his head, not lying with the linen clothes, but wrapped together in a place by itself. **(20:8)** Then went in also that other disciple, which came first to the sepulchre, and he saw, and believed. **(20:9** For as yet they knew not the scripture, that he must rise again from the dead. **(20:10)** then the disciples went away again unto their own home. **(20:11)** But Mary stood without at the sepulchre weeping: and as she wept, she stooped down, [and looked] into the sepulchre, **(20:12)** And seeth two angels in white sitting, the one at the head, and the other at the feet, where the body of Jesus had lain. **(20:13)** And they say unto her, Woman, why weepest thou? She saith unto them, Because they have taken away my Lord, and I know not where they have laid him. **(20:14)** And when she had thus said, she turned herself back, and saw Jesus standing, and knew not that it was Jesus. **(20:15)** Jesus saith unto her, Woman, why weepest thou? whom seekest thou? She, supposing him to be the gardener, saith unto him, Sir, if thou have borne him hence, tell me where thou hast laid him, and I will take him away. **(20:16)** Jesus saith unto her, Mary. She turned herself, and saith unto him, Rabboni; which is to say, Master. **(20:17)** Jesus saith unto her, Touch me not; for I am not yet ascended to my Father: but go to my brethren, and say unto them, I ascend unto my Father, and your Father; and [to] my God, and your God. **(20:18)** Mary Magdalene came and told the disciples that she had seen the Lord, and [that] he had spoken these things unto her.

LUKE

(4:17) And there was delivered unto him the book of the prophet Esaias. And when he had opened the book, he found the place where it was written, **(4:18)** The Spirit of the Lord [is] upon me, because he hath anointed me to preach the gospel to the poor; he hath sent me to heal the brokenhearted, to preach deliverance to the captives, and recovering of sight to the blind, to set at liberty them that are bruised,

(4:19) To preach the acceptable year of the Lord. **(4:20)** And he closed the book, and he gave [it] again to the minister, and sat down. And the eyes of all them that were in the synagogue were fastened on him. **(4:21)** And he began to say unto them, This day is this scripture fulfilled in your ears. **(4:29)** And rose up, and thrust him out of the city, and led him unto the brow of the hill whereon their city was built, that they might cast him down headlong. **(4:30)** But he passing through the midst of them went his way, **(4:41)** And devils also came out of many, crying out, and saying, Thou art Christ the Son of God. And he rebuking [them] suffered them not to speak: for they knew that he was Christ.

(8:28) When he saw Jesus, he cried out, and fell down before him, and with a loud voice said, What have I to do with thee, Jesus, [thou]

Son of God most high? I beseech thee, torment me not.

(23:46) And when Jesus had cried with a loud voice, he said, Father, into thy hands I commend my spirit: and having said thus, he gave up the ghost.

(24:10) It was Mary Magdalene, and Joanna, and Mary [the mother] of James, and other [women that were] with them, which told these things unto the apostles. **(24:11)** And their words seemed to them as idle tales, and they believed them not. **(24:13)** And, behold, two of them went that same day to a village called Emmaus, which was from Jerusalem [about] threescore furlongs. **(24:17)** And he said unto them, What manner of communications [are] these that ye have one to another, as ye walk, and are sad? **(24:18)** And the one of them, whose name was Cleopas, answering said unto him, Art thou only a stranger in Jerusalem, and hast not known the things which are come to pass there in these days? **(24:19)** And he said unto them, What things? And they said unto him, Concerning Jesus of Nazareth, which was a prophet mighty in deed and word before God and all the people: **(24:21)** But we trusted that it had been he which should have redeemed Israel: and beside all this, to day is the third day since these things were done. **(24:22)** Yea, and certain women also of our company made us astonished, which were early at the sepulchre; **(24:23)** And when they found not his body, they came, saying, that they had also seen a vision of angels, which said that he was alive. **(24:24)** And certain of them which were with us went to the sepulchre, and found [it] even so as the women had said: but him they saw not. **(24:25)** Then he said unto them, O fools, and slow of heart to believe all that the prophets have spoken: **(24:26)** Ought not Christ to have suffered these things, and to enter into his glory?

(24:27) And beginning at Moses and all the prophets, he expounded unto them in all the scriptures the things concerning himself. **(24:29)** But they constrained him, saying, Abide with us: for it is toward evening, and the day is far spent. And he went in to tarry with them. **(24:31)** And their eyes were opened, and they knew him; and he vanished out of their sight. **(24:32)** And they said one to another, Did not our heart burn within us, while he talked with us by the way, and while he opened to us the scriptures? **(24:33)** And they rose up the same hour, and returned to Jerusalem, and found the eleven gathered together, and them that were with them, **(24:34)** Saying, The Lord is risen indeed, and hath appeared to Simon. **(24:35)** And they told what things [were done] in the way, and how he was known of them in breaking of bread. **(24:30)** Behold my hands and my feet, that it is I myself: handle me, and see; for a spirit hath not flesh and bones, as ye see me have. **(24:39)** Behold my hands and my feet, that it is I myself: handle me, and see; for a spirit hath not flesh and bones, as ye see me have. **(24:41)** And while they yet believed not for joy, and wondered, he said unto them, Have ye here any meat? **(24:42)** And they gave him a piece of a broiled fish, and of an honeycomb. **(24:43)** And he took [it], and did eat before them. **(24:44)** And he said unto them, These [are] the words which I spake unto you, while I was yet with you, that all things must be fulfilled, which were written in the law of Moses, and [in] the prophets, and [in] the psalms, concerning me. **(24:45)** Then opened he their understanding, that they might understand the scriptures, **(24:46)** And said unto them, Thus it is written, and thus it behoved Christ to suffer, and to rise from the dead the third day:

MARK
(1:18) And straightway they forsook their nets, and followed him.

(3:11) And unclean spirits, when they saw him, fell down before him, and cried, saying, Thou art the Son of God.

(16:12) After that he appeared in another form unto two of them, as they walked, and went into the country.

MATTHEW
(8:29) And, behold, they cried out, saying, What have we to do with thee, Jesus, thou Son of God? art thou come hither to torment us before the time?

(16:12) After that he appeared in another form unto two of them, as they walked, and went into the country. **(16:16)** And Simon Peter answered and said, Thou art the Christ, the Son of the living God. **(16:17)** And Jesus answered and said unto him, Blessed art thou, Simon Barjona: for flesh and blood hath not revealed [it] unto thee, but my Father which is in heaven. **(16:18)** And I say also unto thee, That thou art Peter, and upon this rock I will build my church; and the gates of hell shall not prevail against it. **(16:19)** And I will give unto thee the keys of the kingdom of heaven: and whatsoever thou shalt bind on earth shall be bound in heaven: and whatsoever thou shalt loose on earth shall be loosed in heaven. **(16:21)** From that time forth began Jesus to shew unto his disciples, how that he must go unto Jerusalem, and suffer many things of the elders and chief priests and scribes, and be killed, and be raised again the third day. **(16:22)** Then Peter took him, and began to rebuke him, saying, Be it far from thee, Lord: this shall not be unto thee. **(16:23)** But he turned, and said unto Peter, Get thee behind me, Satan: thou art an offence unto me: for thou savourest not the things that be of God, but those that be of men.

(22:29) Jesus answered and said unto them, Ye do err, not knowing the scriptures, nor the power of God.

(27:32) And as they came out, they found a man of Cyrene, Simon by name: him they compelled to bear his cross.**(27:33)** And when they were come unto a place called Golgotha, that is to say, a place of a skull, **(27:34)** They gave him vinegar to drink mingled with gall: and when he had tasted [thereof], he would not drink. **(27:39)** And they that passed by reviled him, wagging their heads, **(27:43)** He trusted in God; let him deliver him now, if he will have him: for he said, I am the Son of God. **(27:46)** Matthew 27:46 And about the ninth hour Jesus cried with a loud voice, saying, Eli, Eli, lama sabachthani? that is to say, My God, my God, why hast thou forsaken me? **(27:57)** When the even was come, there came a rich man of Arimathaea, named Joseph, who also himself was Jesus' disciple:

(28:12) And when they were assembled with the elders, and had taken counsel, they gave large money unto the soldiers, **(28:13)** Saying, Say ye, His disciples came by night, and stole him [away] while we slept.

2 PETER

(1:16) For we have not followed cunningly devised fables, when we made known unto you the power and coming of our Lord Jesus Christ, but were eyewitnesses of his majesty. **(1:19)** We have also a more sure word of prophecy; whereunto ye do well that ye take heed, as unto a light that shineth in a dark place, until the day dawn, and the day star arise in your hearts: **(1:20)** Knowing this first, that no prophecy of the scripture is of any private interpretation. **(1:21)** For the prophecy came not in old time by the will of man: but holy men of God spake [as they were] moved by the Holy Ghost.

PSALMS

(22:1) My God, my God, why hast thou forsaken me? [why art thou so] far from helping me, [and from] the words of my roaring? **(22:7)** All they that see me laugh me to scorn: they shoot out the lip, they shake the head, [saying], **(22:8)** He trusted on the LORD [that] he would deliver him: let him deliver him, seeing he delighted in him. **(22:13)** They gaped upon me [with] their mouths, [as] a ravening and a roaring lion. **(22:14)** I am poured out like water, and all my bones are out of joint: my heart is like wax; it is melted in the midst of my bowels. **(22:15)** My strength is dried up like a potsherd; and my tongue cleaveth to my jaws; and thou hast brought me into the dust of death.**(22:16)** For dogs have compassed me: the assembly of the wicked have inclosed me: they pierced my hands and my feet.

(22:18) They part my garments among them, and cast lots upon my vesture.

(31:5) Into thine hand I commit my spirit: thou hast redeemed me, O LORD God of truth.

(69:21) They gave me also gall for my meat; and in my thirst they gave me vinegar to drink.

***

WORD INDEX TO VOLUME 1
The Walk to Emmaus

Word Index compiled by tranScriptures of Columbia, S.C.

Bold font - Volume number; Regular font - Page number
A.D. - *anno domini*; C.E.- Common Era
B.C. - Before Christ; B.C.E. - Before Common Era
NT - New Tstament; OT - Old Testament
c. - about; e.g. - for example; i.e. - that is

Church, the Christian: 120 men and women attended the first meeting when Christ Jesus, its Founder, spoke and ate with them; as on the road to Emmaus, he opened the Scriptural prophecy to them, starting again with Moses but then going into the Psalms, emphasizing the suffering Christ **1:**16,17; The *Book of Acts* reports on the primitive C's activity seven weeks (50 days) after Passover and one week after Jesus has ascended, it's the day of Pentecost. Peter delivers the first free lecture sponsored by the First Church of Christ, Jerusalem **1**:28. 3000 new members are taken in as a result **1**:28; Peter together with John deliver a second lecture which, starting with Moses, brings what the earlier prophets had to say about the Messiah as Jesus had done on the road to Emmaus earlier. A major portion of the early preaching was of this sort, an examination of the Scriptures together. The result, 5000 new members counting only the men. Also, Understanding of the Bible enabled healing to occur **1:**29,30. Stephen, the first intellect of the early C, was also chosen to preach to the Jews which was controversial and brought him before the Sanhedrin where he defended himself and was stoned for it, thereby being the first martyr of the primitive church. **1**:30 Philip in Caesarea receives an angel message from God telling him to get to Gaza. There a wealthy Gentile eunuch, an Ethiopian on his chariot is reading Isaiah 53's prophecies about Jesus. The Ethiopian asks Philip to join him in the chariot and to tell him about Jesus. Philip introduces the man to Jesus and his role. After which the Ethiopian asks Philip to baptize him then and there. This apparently is the first member of the black race to become a Christian. **1:**31; Suddeny we find that the Holy Ghost comes to the Gentiles much to the disgruntlment of the Jewish Christians. The results are clear, Christianity is meant to be a universal religion **1:**31; After his road to Damascus experience when Saul became Paul, his preaching and travels often *"brought the whole city together to hear the word of God."* **1:**32; Paul then moved into Europe preaching and reasoning out of the Scriptures. Then came Appolos *"mightily convincing the Jews and showing by the Scriptures that Jesus was the Christ."* **1:**33;

Cleopas: one of the two obscure disciples who were on the walk to Emmaus **1:**5;

Emmaus: a village in Palestine, 3 furlongs, 660 yards, three-eighths of a mile from Jerusalem **1:**3. [In 1748 Moravian settlers in Lehigh County, eastern Pennsylvania, in the foothills of the

Lehigh mountains, established a *Gemeindeort* (Congregation Village), previously known by the Indian name of Maguntchi ("place of bears") and Salzburg. In1761 it was named Emmaus after the biblical village in Palestine, apparently the first place outside of the original village to be so named (Encyclopaedia Britannica, 15th Edition, p. 878, Vol. III, Micropaedia, 1976)]

Eusebius: Bishop of Caesarea (313-339 AD), most important 4th century historian of Christian church who wrote that the other disciple on the road to Emmaus was named Simon, but not Simon Peter **1:**5;

Josephus, Flavius: (AD 37- after 93) Jewish, Pharisee, priest, historian and general **1**:4;

Luke: a two-volume work; the second volume is the *Book of Acts* **1**:15;

Messiah: 1st century Jews' expectation of the M: a king, a ruler, a warrior, a political leader to free Jews from the yoke of any oppressor, who currently was a Roman **1:**8; Prior to 1st Century AD there was no writing about a Messiah who would suffer **1**:16;

SYMBOLS

Angels - archangel, chief angel, Michael, and his angels fought against the dragon in Revelation also Jude where archangel Michael disputed with the devil about the body of Moses; **1:**3 a vision of angels by the women who viewed Jesus' empty tomb **1:**9;

Discovery: the only genuine method of education; religion until recently forgot about discovery and dealt mainly with dogma; the word "Wow!" signifies discovery, i.e., something which is already within consciousness has awakened **1:**3;

Emmaus, walk to - The spark that eventually caught flame in Christianity, spreading throughout the known globe. It was an event of major importance:**1:**3;

Healing - one of two major themes in the Bible that the human mind doesn't comprehend because it can not do either one **1**:10;

Heart, the burning - the feeling the two disciples had after Jesus had opened the Scriptures to them on the road to Emmaus [to this transcriber it is the "Wow" discovery feeling; [see Discovery above.] **1:**15;

It is written - OT prophecy. Jesus' basic rationale for his own life and works which he explained to the two disciples on the Walk to Emmaus when he went through the Scriptures with them **1:**11-16;

Lamb - symbol of John the Baptist's concept of the Son of God.**1:**27,28;

Prophets/prophecy - which hundreds of years before Jesus' advent on earth predicted his arrival; to Jesus P explained currrent events in the light of documents already hundred of years old **1**:9; P is one of two major themes in the Bible that the human mind doesn't comprehend because it cannot do either one; the first P Jesus mentions is "that Christ should suffer"; the speaker mentions the cross and crown in P; since the disciples had expected to see the Messiah as a political leader and king, apparently they had seen only the crown; they needed a Bible lesson concerning himself; on the road to Emmaus Jesus starts at Moses and goes through all the Ps **1:**10 P to the prophet is like a blueprint to an engineer which he could consult to understand the out come of his work; therefore, studying P tells us when to expect its fulfillment **1:**11; Amos (750 BC) was the first literate prophet; Peter much later (95 AD) followed Jesus and said, *"We haven't followed fables; we were eyewitnesses; we also have a more sure word, prophecy, which is not opinion, and it's not private, but holy men of God spoke, moved by the Holy Ghost,"* **1:**13 Later Jesus to his disciples in commending Peter for affirming *"You are the Christ,"* he says, *"Flesh and blood hath not revealed it unto you, but my Father."* **1:**18;

OT Prophecy and NT Fulfillment: Jesus' commandment (John 5:39):*"Search the Scriptures; they are they which speak of me."* **1**:19-29**;**

Example 1: Prophecy of Moses and God in Deuteronomy 18:15, 18 written c.650 B.C. is fulfilled by events in John 6:14 and John 7:40,41, John 12:49,50 written c. 90-100 A.D.**1:**19-22;

Example 2: Prophecy in Psalm 22:1 written

between 1000-165 B.C.) is fulfilled by events on Matthew 27:46 written c.80 or 85 A.D.) **1:**22-24

Example 3: Prophecy in Psalm 22:7,8,13 written between 1000-165 B.C.) Is fulfilled in Matthew 27:39,43 written c. 80 or 85 A.D.)**1:**22-24;

Example 4: Prophecy in Psalm 22:18, written c. 1000-165 B.C.) is fulfilled in Matthew 27::35 written c.80 or 85 A.D. **1:**24;

Example 5: Prophecy in Psalm 69:21 written c. 1000-165 B.C. is fulfilled in Matthew 27:34 written c.80 or 85 A.D.) **1**:24;

Example 6: Prophecy in Psalm 22:14 written between c. 1000-165 A.D.is fulfilled in John 19:34 written between 90-100 A.D **1:**23-25;

Example 7: Isaiah 53:3,5,7,8,9 written between 742-300 B.C. is alluded to in the New Testament **1:**25,27

Example 8: When Jesus went to his hometown synagogue, to honor his visit they handed him the scroll of Isaiah to read which opened to Chapter 61, Verses :1,2, and 3, to wit,*"The Spirit of the Lord God is upon me; because the Lord hath anointed me to preach, to bind up, to proclaim liberty, to comfort, to appoint, to give unto them beauty."* All items in the accepted role of the Messiah. On returning to his seat he announced, *"This day is this Scripture fulfilled in your ears."* For that they tried to throw him off a cliff but he *"walked through the midst of them."* From then on he did not announce his role publicly, but protected it. Occasionally he would announce it privately as when he met the Samaritan woman at the well who said to him, "We know that the Messiah is coming. Jesus responded with, *"I that speak unto thee am he."* **1:**27;

Woman's first-century rights: W were second class citizens, i.e., they were not permitted to bear witness in court; Jesus ignored customs of his day and regarded W as God regarded them **1**:9

***

Passover Lamb Photograph by Gordon N. Converse

SONG OF THE LAMB
Volume 9

by B. Cobbey Crisler

CONTENTS

Notes: The transcript was produced from a tape of an unscripted lecture delivered extempore. Earlier tape versions may differ. Biblical quotations and Hebrew, Greek, Latin, French and German words in the commentary are italicized. Brackets enclose additions by the original Bible translators and the transcriber: such as book names, chapter and verse numbers which the speaker mentioned, but did not cite, some audience comments or questions, and an occasional word or footnote. Some spoken words which appeared to be unnecessary for the reader, such as "and, but, so, turn to, well," etc, were deleted. The Citation Index contains the full text of all King James Bible citations which the speaker cited or mentioned. The purpose of the transcript is to preserve the speaker's words verbatim.

***

BEGIN TAPE 1, SIDE A

When I first arrived, a couple of young men showed up about the same time. They had a Bible in one hand and a frisbee in the other. I had wondered what kind of advanced publicity had gone out. But I did find some biblical authority for it, so before they began to play with the frisbees, I turned to Nehemiah [4:17]. It said, *They which builded on the wall, and they that bare burdens, with those that laded, [every one] with one of his hands wrought in the work, and with the other [hand] held a frisbee.* [Laughter] He seemed to accept that as Scriptural authority, as if he needed it, and out they went to play frisbee. In fact, they were having such a good time, that a half hour before the talk was to begin, he came up to me and said, "How long till we start listening?" [Laughter] It's a good question. Sometimes God asks that question. One gets the idea that one of the main themes of the Bible is, "When will we start listening?"

The Song of the Lamb may be in the process of being sung. Are we hearing it? Where are we supposed to hear it? What is it? And what practical application does it have to us? [Those are] some of the things we're going to investigate today.

But let's see where we got the whole idea of the title, **Song of the Lamb.** It's in the *Book of Revelation*. When you get into the *Book of Revelation*, what do you feel like? Do you get into it often? [Chuckles] You're surrounded by imagery and symbols. Once we're challenged with that kind of search and research, we often just put the Book aside. But the Book itself is a kind of key to the Scriptures which have preceded it. You don't run into too many symbols that have not been used before in the Bible, thus proving out what the Bible sets as its own standard when it states [in Matthew 18:16], *"In the mouth of two or three witnesses shall every word be established,"* so that if it has been said or referred to once in the Bible, here is your second witness, or maybe your third witness to the particular point.

Revelation 15:2. Notice in the midst of this imagery what we are being told, *"And I saw as it were a sea of glass..."* No matter where we go in the natural world we haven't yet come up with *"a sea of glass..."* So, it must be symbolic of something. It's not just glass. What else is happening? It's *"mingled with fire."* What happens to *"glass mingled with fire?"* [Voice: "It melts."] That's right. Even the glass itself is going through some kind of change. Then it says, those *"that had gotten the victory over"* one, two, three, four things: *"the beast," "his image," "his mark, [and] the number of his name."* Does that still leave us somewhat up in the air as far as what that meaning is concerned? Remember, revelation is nothing that I can tell you or you can tell me. Revelation will always be exactly what that title says it is. It is revelation. Therefore, it comes *via* revelation. You never get it dogmatically. Common sense can be applied, however, because common sense, or logic, and revelation, should coincide.

When we're talking about the beast as something that needs to be overcome, that we need to get a victory over, what does that suggest itself? What is it? Beast is another name for animal. What basically keeps you and me as limited as we seem to be? What kingdom do we think we belong to? The animal kingdom. All our textbooks in school inform us of that fact. When we look in the mirror every morning, what stares back at us? A member of the animal kingdom, which we try to groom to the best of our ability. [Laughter] What we can't take care of, we forget, and go on about our business, and let others looking at us suffer.

But, you will notice that it's not only *"the beast"* that, whoever we're referring to on this *"sea of glass,"* not only *"the beast"* that we've got *"the victory over,"* but the image of *"the beast."* Is that what we're looking at in the mirror every day? Do we constantly face the image of "the animal"? Is it in the forefront of your thinking and mine, and how often in a given day ?

Then, we find *"over his mark."* That's an interesting thing, *"mark."* What do you think that might refer to? "The mark of the beast" has been referred to so often. It's like a signature. It was an identitymark, the identity of the animal, worn in effect by you and me. That was the way that often slaves were identified with their master, which is an interesting parallel. Where slaves, who had nothing they could call their own, and were entirely dominated, by owner possessed, had to display such a mark.

It's interesting in the *book of Revelation* we have always a contrast. In the Bible, not just the *book of Revelation*, we have the problem and the solution. Just to give you an example. If the problem was Babel [Genesis 11:9], what was the specific solution given in the Bible for that particular problem? What was the problem at Babel? [Voice: "Confusion."] No one could understand anyone. We don't relate to that? Babel is very ancient indeed! But there is a Biblical solution for Babel. Do you remember what it was? [Voice: "Pentecost."] Pentecost [Acts 2:1. Do you remember what happened at Pentecost? [Voice: "Everybody understood."] Everyone understood. Guess what? Language was no longer a barrier. Not even language could stand in the way of God's communicating to man and man with each other, meeting in that understanding of God.

There is one example. You in your own research in the Scriptures might find other problems and solutions matched in that way.

We have [another] one. If the "mark of the beast" is the problem, what do you think the solution would be?

Revelation 14:1. Notice there's a whole different thing there, isn't there? The *"Father's name written in the forehead."* If that were literal, and you and I had our heavenly Father's name written on our forehead, what would be the first thing anyone meeting us at any given moment of any given day would see? The Father's name. We are identified with the Father. That stands in marked contrast to the mark-of-the-beast. They are two different Greek words. The one that is used for the mark-of-the-beast is the Greek word *charagma.* One of the lexicons said that word can describe a serpent's sting. Imagine the mark-of-the-beast as a serpent's sting. But the other word, the seal-of-God in the foreheads, can mean evidence or proof of God. Nothing will make it's mark or impression on us unless it first reaches where? Our thought, and then impressed further in our hearts and in our lives. The important impression, is not a surface one, but what our lives actually say to ourselves and to others, and even more importantly, to God.

Back in Chapter 15:2 when we see there is a *"sea of glass mingled with fire"* and *"them that had gotten the victory over"* anything connected with the animal, whether it's the bodily image of animalism, whether it is the mark or identity with the animal kingdom, or whether it's *"the number of his name,"* the vast quantity that seem to walk around claiming such kinship to the animal, we find that there is a group here referred to that *"stand on that sea of glass, having the harps of God."*

"Standing on the sea of glass." "A sea of glass," if it were made of glass, what could you do? You could see right through it. Yet what is the most mysterious part of nature today, the thing we probably least understand is the sea, that murky, always moving, unpredictable, to-and-fro motion of the sea. Where do evolutionists tell us you and I came from? There we have the most mysterious aspect of our own origin, covered up, so to speak, in the murky depths of the sea symbolically.

Notice, however, for these who are standing on this sea, it is no longer murky; it is no longer a mystery; it is no longer moving unpredictably. They have a sense of dominion over it, standing on it, and seeing through it.

There's no way you and I can even appreciate where the individual discussed in Chapter 15 was in thought unless we are on the way to perhaps achieving that same kind of goal. Is it possible? Is it impractical?

Is it really something that you and I can do in our daily life, especially with all the pressures and temptations of today? What is the clue the Scripture gives us? It tells us something about what these individuals were knowing, thinking, doing, or living actively that enabled them to cut or sever the animal connection, thus freeing their own origins to where Jesus himself indicated man originated, basing his own revelation of this fact on the Scriptural concept of man, having dominion given to him by God.

[Revelation 15]:3. We find they sing two songs: one is *"the song of Moses"* and the other is *"the song of the Lamb."* Those two songs, whatever they might be, sound like they hold the clue to victory, some hint of the way you and I can proceed in our own lives to sever this animal connection that isn't doing many of us much good any way.

One of the Biblical statements [1 Corinthians 15:22] gives us a choice, *"As in Adam"* what happens? *"All die."* There's your animal connection. But *"even so in Christ shall all be made alive."*

What does *"Lamb"* mean? What is the symbol of *"Lamb"* used in the *book of Revelation?* Does it refer to anything more particular? Who is *"the Lamb"?* It's actually used for a description of Jesus. Therefore, we are automatically turned to whatever his example might be.

Song of Moses and *Song of the Lamb.* Let's see if logic might help us out in some way. If a visitor from Mars arrived and told you that he only had about two minutes to spend with you, but would like very much to know in as brief a summary as possible what the essence, and therefore, the greatest impact of Moses' teachings was, and the same as far as Jesus is concerned. You probably would tell him the Commandments and the Beatitudes.

Haven't Christians linked those two for centuries, and why? Because they sound good? Do they work? [Voice: "Yes."] Believe it or not, that's one of the great problems in theology today. We'll go into that. But, can we suggest for a moment, then, those that had been able to overcome all links to the animal, therefore all limitations that membership in the animal kingdom brings, if they were able to overcome that through the application of *"the Song of Moses"* and *"the Song of the Lamb,"* can we suggest that, perhaps, what is being discussed here, basically, is the Commandments and the Beatitudes?

Where usually is a song? Where do we carry it? We carry it in our heart, don't we? *"The Song of the Lamb."* What was closest to Jesus' heart? What was closest to his thinking? If we had to throw everything else away in the Bible, and if we could reserve the Commandments and the

Beatitudes, do you think we would have the essence of the Biblical teaching still? Even in that brief form? Then what we, perhaps, might regard as *the Song of Moses* is just that, a summary of God's will for man as revealed to Moses. The essence of Moses' teaching is the Commandments. And *the Song of the Lamb,* the essence of Jesus' teaching, the Beatitudes and the Sermon on the Mount.

Suppose God's seal has stamped your individuality and mine uniquely. Still, in studying that seal of our individuality, should we see within it all the aspects of the Sermon on the Mount? Does the Sermon on the Mount identify you and me with God? Do you remember in II Timothy [2:19] when the seal of God is discussed, the author tells us, *"The foundation of God standeth sure, having this seal, The Lord knoweth them that are his."* There must be some kind of identification factor then. Secondly, *"Everyone that nameth the name of Christ depart from iniquity."*

God knows who we are, then, in *"the seal of God."* That's what it means. But also, our response to God is a total commitment to such a seal, and the dwindling away to absolute nothingness of iniquity [by] those who name the name of Christ.

When you read the gospels, how many of you could actually paint a portrait of Jesus after you finished reading them? Could any of us really paint a personal portrait of Jesus? Do you know what time he got up in the morning? Do you know the length of his hair, the color of his eyes, his height, whether he sang tenor, baritone, or bass? Why wouldn't the biographers give us this information? [Voice: "It wasn't important."] That's an interesting response. If it was not important, how was such information conveyed to those who eventually wrote the gospel and passed the tradition of the gospel down before it even became written. Who must have left the impression that such details were not important? Do you think Jesus himself is influencing the very environment of the gospel, and that this brings us very close indeed to the way Jesus thought? Then maybe you and I could rework our own concept of biography in the highest sense? Think of how uplifted one is in reading the gospels. Is it possible that the Sermon on the Mount itself is the best portrait of Jesus one could have? Where we meet him not personally, but right where he was, and is, and ever will be. Because, you remember that one of the descriptions in Hebrews [13:8], we're given a description of Jesus, *"Jesus Christ the same yesterday, and today, and forever."* There's no alteration, then, in aspect.

Listen to what many Christian churches have thought about the Sermon on the Mount. Could this actually be the "Song of the Lamb" if taken in this context? Scholars searching the Sermon on the Mount have come up with point 1, they call it "perfectionist legalism." The second point, that the Sermon on the Mount presents "impossible ideals." The third point, that since Jesus must have known all of this, that it was impossible, that it must have been what Albert Schweitzer [1875-1965] calls an "interim ethic." That Jesus foresaw a disaster or crisis for mankind and we'd better hurry up and try to reach that ideal in a hurry. Those are three concepts about the Sermon on the Mount.

Almost anything you pick up in a scholarly way about Matthew 5 through Matthew 7 will give you an indication of that. That doesn't help us out very much, does it? It doesn't tell us that the Song of the Lamb is something attainable. Do you know what some theologians actually have preached to their congregations as a result? That Jesus was trying to get across to people in the Sermon on the Mount that you and I are doomed to failure anyway and must rely then on the salvation of the cross to make it.

As in all theories, if they aren't simply motivated by human preconceptions and denominational outlining, there is a hint of fact or truth. Certainly, the Sermon on the Mount none of us either individually or collectively are exemplifying. As of this moment we haven't quite made it as far as exemplifying that Sermon on the Mount. Does that mean it's impossible? Has any one done it? Has Jesus actually lived what he's preaching here? Has he practiced? If so, what is his relationship to humanity? What's he told you and me what he could do? In fact, we're supposed to do it. We're supposed to follow him. If he is "the way", that implies that we're supposed to be on it and following him. It would not be very intelligent then to assume that Jesus was inviting us to follow where it was impossible to go, inviting us to sing his song, the Song of the Lamb, and have that song in our hearts, and the seal of our father in our foreheads unless it could be done.

Let's see what is so impracticable about this, if it is.

[Matthew] Chapter 5:1 *"He went up into a mountain:"* This does not necessarily mean a geographical spot because the gospel of Luke [Chapter 6] tells us about this same sermon, doesn't give it in the same words, but everything that is in Luke's sermon is in Matthew's sermon with one or two exceptions.

[Luke 6:12]. Luke says that *"Jesus spent the night before the sermon on the mount in prayer"*

[Luke 6:17] *"And then came down to the plain to deliver the message."* So, from what we gather in the gospels it isn't the place that counts. As a matter of fact, it, again, may be more symbolic. Where would Jesus have been, both in his preparatory phase and in his delivery phase at that altitude that we would symbolize as a mountain?

[Matthew 5:1.] It says that *"when he was set,"* and not until then, *"his disciples came unto him."* That word disciple bears directly on your relationship and mine if we're going to be able to sing the Song of the Lamb. This message is for the disciple.

Are we disciples? We'd better think for some time before we respond, because if we say "Yes," Jesus has all sorts of prerequisites for disciples. And if you go through the gospels, especially the one from the beloved-disciple, John, and underline the identification aspects, discipleship, that Jesus gives, Wow! We'll all wonder where actually we are in terms of that definition. We may be defining it for ourselves, rather than taking Jesus' definition of it. For one thing, you know the word disciple is *mathētēs* in Greek, the root of our word mathematics.

END TAPE 1, SIDE A

BEGIN TAPE 1, SIDE B

Just think of the concept of disciples as mathematicians in a very early basic sense. Is there any more disciplined course in the school curriculum than mathematics? Did he expect his disciples to be mathematical in their approach to living? Is there any relationship between music and mathematics? Music provides the grandeur for the discipline of mathematics. And the Song of the Lamb then would have to have some kind of relationship to mathematics. We find that the word Jesus uses here for disciples relates to learners who constantly practice what they learn. That's your basic meaning for it. A lexicographer describes the Song of the Lamb and the Song of Moses in these words. It's in <u>Thayer's Lexicon</u>, "It is the song which Moses and Christ taught them to sing."

[Matthew] 5:2. Isn't it interesting that we find, *"He opened his mouth, and taught them, saying."* The Song of the Lamb, then, isn't an automatic thing is it? It's not a melody that we hear once and necessarily makes an impression. What must we do with it? We have to learn it, don't we? We have to learn the song.

[Matthew] 5:3-12. Let's take the Beatitudes going from Verse 3 through Verse 12 and just look at them as a group for the moment.

(5:3) Blessed [are] the poor in spirit: for theirs is the kingdom of heaven.

(5:4) Blessed [are] they that mourn: for they shall be comforted.
(5:5) Blessed [are] the meek: for they shall inherit the earth.
(5:6) Blessed [are] they which do hunger and thirst after righteousness: for they shall be filled.
(5:7) Blessed [are] the merciful: for they shall obtain mercy.
(5:8) Blessed [are] the pure in heart: for they shall see God.
(5:9) Blessed [are] the peacemakers: for they shall be called the children of God.
(5:10) Blessed [are] they which are persecuted for righteousness' sake: for theirs is the kingdom of heaven.
(5:11) Blessed are ye, when [men] shall revile you, and persecute [you], And shall say all manner of evil against you falsely, for my sake.
(5:12) Rejoice, and be exceeding glad: for great [is] your reward in heaven: for so persecuted they the prophets which were before you.

Do you see the word "blessed"? That isn't really the meaning of the Greek word [*makariŏs*] used there. It is **"happy."** Much closer to the definition is **"happy."** How many of us every single day are looking for **happiness**? In some way we want to be **happy**. We take various, and sometimes devious, routes to arrive at this objective, in many cases never arriving, because we've gone the wrong way.

Now Jesus said he is the way [John 14:6]. Any Master, who himself has been able to overcome all links to this limiting animal kingdom, severs them completely. Any Master, with the great love of Jesus, would turn around and tell humanity that they can make it as well. If this is Jesus' intention, we have Verses 3 to 11 all beginning with the word **"Happy."** Here is our objective, yet it certainly sounds strange.

"Happy are the poor in spirit, those who mourn, those who are meek, merciful, pure in heart, peacemakers, and those who are persecuted." This is not our normal definition of "the happy set." [Laughter] Is Jesus trying to tell us something? That there is a certain state of mind that might not appear at all on the surface, or while we're living through it, that has any relationship to happiness. But, we are right there on the verge of it, if we would comprehend something.

For instance, *"poor in spirit."* [Verse 3] You know how Goodspeed translates that? "those who feel their spiritual need." If you read through these specific beatitudes, you will notice that every state of mind is a receptive one. Without receptivity you and I are never going to be tuned into any message, let alone Jesus' message. Are we ready to get out of the state of lack, or of grief, or of being stepped all over, or not knowing where our next meal is coming from? These are some of the implications behind the beatitudes. And how often do you and I hunger and thirst, for instance, at least three times a day and sometimes in between meals, right? [Laughter]

If Jesus is actually using that as something that needs to be translated from our own human experience into something higher, how often should we be hungering and thirsting after righteousness? [Voice: "All day."] At least three times a day, right? Do you remember that's how often Daniel turned in prayer. So, we do have that as an example.

"The pure in heart" [Verse 8] only see God. Do you think we can make these standards? Can we actually sing the Song of the Lamb? To be *"pure in heart,"* is that possible? Is it gonna happen over night? Are we working on it? Notice how pollution is one of the major problems today. That's external pollution. What is happening to our pollution within? Where did Jesus say the kingdom of heaven is? Within. How much of it is within us now in our own daily experience?

Do the Beatitudes give us the very power that will enable us, in conjunction with the Commandments, to stand on that *"sea of glass"* [Revelation 15:2] and finally get the dominion, which God has indicated, since the first chapter of Genesis, is a divine right of man.

We talk a great deal about the human rights of man today. Look how little progress we have made in the human rights of man. Think of the divine rights of man. If dominion is a divine right of man,-- and notice it isn't domination that is a divine right of man,-- if dominion is a divine right, who is exercising that divine right for himself or herself? Did Jesus?

Did anyone deserve more to be referred to as "Master" than Jesus? After looking at his entire career in life, did anything master him? It looked like it did for a while. What was Jesus doing for three days in that tomb? [Voice: "Making sure he wasn't sick."] That's right. Wondering whether he was dominated at last? Do you think discouragement might have crept into that tomb? Do you remember in Gethsemane he met that ultimate discouragement through the entire weight of his thought? Is that being pure in heart? Because it's unmixed when you're pure. If thought is unmixed, it's pure, if it's totally committed.

Matthew 6:22. Remember in the Sermon on the Mount what [Jesus] tells you and [me] our outlook should be. How should we look at things? This is one of the greatest, then, disciplines of thought ever constructed and passed along to humanity. It tells us how to look at things. *"The light of the body is the eye: if therefore thine eye be single, thy whole body shall be full of light."* It tells us how to give, how to pray, how to fast, or refuse to give any presence any longer, in thought, to those things which are actually keeping us linked to the animal kingdom.

It tells us even how to communicate, how much silence would occur in this world if we obeyed Chapter 5, Verse 37, *"let your communication be, Yes or No."* Sounds like a good title for a book, *No and Yes.*[Laughter] That may be the very biblical point behind that title, when to say "No" and when to say "Yes" gives you and me access to the greatest power "on earth as in heaven." If we actually know and can follow through on that awareness of when to say "Yes" and when to say "No." The Sermon on the Mount is filled with such practical concepts.

There is no way Jesus must have expected us to immediately exemplify and embody that Song of the Lamb because in Revelation it states that the Song of the Lamb has to be learned. We must learn it. On earth that takes time. It takes effort. It takes our willingness to even want to delve into such a sermon and make it our lifestyle instead of theory.

[Mattthew] 5:48. In fact, Jesus said, "Be ye therefore perfect." Did he end it there? He relates perfection to the model that isn't even in Jesus himself, is it? The model is God. Our perfection, then, comes from God. It's God's song, in a way, then, that we're singing, but revealed through the Lamb's example on earth.

Matthew 6:22 That light of the body, the only way physically that you and I seem to manifest an outward sense of light is through the eye physically. Do you think that Jesus is referring strictly to the physical eye when he states that there's one thing we'd better be very clear about, that our eye has to be single. What does he mean by that? Isn't it interesting that we have two eyes but they operate together? It does depend on the focus.

If that focus is off, if there is double vision, are we single-minded? Do you remember what James tells us double-mindedness is? It's the very devil itself that James [4:7.8; 1:8] indicates is double-mindedness. Can we be double-minded and still be pure in heart? Then it seems that Jesus is telling us that the whole tone of his life and his example must be taken from this purity and single-minded outlook.

Where did Jesus get with his humanhood in embodying the Beatitudes and the Sermon on the Mount? What was he able to do with humanhood, his own humanhood? In other words, is there any real reason why you and I should attempt to embody the Sermon on the Mount? If it's mathematical, there is a result, and it's an equation. In each beatitude you can make an equation out of it.

Matthew 5:3. If I said, for instance, **PS=KH,** [Poor in Spirit = Kingdom of Heaven]. Jesus said, *"Blessed [are] the poor in spirit,"* happy are those who feel their spiritual need" in Goodspeed's translation. Notice that it said, *"for theirs* **is** *the kingdom of heaven."* Where is the kingdom? [Voice: "Within."] We're dealing then with the within aren't we? With our Beatitudes we are looking within, where we actually are; exactly where Jesus looked to see where he actually was every single moment. *"Theirs* **is** *the kingdom of heaven."* You can go through and make an equation out of every beatitude and begin to ask yourselves, was Jesus actually teaching us mathematically more than we knew? Was he utilizing equations in his own life work and arriving at such spectacular results that no one has been able to touch the hem of his garment in a three-year span with practically every-known calamity overcome by mastering his within and seeing the kingdom of heaven there?

If that's where Jesus wanted to see you and me eventually, and if the example of Jesus stands behind every word of the Sermon on the Mount then it is an open secret, what you and I must be working daily to accomplish. We should be satisfied that it's not an overnight thing. As long as that doesn't tempt us to lay down our arms and forget that every single day we can gain more mental territory, more of that kingdom within that Jesus himself was able to do. Progressing daily, that seal-impression on us will eventually conform our identity to look more like Jesus himself in our thinking and in our acts. We won't think perfection is such a far off impossible ideal, but something that, to a degree, each of us can improve upon every single day until we begin to be able to do what Jesus did.

Think of what he did with his humanhood. He negated gravity; three days in the tomb without any oxygen, or food, or drink, he was able single-mindedly, in preference to single-handedly, to have that stone, that stands between you and me and that same resurrection, move away and no longer obstruct our own progress. He was able to stand outside the graves of others and summon them forth. He was dealing with incurable diseases, and instantly restored the individuals to complete health. He took time and space, which are virtual limitations and barriers to the animal kingdom, and instantly moved, a wooden boat and fragile skulls of disciples, the human flesh and bone syndrome, together across the Sea of Galilee, going through at least the sound barrier to do so, with no crash helmet but something within, just like an airplane. Within must have at least the pressure there to equal the pressure without or it would be crushed like an eggshell.

What did Jesus' spiritual pressure from within look like? If the kingdom of heaven for him was within, was there any pressure any greater from without? Was he a laboratory scientist and technician beyond what the world knew? Was that Sea of Galilee, by which he delivered the Sermon on the Mount, a laboratory? It must have been the deepest yearnings ever felt that humanity would follow and realize that this was not only the way, but the way out. Only humanity's greater yearnings could Jesus have given us in this Sermon on the Mount. Have we ever thought of that Sea of Galilee as the greatest laboratory in the history of humanity?

If you study the courses in Jesus curriculum that he taught at that sea, you would see the radical difference that he introduced into our whole concepts of life. That could change our own life so radically that we, too, could wake to realize the limitations we're suffering now are just dream bonds and not real limitations on man at all. How you and I could take such knowledge out of that laboratory of the Sea of Galilee and then obey our Master teacher's instructions, for he said that you and I were to do something with what he taught. He said [Mark 16:15], *"Go ye"* where? [Voice: *"Into all the world."*] There wasn't any limitation there, was there? All the world. *"Go ye into all the world"* and do what?*"Preach the gospel,"* the good news about something. And how our newspapers hunger and thirst for good news. And we in searching the newspapers, hunger and thirst for such good news. Out of that laboratory there came that good news. And he didn't say to his disciples, "Stick around the Sea of Galilee, stay in the laboratory, keep experimenting." "You've seen it work," he said, "Go out, preach, in every corner of the world, this good news."

Then he told his followers, not just to preach the gospel. What else were they to do? Make it practical. Probably every Christian, no matter what their denomination might be, privately to himself or herself says this, in kind of a self-assuring way, in our own private thought. You and I say, "I'm a believer in Jesus Christ." Sometimes those words are exactly what people say.

An you know, you and I are not believers in Jesus Christ, unless you and I fulfill this definition of believers given by Jesus, unless you and I are learning that Song of the Lamb. Because the song included not just preaching, not just words, but active living. The song is not sung simply by mouthing words. The real song of the Lamb must be lived. Our whole life turns into a song that way. It's a song that other people hear. It's a melody that comes right from the heart. Who can ever miss that melody? Who can miss the sincerity? Who can miss that quality of mercy? Who can miss that sensitivity to the spiritual needs of ourselves and others? Who can miss the hungering and thirsting world after righteousness? Who can even allow persecution for one's exemplification of this, stand in the way of such preaching and such action?

Mark 16:17. Here's what Jesus says in the closing chapter of Mark,

"These signs shall follow them that believe." You got that specific definition? You and I cannot say we are believers in Jesus Christ unless these signs are following. It requires the following-of-signs, then, to be believers by Jesus' definition, *"In my name shall they cast out devils."* There's sign Number 1. Sign Number 2, *"They shall speak with new tongues."* Just think of what that kind of communication would bring the world.

[Mark 16:18.] Good news. *"They shall take up serpents."* Not one poisonous, malicious attack can have any power over a real believer in Jesus Christ.

"And if they drink any deadly thing, it shall not hurt them." That's the negating of all the laws of chemistry on the body itself, the neutralizing of harm, our having control through this greater understanding ,exemplified by Jesus, and not being dominated, but having the dominion.

And finally, *"They shall lay hands on the sick, and they shall recover."*

That's what Jesus said are the signs following them that believe. Are those signs following us? [Voice: "Yes."] We better be sure because our lives, then, are part of the Song of the Lamb. We are part of the melody. Remember, when your melody and mine [are] through our lives exemplifying the Sermon on the Mount, do you know what that does to you and me? It's not just melody. There's not one melody that will be an inharmonious element or introduce discord. All our melodies will harmonize, and the great chord that you and I are waiting to hear sounded, that has already been sounded in heaven and needs to be made heard on earth, that great chord of unity which is God's outlook on everyone of us.

God sees all of us in unity. And Jesus, in his Sermon on the Mount, begins his Lord's prayer in exactly that same way [Matthew 6:9]. He requires that you and I be at one from the opening words. We don't have to say the Lord's prayer, and especially, we don't have to mean it. That's up to us, isn't it? But if we begin that great prayer, part of the Song of the Lamb, and say, *"Our Father,"* **like it or not**, that makes us brothers and sisters. Look at the oil poured on the world conditions every time we say, "Our Father," with that conviction and purity of heart that sees *"Our Father"* in Moscow, *"Our Father"* in Teheran, *"Our Father"* in Paris, *"Our Father"* in Cambodia, *"Our Father"* everywhere, in heaven. All of us, brothers and sisters. What a song to have in our hearts and to pray in secret, but which our Father seeth in secret will reward us openly. For the Song of the Lamb will always have its reward. Our job is to make sure that it isn't just words. Our job is to insure that we are learning that Song of the Lamb, for we are not singing it until we live it.

Thank you very much.

[Applause]

END TAPE 1, SIDE B

***

CITATION INDEX TO VOLUME 9
"Song of the Lamb"

Citation Index compiled by tranScriptures of Columbia S.C.

(Books are listed alphabetically)

ACTS
(2:1) And when the day of Pentecost was fully come, they were all with one accord in one place. **(ff 2-47)**

I CORINTHIANS
(15:22) For as in Adam all die, even so in Christ shall all be made alive.

GENESIS
(11:9) Therefore is the name of it called Babel; because the LORD did there confound the language of all the earth: and from thence did the LORD scatter them abroad upon the face of all the earth.

HEBREWS
(13:8) Jesus Christ the same yesterday, and to day, and for ever.

JAMES
(1:8) A double minded man [is] unstable in all his ways.

(4:7) Submit yourselves therefore to God. Resist the devil, and he will flee from you. **(4:8)** Draw nigh to God, and he will draw nigh to you. Cleanse [your] hands, [ye] sinners; and purify [your] hearts, [ye] double minded.

JOHN
(14:6) Jesus saith unto him, I am the way, the truth, and the life: no man cometh unto the Father, but by me.

LUKE
(6:12) And it came to pass in those days, that he went out into a mountain to pray, and continued all night in prayer to God. **(6:17)** And he came down with them, and stood in the plain, and the company of his disciples, and a great multitude of people out of all Judaea and Jerusalem, and from the sea coast of

MARK

(16:15) And he said unto them, Go ye into all the world, and preach the gospel to every creature. **(16:17)** And these signs shall follow them that believe; In my name shall they cast out devils; they shall speak with new tongues; **(16:18)** They shall take up serpents; and if they drink any deadly thing, it shall not hurt them; they shall lay hands on the sick, and they shall recover.

MATTHEW

(5:1) And seeing the multitudes, he went up into a mountain: and when he was set, his disciples came unto him: **(5:2)** And he opened his mouth, and taught them, saying, **(5:3)** Blessed [are] the poor in spirit: for theirs is the kingdom of heaven. **(5:4)** Blessed [are] they that mourn: for they shall be comforted. **(5:5)** Blessed [are] the meek: for they shall inherit the earth. **(5:6)** Blessed [are] they which do hunger and thirst after righteousness: for they shall be filled. **(5:7)** Blessed [are] the merciful: for they shall obtain mercy. **(5:8)** Blessed [are] the pure in heart: for they shall see God. **(5:9)** Blessed [are] the peacemakers: for they shall be called the children of God. **(5:10)** Blessed [are] they which are persecuted for righteousness' sake: for theirs is the kingdom of heaven. **(5:11)** Blessed are ye, when [men] shall revile you, and persecute [you], and shall say all manner of evil against you falsely, for my sake. **(5:12)** Rejoice, and be exceeding glad: for great [is] your reward in heaven: for so persecuted they the prophets which were before you. **(5:37)** But let your communication be, Yea, yea; Nay, nay: for whatsoever is more than these cometh of evil. **(5:38)** Ye have heard that it hath been said, An eye for an eye, and a tooth for a tooth:

(6:9) After this manner therefore pray ye: Our Father which art in heaven, Hallowed be thy name. **(6:22)** The light of the body is the eye: if therefore thine eye be single, thy whole body shall be full of light.

(18:16) But if he will not hear [thee, then] take with thee one or two more, that in the mouth of two or three witnesses every word may be established.

NEHEMIAH

(4:17) They which builded on the wall, and they that bare burdens, with those that laded, [every one] with one of his hands wrought in the work, and with the other [hand] held a weapon.

REVELATION

(14:1) And I looked, and, lo, a Lamb stood on the mount Sion, and with him an hundred forty [and] four thousand, having his Father's name written in their foreheads.

(15:2) And I saw as it were a sea of glass mingled with fire: and them that had gotten the victory over the beast, and over his image, and over his mark, [and] over the number of his name, stand on the sea of glass, having the harps of God. **(15:3)** And they sing the song of Moses the servant of God, and the song of the Lamb, saying, Great and marvellous [are] thy works, Lord God Almighty; just and true [are] thy ways, thou King of saints.

2 TIMOTHY

(2:19) Nevertheless the foundation of God standeth sure, having this seal, The Lord knoweth them that are his. And, Let every one that nameth the name of Christ depart from iniquity.

***

WORD INDEX TO VOLUME 9
"Song of the Lamb"

Word Index compiled by tranScriptures of Columbia, S.C.

Bold font - Volume number, Normal font - Page number
A.D. - *anno domini;* C.E - Common Era
B.C. - Before Christ; B.C.E. - Before Common Era
NT - New Testament, OT - Old Testament
c. - about; e.g. - for example; i.e. - that is

---

heart" -- how much pollution do we have within? **9:**62; in conjunction with the Decalogue, do the B give us the power to stand on the "sea of glass" and finally get dominion, our divine right? **9:**62 each B can make an equation **9:**63,64;

Believers in Jesus Christ - learners of the Song of the Lamb who live the Song and do the works by casting out devils, by speaking with new tongues, by taking up serpents, by drinking deadly things accidentally and not being hurt, by healing the sick, **9:**66;

Decalogue (10 Commandments) - the Song of Moses **9:**57;

Equations, mathematical: Each Beatitude can be made in to an equation **9:**63;

(Matt 5:3) **P**oor in **S**pirit = Theirs is the **K**ingdom of **H**eaven **(PS = KH)**

(Matt 5:4) **T**hey that **M**ourn = **T**hey shall be **C**omforted **(TM = TC)**

(Matt 5:6) **T**he **M**eek - They shall **I**nherit the **E**arth **(TM = IE)**

(Matt 5:7) **H**unger and **T**hirst after **R**ighteousness = **T**hey shall be **F**illed **(HTR = F)**

(Matt 5:8) **P**ure in **H**eart = They shall **S**ee **G**od **(PH = SG)**

(Matt 5:9) **T**he **P**eacemakers = They shall be **C**alled the **C**hildren of **G**od **(TP = CCG)**

(Matt 5:10)They which are **P**ersecuted for **R**ighteousness sake = Theirs is the **K**ingdom of **H**eaven **(PR = KH)**

(Matt 5:11) When men shall Revile/**P**ersecute/Say all manner of Evil against you **F**alsely for my sake (Matt 5:12) Rejoice, and be exceeding glad:for **G**reat is your **R**eward in **H**eaven:for so persecuted the prophets which were before you. **(PF = GRH)**

Gethsemane - a garden east of Jerusalem, near the brook of Kedron; scene of Jesus'agony and betrayal; Calvary, Golgotha, the place where Jesus was crucified; the ultimate discouragement which Jesus met through the entire weight of his thought **9:**62;

God's seal - the Father's name written in the forehead **9:**56; the dwindling away to nothingness of iniquity by those who name the name of Christ, i.e., a total commitment to such a seal is required **9:**58; "Our Father" God sees all us "believers" everywhere in heaven singing the Song of the Lamb in unity **9:**66;

---

the Sermon on the Mount **9:**57; Jesus invites us to sing the SotL, and have that S in our hearts and the Seal of our Father in our foreheads **9:**59; the SotL has to be learned; we must delve into the SotL (Sermon on the Mount) and make it our lifestyle instead of theory **9:**63;

Song of Moses - title comes form Revelation 15:3; those standing on the Sea of Glass sing the SoM also **9:**56,57 essence and greatest impact of Moses was the Decalogue **9:**58;

SYMBOLS END

***

Kidron Valley Olive Grove Photograph by Gordon N. Converse

by B. Cobbey Crisler

THE GETHSEMANE DECISION
Volume 15

by B. Cobbey Crisler

CONTENTS

Notes: The transcript was produced from a tape of an unscripted lecture delivered extempore. Earlier tape versions may differ. Biblical quotations and Hebrew, Greek, Latin, French and German words in the commentary are italicized. Brackets enclose additions by the original Bible translators and the transcriber: such as book names, chapter and verse numbers which the speaker mentioned, but did not cite, some audience comments or questions, and an occasional word or footnote. Some spoken words which appeared to be unnecessary for the reader, such as "and, but, so, turn to, well," etc, were deleted. The Citation Index contains the full text of all *King James Bible* citations which the speaker cited or mentioned. The purpose of the transcript is to preserve the speaker's words verbatim.

***

BEGIN TAPE 1, SIDE A

We are involved not just today. We have been involved ever since the earth dawned for us with **The Gethsemane Decision.** I trust all of us have the Bible in front of us. Most especially written on our hearts. That's where the glow of Scripture must ultimately be seen. It's out from that glow that Scripture will ultimately be shared. When you think of the hearts that burned within those disciples on the Walk to Emmaus, simply because a stranger, who turns out later to be Jesus, refocussed their attention on the Bible. And those two did not stay long at Emmaus, they went back to Jerusalem where they belonged, where the action was, where the resurrection was still in progress, where Jesus was able to say earlier to one of the women who had been the first to witness his resurrection, "Go and tell my disciples that, literally in Greek, I am ascending to my Father and to their Father" [John 20:17].

The moment we use the word decision, I'm certain all of us are aware of the choices daily placed before us. There also seems to be a concomitant fact that every time we look in the mirror, we see the results of our choices. That's kind of scary. Can we change choices if we have made the wrong ones? Do you find the Bible filled with this choice making? How does it open, for instance?

Genesis 1 and Genesis 2 are clearly a choice, aren't they? They contradict each other. We really cannot live with both although most of us are undoubtedly trying. The necessity to make a decision, important decision, relates back to how the pioneer Christian made his decision. Whether he himself has that rock beneath him, as we said, before he made any rules. Or whether he, too, vascilated and was dualistic, and was pulled to and fro according to the motion of Satan in the *Book of Job*.

Let's visit Gethsemane geographically first and then let's visit Gethsemane mentally. We might find that it's not necessary to take a trip there physically at all. But for a few moments stand with me before the very prominent mount upon which Jerusalem was built. That city, whose very name dedicates it to peace and yet whose very history has probably had more conflict associated with it than any other city on the globe. How often Jesus faced that city, a city that he wept over, and simply said "*how often he would have gathered its children, her children, under his wings as a hen does her chickens.*" Then those last few words, *"And ye would not."* [Matthew 23:37; Luke 13:34]

That might expose for us the real enemy within that is dealt with in **The Gethsemane Decision,** the fact that *we* would not. Jesus, prior to going to Gethsemane, as you recall, sang a hymn [Matthew 26:30], prayed with his disciples [Mathew 26:35, 42,44] and for them, as well as for those who were to believe on him through the words of his disciples.

I'm not sure one could point to a more meaningful event in history than when Jesus, about to suffer the cruelty of Gethsemane and Calvary, spends his last moments praying for us whom he had never known physically, for those who believe on his disciples through their words.

On the slope of the Mount of Olives, just as it begins to rise from the Valley of Kidron, a very deep gulley that is a natural defence for the city of Jerusalem. One that enables the city to be secure from that vantage point, the East. No one has ever conquered Jerusalem from the East.

That valley of Kidron separates the Mount of Olives from Jerusalem proper. At the vantage point of that slope if you look back up to the city of Jerusalem, it looms above you, well above you. It's wall today pretty much following the outline of the earlier walls, although most of the construction is of the Turkish period in the 16th century. There above you, you see the entrance to what is called the Golden Gate. It's closed, boarded up, walled up, because a long tradition is that the Messiah would come through that Gate, so the Turks walled it up to prevent the Messiah from entry. Once again that sad action is perhaps an example of those few words, *"Ye would not,"* the rejection of the Messiah. Human nature rejecting the very thing that can save it.

The brook Kidron is dry most of the year, only when the winter rains fill it do you have any kind of indication of water. Across from the city of Jerusalem at night, do we recall that John said that those who came to arrest Jesus snaked down the slope of the city into the valley of Kidron, and they were carrying torches and lanterns? I ask you to imagine what that would've appeared like from the vantage point from the beginning slope of the Mount of Olives where Jesus and his disciples were. It certainly would have been enough to strike fear in the average human heart.

Jesus certainly knew the objective of those who were coming. His disciples were falling in and out of almost a drugged-like stupor which prevented them from being any support whatsoever to their Master. The Gethsemane Decision is one that must be taken alone anyway, individually, alone with God.

The word "Gethsemane" is felt by most Bible scholars to mean "oil press." Why do you think an oil press would be located on the Mount of Olives? Pretty obvious, right? It's at the base of the Mount of Olives so the fruit would have flowed from the slope where the trees were and ended up for pressing purposes at the bottom of the mountain. The symbolic nature of that is probably not lost on any of us. The intense pressure, the olive is placed under between two huge stones where the hulk, the skin, the pulp, all pressed out of condition, distorted, and yet the essence is not caught by the pressure of those stones. It flows out to bless mankind in many ways. Olive oil was used for what back then? Still is in many cases. Anointing was for kings, priests, royalty, and what else? It was used for heat, for light.

Back to Gethsemane. The decision that was made there, the decision obviously was a mental one. We need to conclude as we study the event whether this decision was made for the first time by Jesus at Gethsemane or whether it was consistent with the choices he had made ever since age twelve when he is recorded as telling his human parents that his mission was to "*be about his Father's business*" [Luke 2:49].

What do you think the Gethsemane decision is? [Voice: "to let God's will be made manifest..."] To let God's will. What's the other part of the choice? God's will or our own will, self-will or human will. Does that sound like much of a major choice? It's easy for us, isn't it? Certainly, we do our own will easily. That's no problem at all. This may be why we have not succeeded where Jesus did. Where Jesus became one who could be called "Master." Because nothing ever mastered him. Is the secret to being a follower and a believer of Jesus the straightening out of priorities in our thinking as Jesus established that method? God's will not our own. It's something human nature is not used to. It is radical. If we are facing the basic, primary decision between success and failure, it's whether we are in tune with our own wills or whether we are totally committed to God's will. We should be able to see all kinds of indications of this in Scripture.

In chapters 2 and 3 of Genesis, let's discuss the opening account of the Adam-man and locate the initial problem of humanity, sometimes called "original sin." What do you think it might be? Where did Adam go wrong, in other words? The initial mistake. The whole history of errors, really. God told him something. What did he do about it? God indicated what His will was. Adam just simply proceded to do what he wanted. And then blamed woman for it.

An early rabbi, called Rabbi Jose, indicated this about Adam. He said, "Go and learn from the first man upon whom was laid only one negative commandment, and he transgressed it." He is told not to touch dualism, the tree-of-knowledge-of-good-and-evil. Not to attempt to live with both. Interestingly enough we find Satan defined in those terms later in Job [2:2;7:4], to-and-fro, up-and-down. No commitment there, always in flux, no permanence, no rocks, no conviction. Adam chose to go that route. All humanity has followed him.

In 1 Corinthians 15:22 we hear later of this choice once again, Paul informs us if we insist on going the Adam-way, then the objective, the destination will all end up with death as the common denominator. We might have thought that was the only choice. The Adam-man may never have seen beyond such a choice. But the second part of that verse gives us a radically different decision, *"even so in Christ shall all be made alive."*

Pythagoras [Greek philosopher, mathematician, and religious reformer c. 582-500 B.C.] used to symbolize choices and decisions by the letter Y, Greek [vowel sound] *Upsilon.* And at that intersection we decide to go left or right. Let's apply that Pythagorean Y to this verse. If we went to the left branch of that Y, let's say that's the Adam-route, ultimately it ends in death. If we have an alternative, how can we retrace our steps? Can we leap over? The gap widens as the Y goes further and further *ad infinitum.*

We get further and further away from such a possibility as we keep going the Adam-route. As long as we are on that branch, labelled "Adam," then we're constantly looking at the destination which is what? Death. So our eyes are just filled with nothing but death as we go along that route.

Just simply using that graphic symbol, what must we do if we want to get on the Christ-way? We have to go back and straighten out our choice, don't we? Then move down that other road. It may be slow [on] that other road, but where do our eyes look constantly? To life. There is a practicality to such a choice.

This Adam-problem is something that is not limited to the discussion in Genesis. We find it referred to and alluded to throughout the Bible, as if it represents in symbols the human problem. One Bible commentator in discussing the choice between the Adam-man and the Christ-man, represented by Jesus, indicates that the way these terms are used in the New Testament especially, it looks like the intent is that each one, Adam and Jesus, are representatives of an entirely different human race. They are completely opposite. Humanhood following Jesus is ending up at a destination completely opposed to the destination of the Adam followers. There may be something in humanhood we have barely glimpsed if at all.

Jesus found what humanhood could be when the Divine was behind it every step of the way. There is nothing in Jesus' humanhood that could stop the Divine from manifesting itself on earth as in heaven. This may be our decision we're talking about.

Jesus refused to allow anything to obstruct the divine will from operating on earth. Look what he was able to do with his own humanhood as well as the humanhood of others as a result. He could take his fragile, one would think, human frame, anatomically speaking, through what apparently was at least the sound barrier, if not the light barrier. In no way did his body hamper him when he walked above the water.

He therefore, had dominion, obviously, over what we refer to as a law of gravity. Yet when he subdued gravity through this sense of dominion, gravity had no control over the dominion-man. Notice he was not like our astronauts, weightless as the result of negating gravity. He was still in absolute conrol of every aspect of his being and progressing toward his destination. He didn't have to do it step-by-step because we hear that when he set foot in the boat instantly, not only Jesus, but the comprehension of Jesus could embrace his disciples plus boat, and get all of them through what we feel today, technologically would require heat-resistent metals, crash helmets, oxygen masks, or whatever else in order to preserve the human frame, and get it through such stresses and pressures and tensions. Jesus was used to the pressure of Gethsemane, the olive press. He did not fear what flesh could do to him, obviously.

In Romans 5:14, according to Paul, the Adam-way, the Adam-Choice, *"resulted in death reigning"* absolutely *"from Adam to Moses, even over them that had not sinned after the similitude of Adam's transgression."* This was almost a heredity penalty, the Adam-race walking lockstep to destruction.

Romans 5:19. There is a way out. *"As by one man's disobedience."* Is that pinpointing our problem here? In a sense could we say that original sin is adopting the position that our own personal human self will has priority? Thus, casting out of thought all relationship to God. *"As by one man's disobedience many were made sinners, so by the obedience of one shall many be made righteous."* Does it appear that the Scriptures are telling us that the problem is Adam and the remedy is Christ? This problem-solution relationship makes the Bible almost a textbook with mathematical logic throughout in dealing with what we may consider to be the insoluble problems of the human race.

In Romans 5:21 Paul asks, *"As sin hath reigned unto death, even so might grace reign through righteousness unto eternal life?"* Once again we have that Y set up for us there. It's important to know the enemy if we would be victorious over the enemy. Was Jesus aware of the enemy? If the enemy is self-will, human will, disobedience to God's will, our back is really to God and our eyes towards destruction. Let's pick up a few threads of this as we go through the Bible. When we do this, we may accumulate enough evidence so that we finally recognize more clearly than ever before what Jesus was doing for us in that garden. If he took it from Scripture that his mission was to remedy everything Adam stood for, that's provable in Scripture. All those "ifs," all those theories that we come up with should not be accepted dogmatically, simply as theory.

END TAPE 1, SIDE A

BEGIN TAPE 1, SIDE B

The Scriptures have enough evidence within them that we can come to our own conclusions through the text. We don't need, any of us, to add human opinion to those already that have burdened the Bible for so long.

2 Thessalonians 3:1. "*Let the Word have free course,*" Paul says. That "free course" implies our own immediate access to the source of inspiration behind the Spriptures.

Genesis 49:6. Here we are at the time of Jacob. Jacob with his insight sees the problems resident in the mentalities of each of his children, exposes them as problems for his sons to deal with.

Genesis 49:5. In the case of "*Simeon and Levi*" we find their mental states described "*as instruments of cruelty [in] their habitations.*"

Genesis 49:6. The plea of Jacob is that identity, "O my soul," not be related to that kind of thinking. "*Come not thou into their secret;*" plot is another possible translation of that word; "*unto their assembly,*" getting together even, ganging up to accomplish more iniquity; "*mine honour, be not thou united: for in their anger they*" committed murder; "*they slew a man, and in their selfwill they digged down a wall.*" Let's ask ourselves if that isn't really the history of Babel? Where the chaos of self-wills removed that city. They left off building it. No agreement. The opposite of Pentecost in the Bible. No one understood each other. They All scattered. As my dad puts it to me on occasion in his epigramatic ways, summarizing our problems as a human race, "More Babel than Bible." [Chuckles]

That sense of self-will is associated even with Levi. It's the one who is the founder of the priesthood. Religion itself in its human origins, in presuming to speak for God, or in God's stead, has developed a theology of self-will often rather than God's direction. How interesting that we are reminded just before the Bible ends, in that magnificent *Book of Revelation* [2:7], that it is "*what the Spirit saith unto the churches*" that counts, nobody else. That Spirit, speaking to church as well as individual, can our hearts ever be the same when our hearts are in touch with the Spirit? That breathing of the Holy Ghost, fanning the flames of our heart. That's what got church going after the Walk to Emmaus. It had its human birthday, the Christian church, that is, on resurrection evening. By the hearts burning within the disciples and that first meeting that Jesus addressed. Obviously a church, then, Levitically-oriented church will never be able to unite with the inspired Bible, for it is no better than Babel, if it is building on self-will of each member, either of the hierarchy or the laity.

We were warned fairly early in the Bible about the dangers of this original sin creeping in at every level.

Numbers 16:28. We have a breakthrough in human history. A pioneer called Moses who has discovered a better way but is challenged all the way through by those who would occupy the office of human leader, and in the meantime have forgotten God, is the sole One who directs His people. Moses said, "*The very sign you need to look for in my divine appointing. Here is how you will know that the Lord has sent me to do all these works. I have not done them of mine own mind.*" Is that just simply a phoney humility Moses is manufacturing for the good of his hearers? Or is he actually dealing with the secret of his success?

I'm sure we recall Joseph himself, indicating that, when he was interpreting dreams, or what he was able to do in Egypt, it was God motivating, prompting, directing. Joseph's role was to be obedient to do God's will. Unlike Adam, this is a definite commitment to go another route than Adam's route. So, we have Moses and Joseph indicating that.

But certainly we cannot forget Jesus' statement [John 5:30] very much like that. "*I can of mine own self do nothing.*" How often he repeats this in so many different ways! "*The Son can do nothing of himself except what he seeth the Father do*" [John 5:19]. Here is a man who was able to accomplish everything, to overcome every obstacle the world hurled at him. Yet he explains how this is all possible by a total irrelevance of human mentality, instead of a complete relationship of man to God mentally, so that man's mind turns out really not to be his own, as Moses says. If it's not his, who's is it? It would have to be God's mind. That's where God's will is located.

Perhaps that's what the line in the Lord's Prayer is coaching us daily to think as well as live [Matthew 6:9] "*on earth as it is in heaven.*" That this earth-and-heaven business is again a dualism but "on earth as in heaven" is God's will operative here and now. And look what is possible for man under those circumstances!

When Jesus says, *"I can of mine own self do nothing,"* is he consistent with what Genesis 1 has revealed about the nature of man? Who is man, according to Genesis 1? Image and likeness [Genesis 1:26,27]. If man is image and likeness, then God is what? Original, **the Original**. Nothing originates, then, in the image-and-likeness. Not mind, not love, not thought. Only what is in that Original, according to the logic of the Scriptures, may be found in the image. So when Moses and Jesus can say what is being accomplished or initiated or originated in them at all, they are simply indicating a state of thought that has yielded itself, and completely to the divine, and that's possible on earth. In fact, mandatory for salvation on earth.

And this Gethsemane Decision between God's will and our own will begins to take on major proportions. It has been avoided too long, neglected to long. Often in our own lives we've put off such choices. We've delayed.

Right now we're concentrating on what the problem is.

Numbers 24:13 is Balaam [son of Beor] saying, *"If Balak* [king of the Moabites] *would give me his house full of silver and gold, I cannot go beyond the commandment of the LORD, to do [either] good or bad of mine own mind; [but] what the LORD saith, that will I speak?"* That sound familiar?

In John 12:50 Jesus says, *"Whatsoever I speak therefore, even as the Father said unto me, so I speak.."*

In Deuteronomy 18:18 when God is quoted as giving Moses a prophecy that someone would come, a prophet would come. Notice how God's will is revealed even in advance for humanity through prophecy. What could be a greater manifestation of Love for Love's creation and universe, for Love's product, for the image and likeness of Love on earth struggling to fulfill that likeness, to remove the restrictions humanly from manhood and womanhood, and fill in the divine outline. What could be a greater manifestation of that than the fact that prophecy is with us every step of the way that is advancing towards the divine goal of "on earth as in heaven." In the next reference we'll see how Amos underscores that.

In Deuteronomy 18:18 part of the description of the prophet who is to come, who will remind the people of Moses. We just saw one reminder of that, both Moses and Jesus, indicating that the secret of their success, there accomplishments, is that what is happening has not one ounce origin, initiative, in what we call human mentality. Verse 18 continues this prophet-like-Moses will be filled with *"God's words in his mouth"* and *"he will speak unto them all that God shall command him."* When even *"the words of our mouth"* [Psalm 19:14] are *"ordered by the Lord"* [Psalm 37:23].

In fact, Jeremiah 15:19 tells us at one point that if we are to resemble God, to fulfill this likeness-route, this Christ-way, with life as its objective, Jeremiah says we must *"take forth the precious from the vile,"* this dualism in human mentality. Think of the Lord saying this to you and me individually and collectively, *"Therefore thus saith the LORD, If you return, then I will bring thee again, [and] you will stand before me: and if you take forth the precious from the vile, thou shalt be as my mouth."* Imaging forth what God is saying. Wasn't the prophetic description of Jesus centuries before he came [showing] that no one else could ever have occupied that place? We could hardly get through one day with every word being Godlike in origin. We can't get through a traffic jam that way. [Laughter] The motivation! Here is a man that exactly fits, dovetails, into the pattern of prophecy in Jesus' own experience. Here we have God reminding Jeremiah that's what he must do to fulfill prophecy.

One of the greatest prophetic utterances about man and certainly one of my dad's favorites, is found in Isaiah 13:12. When you remind yourselves of the environment we often awaken to every single morning with the airwaves filled with grizzly news, with the world giving every indication that it is hastening down the Adam-route to self-destruction, [we need] to remind ourselves as well we have a book that is printing good news everyday, and that gospel is what we need to be reading more of, filling our own thoughts more with.

In Isaiah 13:12 just look at the inspired view of manhood. We pick up our newspapers and often get nothing but manhood's abused, womanhood's abused, dispised, degraded, desecrated, wounded, violated, hungry, in pain, incurable. And the Bible says, "holy." *"I will make a man more precious than fine gold."* If that isn't restoration of the dignity of God's manhood, what is? Notice, that's the *"precious"* that God is telling Jeremiah to separate out from the *"vile."* There are our tares and wheat. There is our decision, our **Gethsemane Decision**, and the importance of making the right choices now just for our own salvation, as well as for the world.

[In] Psalms 19:12 the psalmist comes face to face with exactly what God has told Jeremiah to do, to take the precious from the vile. But now comes the practical daily business of accomplishing it. The psalmist here, the psalm attributed to David, asks, *"Who can understand [his] errors? Be rid of them. How can we understand our errors?"* Then the initiative again. It's not a human psychology that get's to the bottom of those errors, according to David. It's prayer next is, "*Cleanse thou me from secret [faults].*" The ignorant aspects of error, the inadvertant go-along in human mentality. The ones that perhaps defy discovery but God's cleansing, baptising activity going on in thought can remove them completely.

Remember that John the Baptist had indicated Jesus' baptism would be one not of water, which rules out all physical application as doing mentality any good, and elevates it to the baptism of the Holy Ghost and fire, a twin baptism. And since ghost is spirit, it's obviously something going on mentally, a deep mental cleansing, a separation, once again, like tares from wheat, like vile from precious, like bad fish from good fish, like the evil fig from the good fig, and all of the illustrations we have in the Bible said this is what the kingdom of heaven is all about. To begin to establish that sense of control over every single thought. Paul said [2 Corinthians 10:5], *"to bring into captivity every thought to the obedience of Christ."* That is not doing our own will. "To bring into captivity every single thought to the obedience of Christ" result? Life! That's the right choice on the Y.

Psalm 19:13. Secret faults, however, are not the only ones David continues, *"Keep back thy servant,"*

They know when one can refer to himself or herself as a servant of God; that's one obedient to God's will. That word is very significant throughout Scripture, especially prophecy. It is quite clear as many of our foremost Bible scholars tell us that Jesus was fully conscious that he was fulfilling the prophecies relating to the suffering servant in the Old Testament.

Psalm 19:13 gives us "*presumptuous [sins],*" as well as the secret faults that need to be cleansed out. Remember what God told Jeremiah [15:19] what's the whole reason for taking the *"prescious from the vile"*? What's the result? [Voice "Cleanse your mouth"] That's right, *"your mouth will be as my mouth."* We will be an absolute reflection of what God is saying. In other words, the Word will be embodied in us as it was in Jesus. *"The Word was made flesh"* [John 1:14] in Jesus' example, embodying God's Word.

It must be pure because taking the precious from the vile unpollutes consciousness. That "*pure river of water of life*" we see as the Bible closes in its final chapter [Revelation 22:1] begins to take on a great significance, because there it is in the Holy City. What's a city but where you and I live? That sense of purity, that city, which is the scriptural description of where we should be living, "*will not allow anything inside its gates that defile or make a lie*" [Revelation 21:27]. Because they would be the devil's instrument.

Anything that makes a lie, that's Jesus' definition of the devil [John 8:44]. Diabolism, dualism, to-and-froism, up-and-downism, out of the Holy City. No one lives in that consciousness in the Holy City. Presumptuous sins, secret faults are not in that sense of living either. David adds [in Psalm 19:13], "*let them not have dominion over me: then shall I be upright, and I shall be innocent from the great transgression.*"

END TAPE 1, SIDE B

BEGIN TAPE 2, SIDE A

Innocence in a court of law entitled you to wear a white garment, never before worn by anyone or anything. When the Bible tells us that fine linen is the righteousness of saints, my dad again pointed out to me, "Remember in fine linen, there's not one single animal element."

We're still working on the problem. We're exposing the problem, defining it, identifying it, and then we will be applying the solution.

1 Kings 19:4. Here is the example of Elijah. You know what a great pioneer Elijah was. He was the first one to raise the dead, for one thing. If we run into problems with some things he might say or do on occasion that we wouldn't agree with, let's always remember that what ever Elijah was confronting in human nature, is the same as what you and I are confronting in human nature. But his understanding was sufficient to restore someone's sense of life after that individual had apparently lost his sense of life.

Elijah, however, at this point, after having raised a child, having silenced false theology, having defeated drought, lack, we find that the resistance is so great to this prophetic accomplishing of God's will on earth, that the prophet himself wants to give it all up. The heavy weight of the world counterbalancing in his own thinking the grace of God. He sits down under a juniper tree, a juniper tree I am sure many of us have been under and requested, "This is it, I want out. Stop the world. I want to get off. *I [am] not better than my fathers.*"

But you know, here we are up against the Gethsemane Decision. Jesus had that hurled at him mentally, too, didn't he? The response was different from Jesus. Or is it Divine Will's prompting? He had to go through something here, deal with the enemies resident in human mentality, and show they could be cast out *"taking forth the precious from the vile"* [Jeremiah 15:19], *"burning the chaff and gathering the wheat into barns"* [Luke 3:17] before he could ascend.

1 Kings 19:8. He went to the right place symbolically. We don't have to buy a ticket to the geographical spot to do the same. *"He goes to Horeb, the mount of God,"* the mount that symbolizes the altitude at which one receives the Commandments. What are the Commandments if not God's will summarized for us: "Thou shalt not." Coming to Horeb Elijah makes a mistake, a mistake that seems to be built into the human character.

1 Kings 19:9. *"He finds a cave and lodges there."* That's presumably part of the evolution of man on earth, the cave man. This is atavism [a reversion to a more primitive type ancestor] to Adam. Nothing could be more remote than Adam. In the middle of a crisis, do we become atavistic? Do we regress to that primitive type? Do we begin to look like jungle beings, animal kingdom residents, rather than of the heavenly kingdom and the Holy City? Cave men had thick skulls. Some of them survived even to our day. [Laughter] Some of those skulls are even leaky. [Laughter] It apparently is not God's will to see His man as a cave man, however. Moving Elijah urgently out of the cave, notice the divine question, *"What doest thou here, Elijah?"* That's not progress on earth, going back to the cave. That's a full retreat. The same kind of thing that we find the Lord God asking Adam [in Genesis 3:9], *"Where are you, Adam?"* The usual response from human beings is, "I really don't know." *"What doest thou here, Elijah?"*

In 1 Kings 19:11 we find all the violent elements associated with nature as well as human nature. The revelation of this event that *the LORD [was] not in any of those violent forms of resistance.*

1 Kings 19:13. But Elijah needs the lesson over again. In that he should appear quite familiar to most of us. "*When Elijah heard [it], he wrapped his face in his mantle, and went out, and stood in the entering in of the cave.*" And look who has to ask the question all over again, *"What are you doing here,* Elijah?"

Isn't this perhaps a further and helpful defining of how you and I can make our own Gethsemane Decision? All of the world's revulsion and resistance to the steady march of the divine facts "on earth as in heaven" have nought of God in them. God's will may be seen not in any of that commotion. *"Be silent, O earth, O flesh,"* the prophet [Zechariah 2:13] said. *"Be still and know that I am God"* [Psalm 46:10]. It is the "*still small voice*" [1 Kings 19:12] then that conveys God's will.

The noises need to be silenced.

We don't need to go into a cave. None of them obviously could have effected Elijah. Rocks were blowing all over the place. The earthquake, fire, very close to where Elijah was standing. God would never have misled Elijah to tell him to stand right there on that mount if there were any potential danger there. Nothing obviously could touch Elijah when he was doing God's will.

Ecclesiastes 12. The necessity for sifting human thought once again. That is the definition, isn't it, of the kingdom of heaven so often in Jesus' [7] parables [in Matthew 13:33,44 45,47,52;20:1,2]? *"The kingdom of heaven is like unto."* We find that it is a sifting, a sorting out, to get rid of what doesn't belong within. Then discover that's where the kingdom is. No longer an anarchy within, a rebellion, a riot within. What is disease but a rebellion against the normal order of the bodily system. Putting down rebellion then in thought and discovering the kingdom, or government, or dominion, or rule, or order, law within us must be the discovery of the ages. Yet it's nothing new because it is the initial gift of God to man in Genesis 1, dominion. You have it, God says. You can't get rid of it. The image cannot remove anything that belongs to the original, no matter how hard the image might try. Can't even make a move that hasn't been sponsored by the original.

Ecclesiastes 12:13,14. *"Keeping God's commandments,"* why? Does that whole Sinai standard not only define for us God's will? But as God's will lived on earth, it is the whole [duty]. Notice, those of you with King James translations, the word *duty* is in italics. That means it's not in the original text. *"The whole of man is the commitment,* then, *to love, honor, revere God, and keep his commandments."* That's way out. In the meantime all this mixture in human mentality requiring a Gethsemane Decision out of us every moment of every day. Which way are we going to go? Back to Adam like a pendulum? Then try to swing across the void back to the Christ man again?

Ecclesiastes 12:14. says *"God will bring every work into judgment."* That word "judgment" in the Greek translation is our word "crisis." Crisis has taken on a different meaning for us than its original Greek. One lexicographer's definition of crisis from the Greek: "Originally the process of separating, distinguishing. Its translation "judgment" in the New Testament, disguises the true meaning of the word which contains no idea of condemnation, but means "separating." So, "crisis" frequently wrongly used in English, should be kept for turning points that necessitate a parting of the ways." Those are our Pythagorean ways, the necessity to make a correct decision. The decision being total committment puts darkness for light, and light for darkness; that put bitter for sweet, and sweet for bitter!

[In] Isaiah 5:20 we find this dualism again, "*Woe unto him that calls evil good, and good evil; that mistakes darkness for light, light for darkness; bitter for sweet, and sweet for bitter!*" We can't even discriminate between the extremes. We've lost that ability, that spiritual sense to discern what should be discarded, dismissed, removed from human consciousness and what needs to be kept.

Isaiah 29:16 very succinctly describes where we are most of the time, namely, "*turning of things upside down.*" Optically that's even the way we see. The explanation is that something in consciousness knows it's upside down and mentally turns it rightside up. That's a marvelous lesson from nature. Because if everything we're looking at, nature is already telling us it's upside down, and something mentally must occur in order to correct it, the complete reverse of it, then how do we know that most of our outlook, even mentally, is not inverted? In fact, the harking back to Adam's formation out of clay in verse 16 that that's the upside down man, like the potter's clay. The attempt to initiate even creation, human beings taking upon themselves things that actually belong to God.

Isaiah 32:2. The horror of the crucifixion, and yet Jesus' ascendency over it in his struggle in the garden, is symbolized again here just in the Scriptural view of man, the dignity of man, his divine destiny, "*A man shall be as an hiding place from the wind.*" Does that remind you of Elijah's situation, not a cave, manhood itself has a built-in divine defense against destruction. "*And a covert from the tempest; as rivers of water in a dry place, and the shadow of a great rock in a weary land.*" In the presence of all these problems manhood is solution itself when imaging the source, or God. Man is the solution in the sense that he is the application of God's solution. Does that allow us to neutralize Gethsemane? Is that perhaps an insight where Jesus was in thought when he was dealing with Gethsemane for all of humanity?

Jeremiah 6:16 is quite clear about the conflict between God's will and self-will of humans. Notice how this comes over and over again in the verses in Jeremiah we're now focussing on. Here is His commandment, *["Thus saith the LORD,] Stand, see, ask.*" Notice all those active mandates there used for verbs. "*See where [is] the good way, and walk therein, and ye shall find rest for your souls. But...*" Here is the human qualification. "*But they said*" what? Isn't that what Jesus testified to when he wept over Jerusalem. Remember, New Jerusalem is the name given to the Holy City. If that's where we're supposed to discover ourselves ultimately living, New Jerusalem, you can see that Jesus was witnessing the Old Jerusalem, perhaps symbolizing all mankind attempting to live in that old sense of struggle and conflict and the inflexible sense of human will. *"We would not."* Even though Jesus would embrace us all, "*We would not.*"

When a prophet says *"Thus saith the Lord,"* he feels that this is pure prompting from Deity with nothing human in it. No tampering with it. No prophetic attempt to edit God's inspiration. "*Thus saith the LORD.*" [This phrase appears 413 times in the OT and is not in the NT]

Jeremiah 6:19 continues where God reveals to him quite specifically evil doesn't really come from God even though it's stated, *"I will bring evil upon this people."* Because the very next line tells where it comes from. It's *"the fruit of their thoughts."* It's something mental. It's coming from an inadequate sense of mentality, a dualistic state, a tree of knowledge of good and evil in the midst of our garden. The problem's stated in verse 19 " *because they have not hearkened unto my words, nor to my law, but rejected it.*" Again the resistance element. Also there is a hope implicit in that. If evil, if what has been visited upon us in our lives can be accurately portrayed as the fruit of our thoughts, all thought needs ever to do is to change itself. To be changed. That's what the word "repentance" means in the New Testament in Greek. To change one's concept of things. To change one's thought about things. It must be a radical change which means going back to our roots, our nativity, our origin. Adam-man, dust-man, or Christ's dominion-man. That decision is important. It may explain all of Jesus remarkable healing work which he considered all of his followers should be able to do or we were not worthy of being called believers in him. *"He that believeth in me..."* [John 11:25].

Notice how glibly Christians today say all that's necessary is to believe in the Lord Jesus Christ and you'll be saved. It's glib. It's true but it's glib, because the definition of the believer in Jesus Christ has been given to us by Jesus himself. If we're not doing the works of Jesus, forget being believers in him. Let's not satisfy ourselves with some kind of theoretical medal we bestow on ourselves. If you go through the gospels and underline every time Jesus tells you who his disciples really are: "thus will you be my disciples," that kind of thing, or " he that believeth in me will do the following things." We will see how far we are from fulfilling his prayer that we follow him through all the obstacles that the world would place in our path.

In Jeremiah 7:23-28 you'll just see the same thing, rehearsed for us.

Jeremiah 7:23 God said, "*Here's God's will. Obey my voice, and look at the results. I wll be your God. You shall be my people.*" That's one of the most magnificent themes in the entire Bible. Prophet after prophet, even the book of *Revelation* bringing it in as a rousing crescendo in the closing measures of the symphony of the Bible, *"I will be your God."* What could be greater than that? *"And you shall be my people."* That relationship! The thinnest edge of a wedge could not get between God and his people then. What is God's will for his people? That they be sick? That they be sinful? That thy die?

If so, what was Jesus doing disobeying God's will when he corrected sin, when he healed disease, and when he raised the dead, and when he told the woman who was all bent over for so many years that Satan had bound her? That's not God's will. Yet how often we hear Christians bowing their heads in a mute resignation in the face of the collapse of the fleshly order in our loved ones or in our own selves, saying, "It must be God's will."? That would negate all of Jesus' earthly mission if it were God's will. It is anti-Christian. It is satanic because Jesus said [in Luke 13:16] *"Satan hath bound her."*

Jeremiah 7:24 *"They hearkened not,"* Welcome back to the human race. [Chuckles] *"nor inclined their ear."*

Jeremiah 7:25 *"Since the day that your fathers came forth out of the land of Egypt."* There's the whole symbol of bondage of the human race.

END TAPE 2, SIDE A

BEGIN TAPE 2, SIDE B

In fact, in the book of *Revelation* you'll find that geography in the Bible is meant to be literal. It's symbolic. We find that two witnesses mentioned in the book of *Revelation* [11:8] *"with their dead bodies lying in the streets of what is spiritually called Sodom and Egypt."* That's what crucified Jesus then, Sodom and Egypt. Where can they be located? Not just on the globe. If Sodom is sensuality in all the perverted self-oriented, self-willed characteristic of the human mind, and if Egypt represents all the blackness and darkness of no inspiration, no revelation and bondage, slavery, what is crucifying renewedly our Lord, our Master, our dominion-man within ourselves, but *"Sodom and Egypt, what are spiritually called,"* as the book of *Revelation* [11:8] indicates?

The necessity of translating Scripture into it's spiritual and original means of communication seems tough to do because we live at the level of the literal. The literal is the letter. The spiritual is the Spirit. That's what breathes through the Bible. Without the Spirit we have what Ernest Renan calls the rust of religion.

Does Jeremiah 18:12 describe your own thoughts at any given day? Here's where human will ultimately brings us into hopelessness. *"They said, There is no hope."* So, where do we go? *"We walk after our own devices, and every one of us does according to the imagination of his evil heart."* That's the human race. And the human race is not going to uplift itself by the rule that goes with the biblical logic that a fountain can rise no higher than itself. The only thing that can elevate anything human is something above it. I think it was Emerson [who] said, "I must stand on higher ground if I would lift you up." Perhaps it's the reverse, "You must stand on higher ground if you would lift me up." This lack of salvation within itself. The ultimate resistance to yielding to the divine. That yielding that Gethsemane illustrates.

Jeremiah 23:10. We don't seem so far from this prophetic description. *"The land is full of adulterers; because of swearing,"* that's the word cursing in Hebrew, *"the land mourneth; the pleasant places of the wilderness are dried up, and their course is evil,"* the word course in Hebrew is violence, *"their violence is evil, their force [is] not right."*

[Jeremiah 23:11] We find that even religiously *"prophet and priest are profane."* How can one be sacred and profane simultaneously? *"In my house,"* right in the midst of church, *"have I found their wickedness, saith the Lord"*.

Jeremiah 23:17. Notice again the conflict between the tares and the wheat, between the precious and the vile. *"The Lord says, You shall have peace."* That's obviously the Lord's will. Who's fighting it? We all pay lip service. We want peace. But *"they say unto every one that walketh after the imagination of his own heart, No evil shall come upon you."* On what is that based? If it's not based on God's revelation and understanding that every Word of God is backed with divine authority it falls to the level of human opinion, which is nothing more than a weather vane.

Jeremiah 30:17. What is God's will as far as health is concerned? *"Restoring it."* *"I will heal thee of thy wounds, saith the Lord."* That's God's will. But unfortunately, the last line. *"This [is] Zion, whom no man seeketh after."* Why? What are we too busy doing? Following in our own line of light with its distortions. Standing in our light with its resultant shadows. There are no shadows in the full noon of God.

Ezekiel 2:3-5. Here is the spirit behind prophecy. Why? If we cut off our links to prophecy, it's as if we are cutting off our very breath, stifling what God has revealed is his will for man and woman on-earth-as-in-heaven.

Ezekiel 2:3. *"Son of man,"* God says to Ezekiel, *"I send you to a rebellious nation."*

Ezekiel 2:4. *"[They are] impudent children and stiffhearted. I send you to them; and you say to them, Thus saith the Lord."*

Ezekiel 2:5. *"Whether they will hear, or whether they will forbear, (for they [are] a rebellious house,) yet they shall know that there hath been a prophet among them."* A prophet showing *"This [is] the way, walk ye in it, turn not to the right hand or to the left."* [Isaiah 30:21]

We've had these beacon lights down through history. *"This is the way."* Jesus not only pointed it out, he lived it. So we know how it can be lived, and more importantly, that it can be done so successfully. When humanity begins to wake up perhaps and makes this Gethsemane decision, following the example of Jesus, we may give up dying and start living. Part of the giving-up of dying, in going back to our original graphic symbol in that Y, would be to stop looking at it. If we're on the Adam route, that's all we're doing. That's all that's out there ahead. Even if we were just still on the left branch of that Y, and we'd turned around and [were] heading back to the intersection, on whatever particular choice we have to make between the spiritual and its reverse influence in thought. Even if we'd just turned around and are still on that route, our backs are to them and we're going back to our choice where, as soon as we turn the corner, we'll be looking at light.

Remember what God said to Ezekiel [18:23]:, *"Have I any pleasure in the death of him that dieth, is that My will? rather than that ye should turn yourselves and live ye?"* Turn, turn the corner. If someone asks you, how do you spell relief? [Chuckles] You might try, "G-O-D." What a relief it must be ultimately for the human will to relinquish finally all of its falsely assumed responsibilities. There is no way you and I can approach God in prayer, or enter the kingdom of heaven, according to Jesus, except as a little child. And that little child trustingly, with small hand in the large one of our divine parent, that is a guaranteed entry into all the dominion that Jesus meant when he said [John 5:30], *"I can do nothing of mine own self."* That childlike innocence, that lamb like power which Jesus so exampified that moved all barriers from the way. How much we must be indebted to that pioneer man who went all the way. And from that ultimate end, turned around and invited us to follow. All the barriers are down.

He said [John 16:33] to his disciples before he went to Gethsemane, *"I have overcome the world."* Telling his disciples to *"Be of good cheer."* And it was Jesus who was facing Gethsemane at that point, not his disciples. They hadn't even comprehended it. But he said, *"Be of good cheer."* What could be a more joyous announcement than the fact that he has overcome the world? A good friend and deep Bible student, Elizabeth Earl Jones, brought out a point to me there that I had missed totally, namely, when Jesus said.*"I have overcome the world,"* implicitly it means you and I are fighting a defeated foe. The pioneer work has been done. We must confirm the work of the pioneer by following his every footstep. No turning to right or to left. The Gethsemane Decision has been made for us. It's been proven to us. The reminder is not to leave the footsteps of the Master.

I promised we would get to Amos. Sometimes it takes a little time to get to Amos. [Laughter] But he's between Joel and Obadiah, if that will help. They call Amos a minor prophet. I don't think he would have appreciated that. His message is quite major.

Amos 3:7 Underscoring what we had referred to before as God's will expressed in prophecy. Here is God's will in advance. We really have very little excuse. It's all been placed before us in detail. In fact, Amos says, *"GOD will do nothing, except he revealeth his secret unto his servants the prophets."* If that really said what it apparently does, it's one of the most radical statements in the entire Bible. And yet, what isn't radical in the Bible. Everything important to God is in prophecy, namely, that man as image needs to know about the Original, as well as the anointed footsteps of the development of the on-earth-as-in-heaven. The implication is that if it isn't [in prophecy], it isn't important. It isn't part of the divine destiny of man and the majestic march out of Sodom, out of Egypt to the final conquest of Canaan, when the promised land within becomes the fulfilled land within, and when we ourselves waken to our role in fulfilling prophecy.

If we are not in the Bible, if that Book has not been designed to reveal to us where we actually are in God's sight, it would clearly be impractical and cruel in misleading us. But the waymarks are there. If the waymarks are there, the way must be there. We can check our positions in the Bible as Jesus did.

Is it written? Is disease ravaging our experience? Has the economy depressed us? Is it written? Where are we? What are we subject to? What's in the original? Where are our Gethsemane Decisions on these subjects? God's will, or our will, or the will of others imposed upon us? The way we make our decisions, if they're that infinite and based in God, will not just simply alter our state of viewpoint but the world's as well. That role of prophecy needs to be appreciated and not shoved into a corner. Part of Jesus concern about Jerusalem was that it was the Jerusalem that killed the prophets, stoned those that were sent unto them. We could be in that very same state of mind, killing prophecy in our thought, stoning the divine messages. What is left in our consciousness that will save?

Let's just review some New Testament passages very quickly on the subject of the problem as well as the counteraction of it.

John 5:30 This cannot be repeated to often. Jesus himself obviously thought that. *"I can of mine own self do nothing. I seek not mine own will, but the will of the Father which hath sent me."* What could the teacher tell us more about the success of his method than that? How clear and how simple it is. Not a contrived humility. William Temple wrote on humility as follows: "Humility does not mean thinking less of yourself than of others. Nor does it mean having a low opinion of your own gifts. It means freedom from thinking about yourself at all."

Think of the lamb as symbolizing Jesus. What a beautiful symbol it is! The Bible's original tongue really is the symbolic spiritual language of inspiration. The lamb is totally dependent on the shepherd.

Still sticking with this idea of selfhood, either expressed through God, or through self-will, as we saw associated in the verses in Simeon and Levi in the *Book of Genesis* [34:25,30;49:5].

John 17:5 Here is part of the last prayer Jesus gave with his disciples before he went out to Gethsemane. *"And now, O Father,"* Here's Jesus talking to his Father. *"Glorify thou me,"* We talk about self-glorification. Look where the only gloriication comes from as far as Jesus is concerned. *"Glorify thou me with thine own self with the glory which I had with thee before this whole world mixture and problem that he had been confronting up to now, and was victorious over." "Glorify thou me with thine own self."* Why that's total immersion, isn't it, as far as baptism is concerned. God's selfhood, the only important identity Jesus accepts. It's God's selfhood that he recognizes is eternal. It has nothing to do with the world and temporary nature of things by the earthly world.

Philippians 2:4,5. Do you recall that the decade of the seventies has more or less gotten the label of being the age doing one's own thing? It shouldn't be limited to the seventies. But it certainly shows that in its surfacing so recently that this original sin of Adam is still very much to be dealt with. *"Look not every man on his own things, but every man also on the things of others"* Then adds immediately, *"Let this mind be in you, which was also in Christ Jesus."* Paul must have known that it was the kind of thinking Jesus did or he wouldn't have said that. *"Let this mind"* implies there may be a resistant element there. *"Let this mind"* just as the Bible opens with *"Let there be light."*

Philippians 2:13 Here's what the mind of God accomplishes for us. *"It is*

God which worketh in you both to will and to do." There's the follow through, the practical follow through "*of [his] good pleasure.*"

Philippians 2:21 Yet having to get back to the point that we need reminding on more than anything else, that Adamic disobedience of the Adamic race, "*For all seek their own, not the things which are Jesus Christ's.*" Is that having the mind which is in Christ? Seeking our own thing? Obviously not. It's the very opposite state. That is Anti-Christ then. That's the Anti-Christ mentality. Whatever opposes the Christ way, and the Christ route, and the Christ example, and the anointed in our lives.

2 Peter 2:10 Here the author is telling us "*those that walk after the flesh in the lust of uncleanness,*" (that's certainly not taking the precious from the vile, is it?) "*despise government.*" The word offered by some lexicographers there is "dominion." That's God's gift in Genesis 1[verse 26]. "*Presumptuous [are they], self-willed, they are not afraid to speak evil of dignities.*" To speak evil of man is to speak evil of dignities. "*I will make a man more precious than fine gold,*" God said [Isaiah 13:12]. A hiding place from the wind, a covert from the tempest.

Isaiah 2:22 "*Cease ye from man, whose breath [is] in his nostrils: for wherein is he to be accounted of?*"

Psalm 8:6 The Psalmist in describing man says, "*Thou madest him to have dominion over the works of thy hands.*" Dominion means what it says and must always stand unqualified by anything. Never can it be "dominion but," "dominion if." The integrity of the Word includes no possibility of subjection or subordination.

END TAPE 2, SIDE B

BEGIN TAPE 3, SIDE A

That dominion is God's gift according to Genesis 1[:26] to each and every one of us.

Even though the word "will" may not appear that often in its noun form, you know what its intent is and can get vast Scriptural lessons from almost every page of your Bible on the subject.

[Psalm 91:1] One of our most meaningful psalms. And note here the alternation between God's will and how human will when conformed to God's will can be translated. "*He that dwelleth*" Where? "*in the secret place of the most High"* Where can we find that? Where are the beacons along that way? Do we have to go outside of ourselves? Where does Jesus say the kingdom of heaven is? Is that *"the secret place of the most high"*? Whose been keeping it secret? [Laughter] If that's God's will, our place where we abide, then let's notice what normally would try to run amuck in our system, namely, human thoughts aimed to fulfill our own selfish objectives, when all those attempts to challenge the supremacy of God are placed under the control of the divine, as Jesus did in Gethsemane.

[Psalm 91:2] Notice "*we begin to say of God, [He is] my refuge and my fortress: in him"* what will I do, what's my will? *"Trust in him."* But that really is God's will for us. And we've identified our will with God's. Then what happens? What does the divine will do for us in that state of at-one-ment?

[Psalm 91:3] *"He will deliver us from the snare, the noisome pestilence."* The *Anchor Bible* translates as "venomous substance."

[Psalm 91:4] Let's examine also what belongs to the divine will. *"He will cover thee."* That's the divine will.*"With his feathers, and under his wings,"* our will "*under his wings, trust. His truth [will be our] shield and buckler."*

Psalm 91:5. What about human will that often has fear in it? Transformed in verse 5, *"Thou shalt not be afraid"* that's not part of the will that is at one with God's will. Do you think that might have represented Jesus' thought in Gethsemane? What we're reading here is not just isolated theory. If this is what works, this is what Jesus was as close as it's possible to be. The word was made flesh for him in Gethsemane. *"Thou shall not be afraid for terror."* And think of terrorism virtually paralyzing our world today. "*[Nor] for the arrow [that]"* by chance tries to find its mark in you.

[Psalm 91:6] "*Pestilence, destruction*"

[Psalm 91:7] The other level of human will commits suicide. *"A thousand"* the average human-will approach *"will fall,"* nothing within it can save it. "*[but] it shall not come nigh thee."*

[Psalm 91:8] Jesus could go all the way through Gethsemane and the cross and grave experience, still knowing that it was not coming nigh him despite what it seemed. He emerged the victor even though during that bleak three-day period many were rejoicing that they had silenced his pioneer efforts forever.

Psalm 91:9 Human will subordinated and relinquished *"Because you have made the LORD, [which is] my refuge, thy habitation."*

[Psalm 91:10] *"Then no evil will befall you."* The divine will is unmixed, hasn't evil in it. If the Original hasn't evil in it, how can it appear in the experience of the image? And *"no plague can come nigh thy dwelling."*

[Psalm 91:11] The divine will of God is to *"give his angels charge over each and every one of us."* Are we ignoring angels? Are we failing to entertain them? Angels, being linked to God, are God's constant uplifting directions to stay on the way. *"This [is] the way"* is an angelic message [Isaiah 30:21].

In Psalm 91:15 look at the divine will coinciding here with the highest sense of human will, at one, *"He shall call upon me."* That's God's will. *"And I will answer him."* That's communication. Apparently that's part of God's will, to clear up all the problems we've been having with communication. When He calls, we respond.

That is just one illustration of what can be done with so many [chapters], particularly of the Psalms, for we find in them David and other of the psalmists, dealing with the conflicts set up in the human arena always between God's still small voice and divine direction and all of the noise that would intervene. It's obvious why Jesus said not only to go into the closet but to shut the door. The "noisome pestilence" needs to be shut out. [Let's] go through the New Testament's defining of the Gethsemane experience.

Matthew 4:10. We'll answer the question, if there is one, whether Jesus for the first time made the Gethsemane Decision in Gethsemane. *"Then saith Jesus unto him, Get thee hence, Satan: for it is written."* Satan, the Satanic influence in thought, obviously dreads more than anything else the citing of the law from Scripture. Once the law is cited, Satanism is found to be illegitimately occupying a place in thought. *"It is written, Jesus said, Thou shalt worship the Lord thy God, and him only shalt thou serve."* Whose will? Not Satan's, not our own, God's will. Right there in that wilderness Jesus showed us how to deal with temptation. Don't wander from Scripture.

If anyone could have made up a very original and unique protest speech to Satan, Jesus could have done it. He chose instead to let the Bible take the blows, and deliver the message, and declare the law, and he stood on the Bible, and never bothered to elaborate on it. Are they always that straight and narrow? Or do we have many, many "siteseeing" tours, roads with detours wandering off hither and yon, making up conversations, when all Jesus wanted to do was dismiss, on the basis of its illegitimacy, any right of an influence opposed to God to dominate thought.

Matthew 4:11. *"The devil left him; angels came and ministered unto him."*

Matthew 7:21. It's not simply because we ask for help from God verbally that we're going to get the heavenly results. *"Not every one that saith unto me, Lord, Lord, shall enter into the kingdom of heaven;"* the one entrance key is *"to do the will of God which is in heaven."*

As we read more and more of this, we begin to see the message as to why Jesus at one point told his disciples [Luke 9:44] *"let these sayings sink down in your ears."* It's that very lack of receptivity or apathy that so often keep us from establishing our priorities and living our priorities, doing the will of God.

In Matthew 12:50 look at one of the fringe benefits of doing the will of God. *"Whoever does the Father's will is directly related to Jesus"* in as close proximity spiritually as you and I might think of in terms of our blood relationships on earth. [When] we're that close to Jesus in thought we can see that relationship to Jesus is a mental spiritual affinity and has nought to do with consanguinity or physicality or blood at all. Doing God's will relates us immediately to him.

Matthew 18:14. If we have ever doubted our importance to God, and the importance of individuality, after the parable [Matthew 18:12] of leaving the ninety-nine in the wilderness and going after that one important individual that went astray, off the way, blind to the prophecies that would have kept him on the way. Nevertheless, the love going back after that lost sheep, and going back over, and over again. Why, because *"It is not God's will that one of these little ones should perish."* We're those little ones. It's not God's will that we perish. If we're committing suicide, that's not God's will. The elements that are leading [us] to such self-destruction can be examined Scripturally. Again the provision of our heavenly Parent showing us the way, and the angels keeping us therein, just doing God's will. How simple it sounds.

Matthew 21:28. Let's see where we fall in this description that Jesus gives. *"A [certain] man had two sons;"* Here is now in the parable God is going to tell his children to do certain things. This is God's will. *"He comes to the first, and says, Son, go work to day in my vineyard."* [Matthew 21:29] *"He answered and said, I will not: but afterward he repented,"* changed his concept about doing his own will *versus* the Father's, *"and he went."*

[Matthew 21:30] *"Now the Father comes to the second one, and says likewise, Go work today in my vineyard, I sure will, Dad, he said, And never stirred, never went."*

Matthew 21:31 asks the question, *"Whether them twain did the will of [his] father?"* Then he proceeds to indicate that the differences "*between even the Pharisees and publicans and harlots."*

Matthew 21:32 *"The Pharisees: 'Sure I'm doing your will. Every day I'll do your will,' and not once are they fulfilling God's definition of His own will. Publicans and harlots:* their very lifestyles denying God, *'I will not do your will.'* Jesus found often more receptivity there than he did in the Levitical thought, the self-willed thought that we saw earlier in Jacob's insight.

Luke 12:32. What is the father's will expressed there? *"It's your Father's good pleasure to give you the kingdom,"* It's a gift. The kingdom is a gift. Dominion is God's gift.

John 1:13. The whole force behind the origin of God's creation is God. Again we've got things upside down like Isaiah says. Whatever is born of God, and if we are the sons of God, the Greek original used there in [John 1] Verse 12 is not *"sons"* but *"children."*

John 1:12. "*To as many as received him."* There's no resistance *in* receptive thought. "*To them gave he authority*, the right in Greek, *to become the children of God."* If we're that close and related to God, then the logic of it states that the children of God can only image forth what the parent has within the parent's nature.

John 1:13 rules out whatever is *"born of blood,"* "bloods" literally in [the] plural. *"Nor of the will of the flesh, nor of the will of man, but of God."* The whole question of doing our Father's will does back to nativity in origin, then. James [1:18], in fact, tells us, *"Of his own will he begat us."* If it's God's will, our examination of what the Scriptures tell us is God's will, will show what we have been created of, and by whom. That rules out blood, flesh, and human will, the will of man.

John 4:34 What else is doing the will of God? *"It's his meat."* It's what nourishes him. When he says, "*To do the will of him that sent me, and to finish his work,"* does that mean that God left something undone that Jesus is going to hasten to Scotch tape together at the latter day or something? That word *"finish"* in Greek really conveys the idea of completing through the fulfilling of the prophetic message. If that is Jesus' meat and we are to follow him, is our meat doing God's will and to finish God's work in that sense, by fulilling it on earth as in heaven?

John 5:21 What about even raising the dead, the last enemy? The original sin, now the terminal sin.*"The Father raiseth up the dead, and quickeneth [them]; even so the Son."* See how Jesus obviously knows that man is image. The Son can do nothing less or more than what he seeth the Father do and it's the Father's will to raise the dead, not to leave man in any state of dormancy, or death, or the grave, or termination of life which in the very divine nature of the Godhead is eternal and therefore must be in the likeness.

John 5:30 where Jesus is saying, *"I seek not mine own will, but the will of the Father which hath sent me."*

John 6:38 surely defines his mission as what? *"Not to do his own will, but to do the will of him that sent me."* And what is the result of such commitment?

John 6:39 *"That everything God had given Jesus,"* by extension, the humanity that now belongs to Jesus and follows Jesus, *"should lose nothing of what God has given."* That's dominion for one thing. Not one single instance of the loss of dominion can occur *"but should raise it up again at the last day."* Last day of what? The last day of any claim to opposition to God. That last day occurs every day. As Paul says [1 Corinthians 15:31], *"I die daily."* To make any sense out of Paul's statement, one must embrace with it the requisite implication that he's resurrected daily. And he's only losing something that doesn't belong to him, that's passing out of his experience, not part of this renewal which he discusses is absolutely necessary.

The choice for Paul [Romans 12:2], *"Be not conformed to this world; but be ye transformed by the renewing of your mind."* Can you carry it further? That's a lot of mental renewal going on there. Rather than world conformity, *"that we may prove what [is] that good, and acceptable, and perfect, will of God."* It's a transforming thing that's going on mentally. It must be an exciting thing to have that transformation and that yielding of human will to the divine going on daily. Losing a little bit of human will's claim to control over us daily and grasping more of our certain reliance on the rock, on God.

John 7:16 *"Jesus says, My doctrine is not mine, but his that sent me."*

John 7:17 Then adds, *"If any man will do his will, he'll know immediately the authority of what Jesus is saying."* He'll be at one with that authority and know that Jesus is not speaking of himself or for himself, but as the Father hath revealed unto him. He is speaking. How do you do it? The Lord said to Jeremiah,[15:19] *"Take forth the precious from the vile and thou shall be as my mouth."* We can't even recognize divine authority unless we have made the commitment to do God's will.

Let's examine how Paul had to face some of this. Let's see how he went through a Gethsemane Decision himself.

Acts 9:6 Right in the middle of the road to Damascus we find Saul's initial question, already showing the promise and the potential in his character. *"Lord, what wilt thou have me to do?"*

Romans 7:18 Where Paul is going to get quite explicit on the subject that it isn't all that easy to do God's will. There's a confusion that would substitute for the dominion-within. He says quite clearly, *"I know that in me (that is, in my flesh,) dwelleth no good thing:* Who needs it if there's nothing good there. Interesting definition of the flesh from Paul. *"To will is present with me;* There's the original sin tied up with flesh. *"But [how] to perform that which is good I find not anywhere in the flesh."*

Remember what Jesus said [Matthew 26:41], *"The Spirit indeed is willing but the flesh is weak."* He said that in Gethsemane.

Romans 7:19 The good that I would I do not: the evil which I certainly don't want to do, I end up doing anyway.

Remember he tells us [1 Corinthians 10:13] there's no temptation that cometh to you that isn't common to man. If it's happening to him, it's happening to us.

Romans 7:20 If I do what I really don't want to do, it's no more I that do it, but sin that dwelleth in me. There's the impulsion of Adam to that tree of knowledge of the good and evil.

Romans 7:22 Here is the distinction. Here is the sifting out, the separation of kingdom from chaos within. *"I delight in the law of God after the inward man:"*

Romans 7:23 *"But I see another law in my members,"* in the bodily aspects, the fleshly aspects of man, *"warring against the law of my mind,"* It's a warfare; it's a battle; no wonder we find *"Michael and the dragon and angels on both sides,* or thoughts on both sides, *in contest"* in Revelation 12:7. That warfare must be fought out, obviously. And the dragon elements which *"bringing me into captivity to the law of sin which is in my members."*

Romans 7:24 *"O wretched man."* It's a wretched condition to be split down the middle by dualism, a kingdom divided against itself; it can't stand. *"Who will deliver me from the body of this death?"* That Adam thing that leads right smack to that objective.

Romans 7:25 *"I thank God."* And here's the answer again, *"through the Christ. So then with the mind I myself serve the law of God; but with the flesh the law of sin."*

Romans 8:6 The dichotomy just as clear, *"to be carnally minded,"* a mind just absolutely filled with flesh, *"[is] death; but to be spiritually minded [is] life and peace."*

Romans 8:7 The carnal mind, what is it? *"Enmity against God."* Human will, fleshly will, impulses, *"enmity against God."* There's the enemy, the enemy within; it's the carnal mind. Paul has said it. But to the spiritually minded, that's the Christ route, and peace. Then the great news.

Romans 8:9 Then the great news. That we really *"are not in the flesh, but in the Spirit, if,"* there's the qualification, *"the Spirit of God live in us,"* only God's Spirit that we are capable of responding to, and doing God's will, motivated by God, prompted by God. I think you will be hard pressed to discover in the initial early chapters of the *Book of Acts*, for instance, any step of progress in church growth, prior to the announcement being made that an individual apostle, or the group itself assembled, was filled with the Holy Ghost. Once filled with the Holy Ghost, the church moves forward. An attempt to move the church forward without the Holy Ghost is human will. The Bible [Revelation 2:7] pleads with man to remember it is what *"the Spirit saith unto the churches"* only that counts. That Spirit should be communicating to every receptive thought on the face of the globe.

1 John 5:14: Just to check our method of praying. If we aren't getting results, we'd better go back and test the method of prayer according to the Scriptural definitions. Remember the prayer in Gethsemane that got results. This is what Jesus had to go through in prayer. *"This is the confidence,"* Already we're being told what the mental state of prayer has to be. Thought has to be filled with confidence. Confidence in whom? In God, *"That we have in Him*, but here's the rub, *"according to God's will, he heareth us."* There it is. It is as simple as that. Even prayer. Prayer is the means by which we conform thought to God's will and listen to be filled with God's will. God's will expressed is always the immediate results. If it isn't God's will for man to be sick, then the result of prayer conforming to God's will is an elimination of sickness from man's experience. It's not in the image. Doesn't even hurt to remove it. Wasn't there.

1 John 5:15 Then it continues. *"If we know that he hear us,"* which we

just agreed to in verse 14, *"If we really know God hears us, whatsoever we ask, we know that we have* already *the petitions that we desired of him."* Can you think of a better way to describe Jesus' prayer before the tomb of Lazarus, for instance. He knew that he had the petition he had desired of God, because he knew that God had heard him. He said it even [John 11:41]. Therefore he asked according to God's will. God's will did not support Lazarus remaining in that tomb, or ever being there. So, *"Lazarus, you come forth"* [John 11:43]. That's his dominion and his right. He does the moving and the activity and the responding. God calls. Man answers. No one need come between God and His man.

If our thesis as presented is accurate, that the implication of Paul's statement [1 Corinthians 15:22], *"As in Adam all die, even so in Christ shall all be made alive"* presents problem and solution, or remedy, then one of the greatest research jobs awaiting all of us is to get back into that problem called Adam which we're all wrestling with.

Just make a list of everything you detect that Adam did wrong mentally and physically. Because, if it is true that Jesus' mission was to remedy the Adam-man and wipe that alternative off the face of man's consciousness, then everything Adam did wrong which was upside down Jesus is going to put right side up and show man is upright. Many things may occur to you, for instance in the initial phases of such a list which we could just touch upon. Adam's problem occurred in what environment? The garden of Eden. Where did Jesus face down and confront that Adam- problem? The Garden of Gethsemane. Is this a coincidence? Is Gethsemane intended to be the remedy for the problems of Eden in our own thinking? I love in that context to remember Isaiah's words [Isaiah 1:29] when he says, *"Ye shall be confounded for the gardens ye have chosen."* Eden, Gethsemane.

Adam's problem, though, is probably symbolized most graphically by what? He had been told not to do something, what was it? *"Not to eat of that tree"* [Genesis 3:3]. Instead he went and did it. The disobedience, doing one's own will, would have to be totally remedied right up with the same even greater peak pressure on a humanhood that had just announced to the world that the way to get out of this Adam-mess is to yield to God's will regardless of the pressure upon you, so [it's] doing God's will *versus* doing one's own will.

The tree of knowledge of good and evil. You know that the New Testament refers several times to the cross as the tree, that they nailed Jesus to the tree [Acts 13:29; 1 Peter 2:24]. Interesting symbolism. The attempt to nail Jesus as if he were one more in the dying race of Adam, to be nailed to death, and that's the termination and the end of anything that he would offer man radically as salvation. Jesus could not be nailed on the cross any more than God's man could be nailed on the cross, and thus his theology was exemplified.

Do you remember, - just things like this to show you how much fun this work can be as well - part of the curse on Adam [Genesis 3:17,18] was that thorns will be brought forth unto him. Did Jesus have to face Adam's thorns on that weekend. *"In the sweat of thy face shalt thou eat bread...dust thou [art], and unto dust shalt thou return"* [Genesis 3:19]. The grave was the pressure of the dust he was to return to. There are many others showing the complete reversal of the Adam. It's as if the highest sense of mind on earth, which has relinquished its right to mind except by reflection, is turning everything right side up just as we do visually. That topic is far from being exhausted. In fact, what can exhaust an infinite reservoir? It's one thing about supply in the Bible. It's never consumed. Therefore, there are no consumers.

We're going to review the actual events of the Gethesmane experience and see some of the differences. What Jesus faced, what he was remedying, why he was there and see that we must, just for gratitude's sake alone, have a stake in that Gethsemane, pioneer work. But then we must take it beyond this. We must go and do likewise.

END TAPE 3, SIDE A

BEGIN TAPE 3, SIDE B

Matthew 26:30 *"When they had sung an hymn, they went out into the mount of Olives."* A hymn before Gethsemane. That shows the value Jesus places on such an uplifting of thought through the conjoining of music and words. The meaning that is often conveyed even more deeply to us when we have that unity of soul expressed by thought in that manner.

Matthew 26:36 *"Jesus comes to a place called Gethsemane,"* the oil press.

Do you think that by going to so many of these preceding verses that we need now look for very little explanation as to the agony of this hour, and the burden Jesus was bearing? With all the world's tradition behind the necessity for doing one's own will, to take that as an escape route and Jesus slams the door on that forever. The only salvation is taking that door that the key of David unlocks, don't try to shut it, the Scriptures indicate. The Scripture is locked. Or we would not have the mention of the need of a key. The key to the Scripture placed into the lock shows that neither the lock nor the key is the ultimately important thing. It's what's behind that door, that open door for man to walk through. But no one gets there except through that door and except through utilizing that key.

Matthew 26:37 *"Peter, James and John fall asleep, in a trance-like sleep."* It's hypnotic.

Matthew 26:38 Even after Jesus had said, *"Tarry ye here, and watch with me."* My mom pointed out a parallel here. I recall hitting my head several times that I'd never seen that. Those words "Tarry ye here" are exactly the words Elijah said to Elisha and Elisha refused to tarry, "As the Lord liveth and as thy soul liveth." Look at that for image and likeness to Original! *"As God lives and as your identity therefore must live, I will not leave thee."* My mother just said, "Just think of how different that Gethsemane experience might have been if the disciples had just learned the lesson of Elisha and carried that Scriptural inspiration with them. Elisha saw the ascension of Elijah because he did not give up. Jesus was left alone in this experience in Gethsemane. The deep sleep that fell upon the original Adam falls upon his descendants.

Matthew 26:39 *"Jesus then goes away about a stone's cast,"* further spiritual distance from his disciples, perhaps, and his prayer, the Gethsemane decision, *"Saying, my Father, if it be possible, let this cup pass from me: nevertheless"* make no mistake where my committment is, *"**not** as I will,"* He told us that was his mission, not to do his own will but to do his father's will. If Gethsemane had broken him, where would we be? *"**Not** as I will, but as thou wilt."* Is that Jesus overcoming the original sin of Adam?

Let's now turn to Mark's version of the event. Something no other gospel records.

Mark 14:36 *"Jesus says, Abba, Father, all things [are] possible unto thee."* He's praying his own Lord's prayer, showing that this is not a prayer that he doesn't participate in himself. *"Abba,"* as some of you may know, is behind every use of Jesus' word "Father" in the gospels. *"Abba"* is the Aramaic word. No other religious thinker or writer before his time had ever used "Abba" for God. *"Abba"* is a child's word. It is "Daddy." It's one of the first two words that a Hebrew and an Arab child learns today. "Abba, Imma [Daddy, Mama or Mommy]"

When he told us we could not enter in to the kingdom of heaven without becoming as a little child, he obviously meant we cannot say the Lord's Prayer effectively without becoming a little child. It's an infant's reliance on God and Jesus goes to his Father as a little child in Gethsemane. When we're making our Gethsemane decisions, we had better follow the example and remember *"Abba,"*

Mark 14:38 *"He states, The spirit truly [is] ready, but the flesh [is] weak."*

Let's go to Luke's version.

Luke 22:42 Luke tells us a few other things. As a matter of fact, [this is] probably the most well known expression of the Gethsemane Decision where Jesus says, *"Nevertheless not my will, but thine, be done."* Remember if the opening line of the Lord's prayer is recalled by "Abba," Our Father, *"Abba"* being the original behind it.

[Luke 11:1,2] Look at *"Thy will be done"* in the Lord's Prayer. Why is it there? The prayer that Jesus himself gave us in response to the question, *"Lord, teach us to pray."*

[Matthew 6:9] *"After this manner therefore pray ye." "Abba."* Immediately be a little child and be sure you're committed to God's will being done.

Look at that discipline requiring human thought to conform and yield to the divine when all outlines and barriers around mentality as we have become accustomed to it fall away and we find no limitations to thought or mind at all if we are the image of the mind of God. *'Not my will but thine be done.*" is Jesus using his own prayer in Gethsemane. If that Lord's Prayer can carry one through Gethsemane, it can carry one through anything. The *Theological Dictionary of the New Testament* says this,

> "Humanly he has the possibility of an independent will. But this will exists only to be negated in face of the divine will. It's perfect agreement with the divine will finds expression in the declaration of its negation." And also adds, "The third petition of the Lord's prayer in Gethsemane expresses not merely submission but consent to a comprehensive fulfillment of God's will in keeping with the hallowing of His name and the coming of His kingdom. It thus implies an ultimate and basic attitude on the part of the one who prays. It agrees exactly with the petition of the Son in Gethsemane. And again from the same *Theological Dictionary of the New Testament*, "What is meant in this statement *'Not my will but thine be done'* is the active divine resolve which cannot remain in the sphere of thought but demands action everywhere. We have the impression [in the Scriptures] that nothing human but only this divine will can provide the impulse of the execution of the plan of salvation."

We discussed at some length a decision, a question, a choice that could have taken a fraction of a second if it were not for the human mind's built-in resistance that we see the ample testimony to be throughout the Scriptures. The necessity for inculcation to get the point over, and over, and over to us is obvious in studying the works of our master teacher Jesus in the New Testament, but also seeing the examples before him in the Old Testament. Gethsemane is the press, the oil press. Like Jesus, we must have oil within us. The pressure is still on. If Gethsemane is the press, can we say and be backed up by Scripture, that not my will but thine be done is the oil? If so, that's the Christ-oil. The word Christ is based upon the Greek word for oil. That's what poured out of Jesus' experience at Gethsemane. What is it designed to do? To anoint, to heal, to feed, to cleanse. If the pressure of Gethsemane is upon us, what is oil designed to do? Do we find in our character anything unlike that Christ-anointed example? Is that human will that needs to be crushed out forever?

We think we're in an oil crisis today. The pressure is on. But Gethsemane's purpose has a divine result regardless of what the world can bring to bear upon you and me, Jesus could say in part of that hymn that he sang before Gethsemane which is locatable in the later psalms, is still sung today at Passover, that he needed not to fear what man or flesh could do. Out of that experience flowed the oil that is still blessing us, is still being utilized. We're not in an oil crisis today if we're in the way with Jesus. We may be at a "parting of the ways," the meaning of the of the word crisis. We may be challenged regularly and often to make our right decisions, our right choice, our Gethsemane decision.

Then, the result of no longer bowing down to a human will, no longer seeing within us any domination by others through their human will, but filled with the Holy Ghost's own message, the angel that strengthens Jesus at that moment, according to Luke. That angel awaits to strengthen us today. The world with its creaky joints awaits, needs, yearns, for more Christ oil to be poured from the thoughts and lives of those who have made the decision, are continuing to make the decision, and are moving from Gethsemane at the base of the Mount of Olives to the summit of the Mount of Olives where Jesus himself ascended. We never have to budge from that mount. It represents both cross and crown, both problem and solution. And therefore that oil which negates the experience of the cross and delivers the crown shows us that those two symbols, as precious as they are in Scripture, are inseparable. If the cross represents the problem, and the crown the solution, then intertwined they deliver that simple message to me, problem solved. That is the result of the Gethsemane decision.

by B. Cobbey Crisler

Thank you very much.

[Applause]

END TAPE 3, SIDE B.

***

CITATION INDEX TO VOLUME 15
The Gethsemane Decision

Citation compiled by tranScriptures of Columbia, S.C.

(Books are listed alphabetically)

ACTS
(9:6) And he trembling and astonished said, Lord, what wilt thou have me to do? And the Lord [said] unto him, Arise, and go into the city, and it shall be told thee what thou must do.

(13:29) And when they had fulfilled all that was written of him, they took [him] down from the tree, and laid [him] in a sepulchre.

AMOS
(3:7) Surely the Lord GOD will do nothing, but he revealeth his secret unto his servants the prophets.

1 CORINTHIANS
(10:13) There hath no temptation taken you but such as is common to man: but God [is] faithful, who will not suffer you to be tempted above that ye are able; but will with the temptation also make a way to escape, that ye may be able to bear [it].

(15:22) For as in Adam all die, even so in Christ shall all be made alive. **(15:31)** I protest by your rejoicing which I have in Christ Jesus our Lord, I die daily.

2 CORINTHIANS
(10:5) Casting down imaginations, and every high thing that exalteth itself against the knowledge of God, and bringing into captivity every thought to the obedience of Christ;

DEUTERONOMY
(18:18) I will raise them up a Prophet from among their brethren, like unto thee, and will put my words in his mouth; and he shall speak unto them all that I shall command him.

ECCLESIASTES
(12:13) Let us hear the conclusion of the whole matter: Fear God, and keep his commandments: for this [is] the whole [duty] of man. **(12:14)** For God shall bring every work into judgment, with every

secret thing, whether [it be] good, or whether [it be] evil.

EZEKIEL
(2:3) And he said unto me, Son of man, I send thee to the children of Israel, to a rebellious nation that hath rebelled against me: they and their fathers have transgressed against me, [even] unto this very day. **(2:4)** For [they are] impudent children and stiffhearted. I do send thee unto them; and thou shalt say unto them, Thus saith the Lord GOD. **(2:5)** And they, whether they will hear, or whether they will forbear, (for they [are] a rebellious house,) yet shall know that there hath been a prophet among them.

(18:23) Have I any pleasure at all that the wicked should die? saith the Lord GOD: [and] not that he should return from his ways, and live?

GENESIS
(1:26) And God said, Let us make man in our image, after our likeness: and let them have dominion over the fish of the sea, and over the fowl of the air, and over the cattle, and over all the earth, and over every creeping thing that creepeth upon the earth. **(1:27)** So God created man in his [own] image, in the image of God created he him; male and female created he them.

(3:3) But of the fruit of the tree which [is] in the midst of the garden, God hath said, Ye shall not eat of it, neither shall ye touch it, lest ye die. **(3:9)** And the LORD God called unto Adam, and said unto him, Where [art] thou?

(3:17) And unto Adam he said, Because thou hast hearkened unto the voice of thy wife, and hast eaten of the tree, of which I commanded thee, saying, Thou shalt not eat of it: cursed [is] the ground for thy sake; in sorrow shalt thou eat [of] it all the days of thy life; **(3:18)** Thorns also and thistles shall it bring forth to thee; and thou shalt eat the herb of the field; **(3:19)** In the sweat of thy face shalt thou eat bread, till thou return unto the ground; for out of it wast thou taken: for dust thou [art], and unto dust shalt thou return.

(34:25) And it came to pass on the third day, when they were sore, that two of the sons of Jacob, Simeon and Levi, Dinah's brethren, took each man his sword, and came upon the city boldly, and slew all the males. **(34:30)** And Jacob said to Simeon and Levi, Ye have troubled me to make me to stink among the inhabitants of the land, among the Canaanites and the Perizzites: and I [being] few in number, they shall gather themselves together against me, and slay me; and I shall be destroyed, I and my house.

(49:5) Simeon and Levi [are] brethren; instruments of cruelty [are in] their habitations.**(49:6)** O my soul, come not thou into their secret; unto their assembly, mine honour, be not thou united: for in their anger they slew a man, and in their selfwill they digged down a wall.

ISAIAH
(1:29) For they shall be ashamed of the oaks which ye have desired, and ye shall be confounded for the gardens that ye have chosen.

(2:22) Cease ye from man, whose breath [is] in his nostrils: for wherein is he to be accounted of?

(5:20) Woe unto them that call evil good, and good evil; that put darkness for light, and light for darkness; that put bitter for sweet, and sweet for bitter!

(13:12) I will make a man more precious than fine gold; even a man than the golden wedge of Ophir.

(29:16) Surely your turning of things upside down shall be esteemed as the potter's clay: for shall the work say of him that made it, He made me not? or shall the thing framed say of him that framed it, He had no understanding?

(32:2) And a man shall be as an hiding place from the wind, and a covert from the tempest; as rivers of water in a dry place, as the shadow of a great rock in a weary land.

JAMES
(1:18) Of his own will begat he us with the word of truth, that we should be a kind of firstfruits of his creatures.

JEREMIAH
(6:18) Thus saith the LORD, Stand ye in the ways, and see, and ask for the old paths, where [is] the good way, and walk therein, and ye shall find rest for your souls. But they said, We will not walk [therein]. **(6:19)** Hear, O earth: behold, I will bring evil upon this people, [even] the fruit of their thoughts, because they have not hearkened unto my words, nor to my law, but rejected it.

(7:23) But this thing commanded I them, saying, Obey my voice, and I will be your God, and ye shall be my people: and walk ye in all the ways that I have commanded you, that it may be well unto you. **(7:24)** But they hearkened not, nor inclined their ear, but walked in the counsels [and] in the imagination of their evil heart, and went backward, and not forward. **(7:25)** Since the day that your fathers came forth out of the land of Egypt unto this day I have even sent unto you all my servants the prophets, daily rising up early and sending [them]: **(7:26)** Yet they hearkened not unto me, nor inclined their ear, but hardened their neck: they did worse than their fathers. **(7:27)** Therefore thou shalt speak all these words unto them; but they will not hearken to thee: thou shalt also call unto them; but they will not answer thee. **(7:28)** But thou shalt say unto them, This [is] a nation that obeyeth not the voice of the LORD their God, nor receiveth correction: truth is perished, and is cut off from their mouth.

(15:19) Therefore thus saith the LORD, If thou return, then will I bring thee again, [and] thou shalt stand before me: and if thou take forth the precious from the vile, thou shalt be as my mouth: let them return unto thee; but return not thou unto them.

(18:12) And they said, There is no hope: but we will walk after our own devices, and we will every one do the imagination of his evil heart.

(23:10) For the land is full of adulterers; for because of swearing the land mourneth; the pleasant places of the wilderness are dried up, and their course is evil, and their force [is] not right. **(23:11)** For both prophet and priest are profane; yea, in my house have I found their wickedness, saith the LORD. **(23:17)** They say still unto them that despise me, The LORD hath said, Ye shall have peace; and they say unto every one that walketh after the imagination of his own heart, No evil shall come upon you.

(30:17) For I will restore health unto thee, and I will heal thee of thy wounds, saith the LORD; because they called thee an Outcast, [saying], This [is] Zion, whom no man seeketh after.

JOB
(1:17) And the LORD said unto Satan, Whence comest thou? Then Satan answered the LORD, and said, From going to and fro in the earth, and from walking up and down in it.

(2:2) And the LORD said unto Satan, From whence comest thou? And Satan answered the LORD, and said, From going to and fro in the earth, and from walking up and down in it.

(7:4) When I lie down, I say, When shall I arise, and the night be gone? and I am full of tossings to and fro unto the dawning of the day.

JOHN
(1:12) But as many as received him, to them gave he power to become the sons of God, [even] to them that believe on his name:

(1:13) Which were born, not of blood, nor of the will of the flesh, nor of the will of man, but of God. **(1:14)** And the Word was made flesh, and dwelt among us, (and we beheld his glory, the glory as of the only begotten of the Father,) full of grace and truth.

(4:34) Jesus saith unto them, My meat is to do the will of him that sent me, and to finish his work.

(5:19) Then answered Jesus and said unto them, Verily, verily, I say unto you, The Son can do nothing of himself, but what he seeth the Father do: for what things soever he doeth, these also doeth the Son likewise. **(5:21)** For as the Father raiseth up the dead, and quickeneth [them]; even so the Son quickeneth whom he will. **(5:30)** I can of mine own self do nothing: as I hear, I judge: and my judgment is just; because I seek not mine own will, but the will of the Father which hath sent me.

(6:38) For I came down from heaven, not to do mine own will, but the will of him that sent me. **(6:39)** And this is the Father's will which hath sent me, that of all which he hath given me I should lose nothing, but should raise it up again at the last day.

(7:16) Jesus answered them, and said, My doctrine is not mine, but his that sent me. **(7:17)** If any man will do his will, he shall know of the doctrine, whether it be of God, or [whether] I speak of myself.

(8:44) Ye are of [your] father the devil, and the lusts of your father ye will do. He was a murderer from the beginning, and abode not in the truth, because there is no truth in him. When he speaketh a lie, he speaketh of his own: for he is a liar, and the father of it.

(11:25) Jesus said unto her, I am the resurrection, and the life: he that believeth in me, though he were dead, yet shall he live: **(11:41)** Then they took away the stone [from the place] where the dead was laid. And Jesus lifted up [his] eyes, and said, Father, I thank thee that thou hast heard me.

(12:50) And I know that his commandment is life everlasting: whatsoever I speak therefore, even as the Father said unto me, so I speak.

(16:33) These things I have spoken unto you, that in me ye might have peace. In the world ye shall have tribulation: but be of good cheer; I have overcome the world.

(17:5) And now, O Father, glorify thou me with thine own self with the glory which I had with thee before the world was.

(20:17) Jesus saith unto her, Touch me not; for I am not yet ascended to my Father: but go to my brethren, and say unto them, I ascend unto my Father, and your Father; and [to] my God, and your God.

1 JOHN

(5:14) And this is the confidence that we have in him, that, if we ask any thing according to his will, he heareth us: **(5:15)** And if we know that he hear us, whatsoever we ask, we know that we have the petitions that we desired of him.

1 KINGS

(19:4) But he himself went a day's journey into the wilderness, and came and sat down under a juniper tree: and he requested for himself that he might die; and said, It is enough; now, O LORD, take away my life; for I [am] not better than my fathers. **(19:8)** And he arose, and did eat and drink, and went in the strength of that meat forty days and forty nights unto Horeb the mount of God. **(19:9)** And he came thither unto a cave, and lodged there; and, behold, the word of the LORD [came] to him, and he said unto him, What doest thou here, Elijah?

(19:11) And he said, Go forth, and stand upon the mount before the LORD. And, behold, the LORD passed by, and a great and strong wind rent the mountains, and brake in pieces the rocks before the LORD; [but] the LORD [was] not in the wind: and after the wind an earthquake; [but] the LORD [was] not in the earthquake: **(19:12)** And after the earthquake a fire; [but] the LORD [was] not in the fire: and after the fire a still small voice. **(19:13)** And it was [so], when Elijah heard [it], that he wrapped his face in his mantle, and went out, and stood in the entering in of the cave. And, behold, [there came] a voice unto him, and said, What doest thou here, Elijah?

LUKE

(2:49) And he said unto them, How is it that ye sought me? wist ye not that I must be about my Father's business?

(3:17) Whose fan [is] in his hand, and he will throughly purge his floor, and will gather the wheat into his garner; but the chaff he will burn with fire unquenchable.
(11:1) And it came to pass, that, as he was praying in a certain place, when he ceased, one of his disciples said unto him, Lord, teach us to pray, as John also taught his disciples. **(11:2)** And he said unto them, When ye pray, say, Our Father which art in heaven, Hallowed

be thy name. Thy kingdom come. Thy will be done, as in heaven, so in earth.

(12:32) Fear not, little flock; for it is your Father's good pleasure to give you the kingdom.

(13:16) And ought not this woman, being a daughter of Abraham, whom Satan hath bound, lo, these eighteen years, be loosed from this bond on the sabbath day? **(13:34)** O Jerusalem, Jerusalem, which killest the prophets, and stonest them that are sent unto thee; how often would I have gathered thy children together, as a hen [doth gather] her brood under [her] wings, and ye would not!

(22:42) Saying, Father, if thou be willing, remove this cup from me: nevertheless not my will, but thine, be done.

MARK
(14:36) And he said, Abba, Father, all things [are] possible unto thee; take away this cup from me: nevertheless not what I will, but what thou wilt. **(14:38)** Watch ye and pray, lest ye enter into temptation. The spirit truly [is] ready, but the flesh [is] weak.

MATTHEW
(4:10) Then saith Jesus unto him, Get thee hence, Satan: for it is written, Thou shalt worship the Lord thy God, and him only shalt thou serve. **(4:11)** Then the devil leaveth him, and, behold, angels came and ministered unto him.

(6:9) After this manner therefore pray ye: Our Father which art in heaven, Hallowed be thy name.

(7:21) Not every one that saith unto me, Lord, Lord, shall enter into the kingdom of heaven; but he that doeth the will of my Father which is in heaven.

(12:50) For whosoever shall do the will of my Father which is in heaven, the same is my brother, and sister, and mother.

(13:33) Another parable spake he unto them; The kingdom of heaven is like unto leaven, which a woman took, and hid in three measures of meal, till the whole was leavened. **(13:44)** Again, the kingdom of heaven is like unto treasure hid in a field; the which when a man hath found, he hideth, and for joy thereof goeth and selleth all that he hath, and buyeth that field. **(13:45)** Again, the kingdom of heaven is like unto a merchant man, seeking goodly pearls: **(13:47)** Again, the kingdom of heaven is like unto a net, that was cast into the sea, and gathered of every kind: **(13:52)** Then said he unto them, Therefore every scribe [which is] instructed unto the kingdom of heaven is like unto a man [that is] an householder, which bringeth forth out of his treasure [things] new and old.

(18:12) How think ye? if a man have an hundred sheep, and one of them be gone astray, doth he not leave the ninety and nine, and goeth into the mountains, and seeketh that which is gone astray? **(18:14)** Even so it is not the will of your Father which is in heaven, that one of these little ones should perish.

(20:1) For the kingdom of heaven is like unto a man [that is] an householder, which went out early in the morning to hire labourers into his vineyard.
Matthew 20:2 And when he had agreed with the labourers for a penny a day, he sent them into his vineyard.

(21:28) But what think ye? A [certain] man had two sons; and he came to the first, and said, Son, go work to day in my vineyard. **(21:29)** He answered and said, I will not: but afterward he repented, and went. **(21:30)** And he came to the second, and said likewise. And he answered and said, I [go], sir: and went not. **(21:31)** Whether of them twain did the will of [his] father? They say unto him, The first. Jesus saith unto them, Verily I say unto you, That the publicans and the harlots go into the kingdom of God before you.

(21:32) For John came unto you in the way of righteousness, and ye believed him not: but the publicans and the harlots believed him: and ye, when ye had seen [it], repented not afterward, that ye might believe him.

(23:37) O Jerusalem, Jerusalem, [thou] that killest the prophets, and stonest them which are sent unto thee, how often would I have gathered thy children together, even as a hen gathereth her chickens under [her] wings, and ye would not!

(26:30) And when they had sung an hymn, they went out into the mount of Olives. **(26:35)** Peter said unto him, Though I should die with thee, yet will I not deny thee. Likewise also said all the disciples. **(26:36)** Then cometh Jesus with them unto a place called Gethsemane, and saith unto the disciples, Sit ye here, while I go and pray yonder. **(26:37)** And he took with him Peter and the two sons of Zebedee, and began to be sorrowful and very heavy. **(26:38)** Then saith he unto them, My soul is exceeding sorrowful, even unto death: tarry ye here, and watch with me. **(26:39)** And he went a little further, and fell on his face, and prayed, saying, O my Father, if it be possible, let this cup pass from me: nevertheless not as I will, but as thou [wilt]. **(26:40)** And he cometh unto the disciples, and findeth them asleep, and saith unto Peter, What, could ye not watch with me one hour? **(26:41)** Watch and pray, that ye enter not into temptation: the spirit indeed [is] willing, but the flesh [is] weak. **(26:42)** He went away again the second time, and prayed, saying, O my Father, if this cup may not pass away from me, except I drink it, thy will be done. **(26:44)** And he left them, and went away again, and prayed the third time, saying the same words.

NUMBERS

(16:28) And Moses said, Hereby ye shall know that the LORD hath sent me to do all these works; for [I have] not [done them] of mine own mind.

(24:13) If Balak would give me his house full of silver and gold, I cannot go beyond the commandment of the LORD, to do [either] good or bad of mine own mind; [but] what the LORD saith, that will I speak?

1 PETER

(2:24) Who his own self bare our sins in his own body on the tree, that we, being dead to sins, should live unto righteousness: by whose stripes ye were healed.

2 PETER

(2:10) But chiefly them that walk after the flesh in the lust of uncleanness, and despise government. Presumptuous [are they], selfwilled, they are not afraid to speak evil of dignities.

PHILIPPIANS

(2:4) Look not every man on his own things, but every man also on the things of others. **(2:5)** Let this mind be in you, which was also in Christ Jesus: **(2:13)** For it is God which worketh in you both to will and to do of [his] good pleasure. **(2:21)** For all seek their own, not the things which are Jesus Christ's.

PSALMS

(8:6) Thou madest him to have dominion over the works of thy hands; thou hast put all [things] under his feet:

(19:12) Who can understand [his] errors? cleanse thou me from secret [faults]. **(19:13)** Keep back thy servant also from presumptuous [sins]; let them not have dominion over me: then shall I be upright, and I shall be innocent from the great transgression. **(19:14)** Let the words of my mouth, and the meditation of my heart, be acceptable in thy sight, O LORD, my strength, and my redeemer.

(37:23) The steps of a [good] man are ordered by the LORD: and he delighteth in his way.

(46:10) Be still, and know that I [am] God: I will be exalted among the heathen, I will be exalted in the earth.

(91:1) He that dwelleth in the secret place of the most High shall abide under the shadow of the Almighty. **(91:2)** I will say of the LORD, [He is] my refuge and my fortress: my God; in him will I trust. **(91:3)** Surely he shall deliver thee from the snare of the fowler, [and] from the noisome pestilence.

(91:4) He shall cover thee with his feathers, and under his wings shalt thou trust: his truth [shall be thy] shield and buckler.Psalm 91:5 Thou shalt not be afraid for the terror by night; [nor] for the arrow [that] flieth by day; **(91:5)** [Nor] for the pestilence [that] walketh in darkness; [nor] for the destruction [that] wasteth at noonday. **(91:7)** A thousand shall fall at thy side, and ten thousand at thy right hand; [but] it shall not come nigh thee. **(91:8)** Only with thine eyes shalt thou behold and see the reward of the wicked. **(91:9)** Because thou hast made the LORD, [which is] my refuge, [even] the most High, thy habitation; **(91:10)** There shall no evil befall thee, neither shall any plague come nigh thy dwelling. **(91:11)** For he shall give his angels charge over thee, to keep thee in all thy ways. **(91:15)** He shall call upon me, and I will answer him: I [will be] with him in trouble; I will deliver him, and honour him.

REVELATION

(2:7) He that hath an ear, let him hear what the Spirit saith unto the churches; To him that overcometh will I give to eat of the tree of life, which is in the midst of the paradise of God.

(11:8) And their dead bodies [shall lie] in the street of the great city, which spiritually is called Sodom and Egypt, where also our Lord was crucified.

(12:7) And there was war in heaven: Michael and his angels fought against the dragon; and the dragon fought and his angels,

(21:27) And there shall in no wise enter into it any thing that defileth, neither [whatsoever] worketh abomination, or [maketh] a lie: but they which are written in the Lamb's book of life.

ROMANS

(5:14) Nevertheless death reigned from Adam to Moses, even over them that had not sinned after the similitude of Adam's transgression, who is the figure of him that was to come. **(5:19)** For as by one man's disobedience many were made sinners, so by the obedience of one shall many be made righteous. **(5:21)** That as sin hath reigned unto death, even so might grace reign through righteousness unto eternal life by Jesus Christ our Lord.

(7:18) For I know that in me (that is, in my flesh,) dwelleth no good thing: for to will is present with me; but [how] to perform that which is good I find not. **(7:19)** For the good that I would I do not: but the evil which I would not, that I do. **(7:20)** Now if I do that I would not, it is no more I that do it, but sin that dwelleth in me. **(7:22)** For I delight in the law of God after the inward man: **(7:23)** But I see another law in my members, warring against the law of my mind, and bringing me into captivity to the law of sin which is in my members. **(7:24)** O wretched man that I am! who shall deliver me from the body of this death? **(7:25)** I thank God through Jesus Christ our Lord. So then with the mind I myself serve the law of God; but with the flesh the law of sin.

(8:6) For to be carnally minded [is] death; but to be spiritually minded [is] life and peace. **(8:7)** Because the carnal mind [is] enmity against God: for it is not subject to the law of God, neither indeed can be. **(8:9)** But ye are not in the flesh, but in the Spirit, if so be that the Spirit of God dwell in you. Now if any man have not the Spirit of Christ, he is none of his.

(12:2) And be not conformed to this world: but be ye transformed by the renewing of your mind, that ye may prove what [is] that good, and acceptable, and perfect, will of God.

2 THESSALONIANS

(3:1) Finally, brethren, pray for us, that the word of the Lord may have [free] course, and be glorified, even as [it is] with you:

ZECHARIAH

(2:13) Be silent, O all flesh, before the LORD: for he is raised up out of his holy habitation.

***

WORD INDEX TO VOLUME 15
The Gethsemane Decision

Word Index compiled by tranScriptures of Columbia, S.C.

Bold font - Volume number; Normal font - Page number
A.D. - *anno domini;* C.E. - Common Era
B.C. - Before Christ; B.C.E. - Before Common Era
NT - New Testament; OT - Old Testament
c. - about; e.g.; for example; i.e., - that is

Bible: choices and contradictions, e.g between Genesis 1 and Genesis 2 **15:**78;

Emerson, Ralph Waldo: 19th century American writer who said, either "I must stand on higher ground, if I would lift you up" or "You must stand on higher ground, if you would lift me up." **15**:94;

Kidron brook = dry most of the year except when for rains, **15**:79;
Kidron valley = a very deep gulley which is a natural defense of Jerusalem;**15:**79;

Levi - founder of the Hebrew biblical priesthood **15**:83;

Symbolism: the necessity of translating Scripture into its spiritual and original means of communication. The literal is the letter. The spiritual is the Spirit, which breathes through the Bible. Without the spirit there is what has been called "the rust of religion." **15:**93,94;

SYMBOLS

Anointing - (of oil) was for kings, priests, royalty, as well as for heat and light **15**:80;

Atavism - reverting to a more primitive type of ancestor, i.e., to the cave man, to jungle beings, animal kingdom residents, also to Adam **15:**89;

Babel - the chaos of self-wills **15:**83;

Bible - the book designed to reveal the waymarks where one is in God's sight; so that one can check his position in the Bible as Jesus did **15:**96;

Calvary - Golgotha, a hill near Jerusalem where Jesus was crucified. **15:**79;

Disease - a rebellion against the normal order of the bodily system **15:**90;

Dominion - God's gift to each of us according to Genesis 1, some lexicographers say it means "government"; however, the word means what it says; it must always stand unqualified by anything; never can it be "dominion but," or "dominion if." The integrity of the Word includes no possibility of subjection or subordination. **15:**98;

Egypt, Land of - the whole symbol of bondage of the human race **15:**93; E represents all blackness and darkness of no inspiration, no revelation, and bondage slavery; what is crucifying renewedly our Lord, our Master, our dominion-man within ourselves **15:**93;

Gethsemane - meaning "oil press;" a garden east of Jerusalem, at the base of the Mount of Olives, near the Kidron brook, where Jesus suffered; the olive is placed under intense pressure between two huge stones where the bulk, the pulp, all pressed out of condition and distorted, yet the essence is not caught by the pressure of the stones; symbolically it represents the intense pressure Jesus was under, yet his essence was not harmed by the pressure he suffered. His essence flowed out to bless mankind in many ways **15**:79,80; G illustrates the ultimate yielding to the divine **15:**85,95; G also illustrates what Jesus faced and what he was remedying by that experience. G was the "oil press," symbolic of the tremendous pressure of the world's Adamic tradition behind the necessity for doing one's own will *versus* doing God's will, Jesus route to salvation. **15:**110 Like Jesus, we must have oil within us. The pressure is on. **15:**110;

Gethsemane Decision/Choice - Jesus had made ever since age 12 when he told Mary and Joseph that his mission was to *"be about his Father's business."* a choice: to let God's will **or** human will/self-will be manifested; the straightening out of priorities in thinking; the basic, primary decision between success and failure; the total commitment to God's will; **15:**80; As seen throughout the Bible: Paul's *"Let the Word have free course."* and the cases of Jacob, and of Simeon and Levi **15:**83;

GD is between God's will and our own will. **15:**84; Jesus, up against the GD, had to deal with the enemies resident in mortal mind, i.e., "taking the precious from the vile" and "burning the chaff and gathering the wheat into barns" **15:**86; The commotion and noises of the world's revulsion and resistance to the divine facts need to be silenced; it is the still small voice that convey's God's will in defining how we can make our own GD **15:**90; Putting down rebellion (see "disease" above) in thought and discovering within the kingdom/government/dominion and rule/order/law is the discovery of the ages. In Genesis 1 dominion is God's, the Original's, gift to man, the image **15:**90;.GD has been made for us; it has been proven to us; we are reminded not to leave the Master's footsteps **15:**96; Jesus makes the GD for the first time citing Scriptural law, "for it is written," and showing how to deal with temptation **15:**100;

In the middle of the road to Damascus Saul made the GD to do God's will **15:**28; Beginning with the "Original sin" that's tied up with the flesh which is "weak, along with evil's temptation, and "the sin that dwells within," then comes the war between "the law in my members" against "the law of God after the inward man" which separates within the kingdom from chaos, which find angel-thoughts on both sides (Michael's and the dragon's), causing a wretched condition with one's consciousness split down the middle by dualism, a kingdom divided against itself; thus in the battle, with my consciousness I serve the law of God and with the flesh I serve the law of sin; I know two things: (1) to be carnally minded is enmity against God and leads to death, and (2) that to be spiritually minded is life and peace. **5:**105; Then comes the great news: if the Spirit of God lives in me, and respond only to God's will and do God's will, and am motivated by God, and prompted by God, I am not in the flesh but in the Spirit **15:**105; Gethsemane's purpose has a divine result regardless of what the world has to bring on you and me. If we are on Jesus' way, we are not in an "oil crisis," but we may be at a "parting of the ways" (see Pythagoras below) and may be challenged regularly and often to make our right decisions, our right choice, our Gethsemane decision.**15:**110; If the cross represents the problem, and the crown the solution, intertwined, they deliver the simple message, problem solved. That is the result of the GD. **15:**110.

Gethsemane prayer - the means by which we conform thought to God's will and listen to be filled with God's will; **(1)** A consciousness filled with **confidence** is the mental state of prayer; Since it isn't God's will for man to be sick, the result of prayer conforming to God's will is an elimination of sickness from man's experience. It's not in the image; it doesn't even hurt to remove it; it wasn't there **(2)** Before the tomb of Lazarus, Jesus **knew that God had heard him**; Jesus had prayed according to God's will; God's will did not support Lazarus' remaining in the tomb, or ever being there; So, "*Lazarus, come forth.*" That was his dominion and his right. God calls. Man answers. **15:**106;

Glory and glorify - God's eternal selfhood, the only identity Jesus accepted **15:**97;

God's will - doing His will relates us immediately to Him. **15:**101; If you agree to do His will, do it, don't be self-willed and hypocritical and slack off. **15:**102; G'sW shows of what we have been created , and by Whom, which rules out blood, flesh, human will, the will of man; Jesus' nourishing food is doing G'sW. [As the Original sin, human self-will, as self-destructive, leading to the "terminal sin" of death,] G'sW is not to leave man in any state of dormancy, death, or the grave, or termination of life. **15:**103 Unless one makes the commitment to do G'sW, one can't even recognize divine authority. **15:**109;

Golden Gate - where long tradition has it that the Messiah would come through this Gate, which the Turks in the 16th century walled up to prevent that happening. **15:**79;

Gravity, law of - Jesus dominion over G **15:**82;

Holy City - heavenly kingdom **15:**88;

Horeb - the mount of God, that symbolizes the altitude at which one receives the Commandments **15:**89;

Humanhood - Humanhood following Jesus, ends up at a destination completely opposed to the destination of the Adam followers. (See Pythagoras in SYMBOLS) Symbolically, this is the human dilemma. Jesus found what humanhood could be when the Divine was behind every step of the way. There was nothing in Jesus' humanhood that could stop the divine from manifesting itself on-earth-as-it-is-in-heaven. Jesus refused to allow anything to obstruct the Divine Will from operating on earth. **15:**81;

Judgment - a Greek word translated into English as "crisis," which means "separating," i.e, the turning points that necessitate a parting of the ways, e.g., separating chaff from wheat, taking forth the precious from the vile, bringing every thought into captivity to the obedience of Christ. **15:**90;

Key to the kingdom of heaven - "to do the will of God which is in heaven". **15:**101; God's gift is the kingdom and dominion **15:**102; when Jesus told us we could not enter the kingdom of heaven without becoming as a little child, he meant that we could not say the Lord's Prayer effectively without becoming a lttle child. When making our Gethsemane Decisions we had better follow his example and remember "Abba"/"Imma" **15:**108

Lamb - symbol of Jesus; the L is totally dependent on the shepherd **15:**97;

Mount of Olives - separated from Jerusalem by the Kidron Valley, where Jerusalem looms above. On its slope one can look back up at Jerusalem. Those who came to arrest Jesus used it to snake down its slope carrying torches and lanterns. **15:**79;

"The Original" - God when man is the image and likeness. **15:**85;

"Original sin" - the initial problem of humanity: God told the Adam-man what His will was, not to touch dualism, the tree of knowledge of good and evil; Adam proceeded to do what he wanted to do and then blamed woman for it. Adam chose Satan's route, defined in Job: attempting to live with both, to-and-fro, up-and-down, no commitment, always in flux, no permanence, no rock, no conviction. All humanity has followed him. Later Paul notes that if one insists on the Adam-way, the objective, the destination ends up with death as the common denominator with the added choice, *"even so in Christ shall all be made alive."* **15:**80,81; also **15**:5 OS is self-will **15:**82; Since "doing one's own thing" is the label of the decade of the 1970's, the original sin of Adam is still very much to be dealt with; it is the Anti-Christ mentality, whatever opposes the Christ way/route/example and the anointed in our lives **15:**98; Jesus' overcoming of the original sin of Adam, "Not as I will, but as Thou wilt." **15:**108;

Prophecy - P reveals God's will in advance to humanity **15:**10;

Psalm 91 - commentary on one of the most meaningful psalms dealing with conflicts in the human arena between God's still small voice and divine direction and all of the noise which would intervene, in this case between God's will and how human will can be conformed to God's will. **15**:100;

Pythagoras - Greek philosopher, mathematician, and religious reformer (ca. 582-500 B.C) who symbolized choices/decisions by the Greek letter *upsilon (Y)*. e.g., let the Adam-choice be the left branch of the Y, ultimately ending in death. Let the right branch represent another choice, the Christ-path, leading to life. The gap between the branches widens the further along the branch one goes *ad infinitum*. Furthermore, one's eyes/consciousness tend to rest constantly on whichever path one takes. **15:**81 Notice the conflict between "taking forth the precious from the vile", and between "burning the chaff/tares and gathering the wheat into barns," in "bringing into captivity every thought to the obedience of Christ" which are represented by the two-branched Y. **15:**86,87;

Receptivity and lack of receptivity - apathy keeps one from establishing priorities in living and doing God's will which immediately relates one to God. **15:**101; Receptivity to God's will enables one to become a child of God and to image forth what is in the Parent's nature. **15:**102;

Repentance - to change one's concept of things **15:**92;

Selfhood - an idea which is expressed through God or though self-will. **15:**97;

Self-will - theology of self will **15:**7; Levi and self-will **15:**83; "Leviticially-oriented" church is no better than Babel **15:**83,84; Original Sin is S-w **15:**84; human will ultimately bring hopelessness, the lack of salvation within itself, the ultimate resistance to yielding to the divine, the yielding that Gethsemane illustrates **15:**94; God sends the prophet Ezekiel to show "the way" to the self-willed rebellious children of Israel who keep looking after the left Adam route of branch of the Pythagorean Y **15:**95;

Sodom - represents sensuality in all the perverted self-oriented, self-willed characteristic of the human mind. **15:**93;

END SYMBOLS

Temple, William: who wrote, "Humility does not mean thinking less of yourselves than of others. Nor does it mean having a low opinion of your own gifts. It means freedom from thinking about yourself at all." **15:**97;

***

Seaside Amphitheater Photograph by Gordon N. Converse

by B. Cobbey Crisler

HOW CHRIST JESUS SAW HIMSELF
Volume 23

by B. Cobbey Crisler

CONTENTS

Notes: The transcript was produced from a tape of an unscripted lecture delivered extempore. Earlier tape versions may differ. Biblical quotations and Hebrew, Greek, Latin, French and German words in the commentary are italicized. Brackets enclose additions by the original Bible translators and the transcriber: such as book names, chapter and verse numbers which the speaker mentioned, but did not cite, some audience comments or questions, and an occasional word or footnote. Some spoken words which appeared to be unnecessary for the reader, such as "and, but, so, turn to, well," etc, were deleted. The Citation Index contains the full text of all King James Bible citations which the speaker cited or mentioned. The purpose of the transcript is to preserve the speaker's words verbatim.

***

BEGIN TAPE 1, SIDE A

Ladies and Gentlemen, we're going to explore a very significant subject this morning under the title ***How Christ Jesus Saw Himself.*** I suppose that you might consider what we are about to examine. Because I must add, it's not a matter for discussion. It is a matter for examination of what the gospel texts actually indicate. We might consider it, however, one of the most controversial contemporary topics during the time of the gospels and it has continued to have that element of controversy swirl about it.

Isn't it remarkable that, despite the fact that most religions that name the name of Christ, dedicate themselves ostensibly to the words and works of Jesus, that still, in the background, and sometimes hauntingly invading the commitment of these churches, is still this unresolved question, at least unresolved to those debating the issue, of "Who is Jesus?"

This nagging issue is one that it is impossible not to confront when you're reading through the gospels. It is almost as if that is the priority question; and Jesus has to deal with this, either mentally in a dialogue, [or] in sometimes reading the thoughts of those around him, in order to try to set it at rest, before he could even get down to the exemplification of his mission. We'll note that the purity of the answer to who is Jesus of Nazareth, or Jesus the Christ, or Christ Jesus. He's called that in all three of those ways. But, purity of the answer to the question "Who is this man?" is going to come through what he tells us.

That fact alone would almost shelve many of the books on the subject that have laden shelves for so long. Because most of the books are filled with human opinion, theological notions, traditional views, students passing down through the years what their teachers have told them. Look at the varied views, for example, just in the Bible. Can you think of any? The extremes?

[Voice:"Beelzebub."] Beelzebub, that he cast out devils through Beelzebub, the prince of the devils [Matthew 12:24; Mark 3:22; Luke 11:15]. That he was an instrument of the devil. There's one view. *"Isn't this the son of the local carpenter?"* was asked him in Nazareth [Matthew 13:55; Mark 6:3]. Some say you are Isaiah;*"some say you are Isaiah, Jeremias;" "some say you are John the Baptist"* reincarnated [Matthew 14:2; 16:14; Mark 8:28; Luke 9:19]. Anything else?

They called him a winebibber [Matthew 9:11;11:19; Luke 7:34]. They called him a glutton [Matthew 11:19; Luke 7:34]. They called him a friend of publicans and sinners [Matthew 11:19; Mark 2:16; Luke 5:30;

7:34; 15:1,2]. Thomas doubted that he was even facing Jesus [John 20:27,28]. In an extreme reaction to the shock that he really now thinks it's Jesus, Thomas calls him, *"My Lord and my God."* Can he be all those things? Is this human opinion trying to get to him, at him, get some kind of handle on this man?

A blasphemer, he was called by some of the Jews of his period [Mark 2:6,7; Luke 5:21]. You can imagine how dearly he was thought of by the family at Bethany, for example, after the raising of Lazarus [John 12:1-3]. Even his disciples' opinions ran either too high or too low.

Jesus is rarely hit in the Bible. Everybody's aiming at him but he's rarely hit. Misunderstanding seems to be the rule rather than the exception. Even on the cross, who he is, is the question that tauntingly is thrown up at him from those who walked by the base of that cruel instrument of execution [Matthew 27:37,39-42; Mark 15:29-32; John 19:19].

Realizing this, and the fact that it has reached well into our century, where we have denominations under the name of Christ, some considering Jesus to be God, others considering Jesus to be the Son of God. Some writing books about Jesus being a magician, (and this a Christian author.)

The Jews, undergoing many changing concepts, for an example, from an article in The New York Times, "There has been in Jewish history a form of an antigospel, *Toledo Jeshu*, the history of Jesus, which showed Jesus as a practitioner of black magic. Editions of this document were published as late as the turn of this century." But, as *The Times* article says, "After centuries of relative silence by Jews on the subject of Jesus, including periods when the mention of the name was rare or even forbidden, some recently stepped-up efforts are reclaiming the first-century figure as an exemplary, deeply religious Jew, deserving of a high place in Jewish history." Here come the qualifications. "The new view is that Jesus was an observant Jew, not the Messiah. He had a powerful moral message rooted in the Hebrew scriptures, but whose role was misinterpreted by Christians."

[Notice] Dr. Pinchas Lapide, an Israeli religious scholar, who just said, "We Jews are very proud of our Einsteins, Heinrich Heines, and Sigmund Freuds. We ought to be much prouder of Jesus." He continues, "Jesus was as faithful to the Law as I would hope to be. I even suspect that Jesus was more faithful to the Law than I am, and I am an orthodox Jew." Martin Buber, I'm sure many of you know of him, he wrote, "From youth on I felt Jesus to be my elder brother. Jesus deserved a large place in Judaism. And this place can be described by none of the customary categories."

Once again, we have a target, either out of range here or unable to be hit. So can we honestly respond to this still unresolved question of who Jesus is? How do we know this? Jesus gives a very simple summary of this in Matthew 11, Verse 27. It is so simple, as so many of Jesus' instructions are. In fact, wouldn't you say that the simplicity of Jesus' teaching constitutes its radical nature? In Verse 27, beginning after the colon to the semicolon, *"and no man knoweth the Son, but the Father."*

If there is no appeal from that statement, Jesus is telling you and me categorically, that the only one who can define the Son, who knows the Son, is God, the Father. Where would logic lead you and me from there, or anyone from there? To whom must we go? We must go then to the Father. Where can we meet the Father? Where can we get this kind of information?

Note that even the title of this course is somewhat in question, "How Christ Jesus Saw Himself"? If Jesus is now telling us that he saw himself as the Father saw him, it would seem that there is no other resort for you and me than to dig deeply into what has been revealed from the Father on this subject. That only will free it from human opinion, from conflict, from controversy, and lift the identity of Jesus above the human to the divine definition. Which also must give us the reason for his mission and the details that he had to carry out in order to fulfill that mission.

Let's meet Jesus at age twelve in Luke 2, Verse 49. We discover that this twelve-year-old boy already in one way was having to resort to the Father for the explanation of his role, even to his own human parents. He asks the question, *"How is it that ye sought me?"* Seeking Jesus. How is it that you and I seek him? This boy of twelve says, *"Don't you understand that I must be about my Father's business?"* Once again, we find his whole occupation, his career, his commitment, all to seek their meaning, we must seek it in the Father. What is the Father's revealed concept of the mission of this controversial man Jesus?

Are we ready for real precision in approaching this topic to show us that the information is there? It is not cloudy. It is direct. To John 5, from Verse 31 through 39 we have five proposed witnesses to Jesus' identity and mission. Let's see what Jesus himself does with them because now we are listening to what at least the gospel indicates is Jesus himself telling us.

Number one, Verse 31, self-witness, how good is it? *"If I bear witness of myself, my witness is not true."* Is that consistent with what we have read in the two previous selections [Matthew 11:27; Luke 2:49]? The only one who knows the Son is the Father. So the Son can't really bear witness of himself. Before we totally conclude that is an accurate statement, we must go further and examine some of the other options and also what Jesus has to say a little later on the same topic. As of now, it seems quite clear that Jesus is ruling out self-witness completely. *"My witness is not true"* if it is based on his own idea or opinion of himself.

Verse 32 adds what? *"There is another."* This would answer the question whether there's only one witness to this event and that's yourself. *"There is another that beareth witness of me; and I know that the witness which he witnesseth of me is true."*

Verse 33 mentions whom? John the Baptist. *"Ye sent unto John, and he bare witness unto the truth."* Is Jesus resting his case on the testimony of John the Baptist? He mentions it, but why? And he explains that. First in Verse 34, *"I receive not testimony from man."* He is rejecting anyone on earth attempting to explain who he is. He, however, mentions John's witness to him because, in Verse 35, he states, *"He was a burning and a shining light and you were willing for a while to rejoice in his light."* They had respected John the Baptist up to a point. They had listened to much of his message and he had born witness to Jesus. Jesus mentions, as number two after self-witness, the witness of John the Baptist. He does not give it priority, however, in the list.

Because the next thing is Verse 36. And the third form of witness is what? [Voice: "The works."] How is that compared to John the Baptist's witness? Greater witness than that of John, *"for the works which the Father hath given me to finish, the same works that I do, bear witness of me, that the Father hath sent me."* Jesus is serious in this revelation of where one goes to comprehend his nature and mission. He's even dealing in comparatives that he mentions John, but the greater witness is the works. Rejecting self-witness, accepting in appreciation and gratitude John the Baptist's clear witness of Jesus and preparatory role, he now goes to the point of, *"if you want to know who I am, take the works. Let the works tell you who I am because those works were given to me,"* Jesus is saying, *"by the Father."*

Verse 37, *"The Father himself, which hath sent me, hath borne witness of me. Ye have neither heard his voice at any time, nor seen his shape."* What do you think that might refer to, *"The Father himself, which hath sent me, hath borne witness of me"*? [Voice: *"This is my beloved son."*] How many times did that occur? *"This is my beloved son"* was a statement made at the transfiguration [Matthew 17:5; Mark 9:7; Luke 9:35; 2 Peter 1:17], but it was made earlier at the baptism [Matthew 3:17].

[Response to inaudible voice] The whole question was at the crux of the temptation in the wilderness, and we will examine that: The whole idea of whether that statement is revealed by God is valid. That's what Satan leans on, *"if thou be the Son of God"* [Matthew 4:3]. God didn't reveal Jesus' sonship with an "if" attached to it. Where did the "if" come from? This is what we'll be examining. There are moments in Jesus' career where we have what seems a direct communication, born witness to by others around, but it is not clear whether the others around actually hear the articulation.

In John 12, Verses 27 through 30, Jesus is praying, deeply troubled about what lies ahead of him, asking, *"What shall I say? Father, save me from this hour: but for this cause came I unto this hour."* Jesus prays [in Verse 28], *"Father, glorify thy name. Then came there a voice from heaven, [saying,] I have both glorified [it], and will glorify [it] again."* Then [in Verse 29] all it states, *"The people therefore, that stood by, and heard [it], said that it thundered: others said, An angel spake to him."* [In Verse 30] *"Jesus answered and said, This voice came not because of me, but for your sakes."* We have examples of a breakthrough in a sense here of something that sounded like a voice, but was not articulate to those who were simply not at the level, one who were listening to such divine communication.

Going back to John 5, Verse 39, we have the fifth form of witness which we are engaged in today. [Voice:"The fourth is the Father?"] The fourth is the Father in Verse 37 and the fifth in Verse 39, *"Search the scriptures;"* for two reasons: *"eternal life; and they are they which testify of me."*

So far, then, in response to the course title, "How Christ Jesus Saw Himself," where is he directing our attention? Where is he telling us to find him? The works, the revealed Scripture, what the Father has said to him directly. Don't neglect John the Baptist because his witness is true, and the matter of self-witness which we have just put aside for the moment.

Notice in Verse 39 when Jesus says, *"Search the scriptures,"* that he gets specific in Verse 46. He says, *"Had ye believed Moses, ye would have believed me."* Wouldn't that have saved a lot of time and effort? Look at the faith of Jesus. The word of God revealed to Moses is absolutely consistent no matter that twelve hundred years have intervened between the careers of the two men. It doesn't matter about the careers of the two men. It's God's word, then, that is absolutely invariable *"without a shadow of turning"* as James [1:17] would have said.

Then he adds those four words in Verse 46 [in John 5], *"he wrote of me."* That is a thing that is incredible to the human mind, isn't it? In fact, it's that kind of remark that narrowed Jesus' following every now and then. *"He wrote of me."* Moses was the hero [of] the Jewish history! To have someone claim that Moses, leaving aside for the moment that the weathermen then, no more than weathermen now, can even tell us what's going to happen twenty-four hours from now; this is twelve hundred years! Leaving that aside, there still is the burning issue whether Moses, the hero, would have thought of a carpenter? Whose birth was somewhat questionable? In a town that no other historian ever mentions, including Josephus who was in charge of Galilee, up to the time of the appearance of Jesus himself, Nazareth?

Remember the remark by one of the disciples [in John 1:46], *"Can any good thing come out of Nazareth?"* How obscure can you get? But how well-known and revered was Moses? When you compare Moses to Jesus at the time that such a thing would have been mentioned, *"He wrote of me,"* you can see that it's loaded with a presumption here, as far as the hearer is concerned. No matter how true it might have been as far as Jesus was concerned.

END TAPE 1, SIDE A

BEGIN TAPE 1, SIDE B

[In John 5,] Verse 47 again Jesus says, "*If you believe not his writings, how shall ye believe my words*?" Let's see what Jesus might have had in thought here when he is referring specifically to the fact that Moses wrote of him. In Deuteronomy 18, Verse 18, God is quoted. What is the information, the expectation, the prophecy contained in Verse 18? It's quite detailed.

Number One, *"I will raise them up a Prophet."* Whoever is the one referred to here to qualify as the fulfiller of this prophecy, the individual would have to be himself a prophet. And what else? *"From among their brethren,"* which would mean also that he would have to be Jewish, "*like unto thee,"* that there would be similarities between Moses' career and Jesus' career.

The next point? *"God will put His words into his mouth,"* so that when the one who is fully capable of fulfilling this, and is divinely appointed to do so, opens his mouth, it's as if you were listening to the pure revelation from God Himself. This prophet will not stand in the way of God's message. He will not alter it. He will not manipulate it. How many could possibly fulfill that?

Even in the obligations that you and I have to our most dearly loved ones on earth today, something of us enters into our faithful pursuit of assignments they have given to us. Our attitude and outlook, even towards them, is colored by our own opinions.

Yet, this prophet will have God's words in his mouth, *"He shall speak unto them all that I shall command him,"* leaving nothing out. And there will be a great danger to the human race if humanity will not listen. Verse 19, *"It shall come to pass, [that] whosoever will not hearken unto my words which he shall speak in my name, I will require [it] of him."*

Let's pick up an intermediary Verse in Luke 16:31, *"He said unto him, If they hear not Moses and the prophets, neither will they be persuaded, though one rose from the dead."*

How important, then, is the Scriptural depiction of the Master's mission? It's right up there with the evidence of being raised from the dead. If we are not prophetically attuned, prophetically oriented, if we do not realize that Israel itself was sustained and saved by the prophetic thought, rather than the priestly thought, -- this statement is made throughout the Old Testament: *"By a prophet was Israel preserved,"* [e.g., Hosea 12:13] -- if we don't recognize that, it's not the prophets themselves and their own opinions that we're relying on, it's their total yielding to what God is telling them.

So, we go back to the prophets in order to listen to God telling human consciousness where it is, where it needs to be, and announcing its prophets and the Savior to come, so that we need be in no doubt when the fulfillment time arrives. Jesus can say that strongly, *"if we are not listening to the prophetic word of God, even if someone is raised from the dead, they won't be persuaded."* Is that the case? Jesus rose from the dead, but what happened? Did that immediately persuade the race?

John 6:45. Here is one of those preliminary, preparatory statements that you find so often in the gospels, *"It is written in the prophets."* What's written? *"And they shall be all taught of God."* Even taught of God who Jesus is? Can't we just listen to Jesus on that subject alone, or the erudite theologians who for centuries have concentrated their efforts in describing Jesus, or our own opinions? Jesus, the greatest teacher known in human history, goes back to the prophet Isaiah [54:13] to say, they *"[shall be] all taught of God."* Look at the conclusion he reaches in the next sentence [of John 6:45], *"Every man therefore that hath heard, and hath learned of the father, cometh unto me."* Father first, and then we find Jesus.

Now, we're going to get to this idea of Jesus' self-witness, whether it is totally of no value. He had said that it was not true. [In] John 8, Verse

13, the Pharisees charge Jesus with self-witness, basing it upon that Jewish concept that was also brought out.

"You bear record." The Greek word is the same as witness [*martyrs*]. *"Thou bearest record of thyself, thy record is not true."* Same point that Jesus had made. *"If I bear witness of myself, my record is not true."* Pharisees are saying the same thing. It looks like they have Jesus in the corner. Caught him in a contradiction? Let's see what happens.

Jesus responds, Verse 14, *"Though I bear record of myself, [yet] my record is true."* It still looks like we've caught him in a contradiction. And yet Verse 17 states, *"It is also written in your law, that the testimony of two men is true."* You need an endorsement. One witness cannot stand alone. Even in the *Bible* we are told about two witnesses all the way through [e.g., Deuteronomy 17:6; Revelation 11:3], the prophesied two witnesses. One would not be enough.

[In] Verse 18 [of John 8] Jesus says, *"I am one that bear witness of myself."* Standing alone, it would have no value. You could rule it out. What's the next statement? *"The Father that sent me beareth witness of me."* Jesus is willing to have every item which could be labeled self-witness thoroughly explored by searchers of the Scriptures, for example, for endorsement, for another witness, for the Father's witness to this same statement. Otherwise, it's not true.

What are we seeing about the theology of Jesus already? Everything flows out from where? [Voice:"God."] Nothing is initiated by Jesus, nothing, not the healing, not the works, not his words, not his mission, not the depiction of his character, not his prophesied role. Everything flows out from the Father. All the information comes from the Father. Has Christendom looked to the Father for the answers to these controversial questions about who Jesus is? If they had, all of these aimings wildly at the target of Jesus' identity would have landed, because only the Father knoweth the Son.

We are not through with what Jesus says can bear witness to him. Why was John the Baptist's witness valuable that he even mentioned it? That's human testimony. It couldn't stand on its own, could it? They had faith in John, but any student could have any faith in any teacher. That still wouldn't necessarily make what the teacher is saying true. [Voice question not clear.] That John's prophecy was exactly in accord with the Father's revelation.

Do you remember that's what got Peter his medal from Jesus? That it was not *"flesh and blood that revealed [it] unto Him, but my Father which is in heaven"* [Matthew 16:17]. That's exactly the consistent kind of commitment that the Master himself had. He took all that would occur to him back to the Scriptures, back to the Father's revelation, to see whether it was written before he would act upon it or even think it.

In John 15, Verse 26, we have what we might refer to as the sixth possible witness. That is what? The Comforter. Which shows that when the Comforter comes, whenever and whatever that may be, that the Comforter is an authentic witness of Jesus role and mission. Jesus says, *"The Comforter when it is come, whom I will send you from the Father."*

The Comforter really is, again, an outcome of the Father. Therefore, it is manifesting the Father's revelation. It is not mixed in with human opinion. This Comforter is *"the Spirit of truth, which proceedeth from the Father."* That would have to be in order for the Comforter really to be legitimately included in this list. Then he tells us, *"He shall testify of me,"* the same words again, *"He shall bear witness of me."*

So, when the Comforter, no matter when that might be, down the future from the time that Jesus is uttering this, would be testifying of Jesus. The very heart and soul of the Comforter's message would be to resurrect the teachings of Jesus in which we could understand his role better than before. That's one of the prophesied missions of the Comforter, to testify of Jesus.

In Verse 27, the seventh possible witness, *"You also shall bear witness, because ye have been with me from the beginning."* Who are they? Disciples. Did they? We're actually reading out of a book that's attributed to one of the disciples.

This bearing witness has a strict form to it. We, as usual, are going to have difficulty, if, when in doubt, we don't read the instructions. The instructions that we need to listen to are Jesus' own list of what bears witness to him. This is how Christ Jesus saw himself, only through the eyes of the Father and the Father's revelation.

Matthew 3:16 What's our rule of march here? If we are going to pursue this topic according to Jesus' own rules, when we read Jesus saying, *"I am this or I am that,"* what should we seek? The Father's witness to that, not just simply self-witness. What do we come up with? See if there really is an enriching revelation that will tell us exactly what we need to know.

Therefore, be with him where he is in fulfillment of his prayer [in John 17:24], *"Father, that they may be with me where I am."* Jesus has just said [in John 5:39], *"Search the scriptures; they are they which testify of me."* If we're going to fulfill his prayer to be with him where he is, he's told us you can find me in the Scriptures. Let's be with him where he is.

This is where God has placed him.

When one stops to think of it, the human mind could never have done something like this. The human mind finds it impossible to predict five minutes from now what is going to happen. But here, according to Jesus himself, is his great conviction that the delineation of his individuality and his mission is untouched in Scriptural prophecy, and had been there for centuries before Jesus appeared in the appointed time to fulfill these details. The blueprint was there, left by the Divine Architect. Therefore, we should be able to check that blueprint thoroughly with what the career of Jesus gives us in the gospels, to see if they honestly relate to one another as prophecy and fulfillment.

In Matthew 3, Verse 16, When Jesus is baptized, coming *"straightway out of the water,"* there is a divine announcement. He sees *"the Spirit of God descending like a dove, and lighting upon him."*

To fill in the witnessing to this kind of event we are going elsewhere, because what's identifying Jesus here is what? What aspect of God's nature do we see here? Spirit. You know that is the root of the whole word inspiration. Consequently, one recognizes that if Spirit represents the motive of his career, it's an inspired career. We discover that it appears like a dove that has been used as a symbol of the Holy Ghost, or the Holy Spirit.

It's how the entire Bible begins [Genesis 1:2] because *"the Spirit of God moved upon the face of the waters."* It's almost as if we are getting this genesis of God's creation, that first chapter, applied on earth. The Spirit is moving on these waters in which Jesus is standing. There is a Spirit-genesis here. Look what happened in Genesis 1 in those brief verses when creation is depicted for us.

Does this suggests that Jesus has something fundamental in his mission, namely to show man his true genesis in God? The Spirit of God is not there for any idle reason, *"descending like a dove."* As a matter of fact, commentators have translated that opening part of Genesis, that Spirit moving like a dove suggests in the Hebrew the brooding over of a bird, *"and lighting upon him."*

John 3:34. In speaking of the Spirit, is this just a temporary endowment? Is this a dramatic exercise to impress those who are standing around, or does this go deeply into the meaning? Is God defining Jesus' purpose in this event? Should we be translating this from the very imagery of what is being revealed here? We don't need it in words, or do we? Cannot we get communications through the symbolism of the Bible, which is the real native tongue of the Bible?

In Verse 34 of John 3, Jesus, or John the Baptist, scholars are dubious about who is saying this. On the chance that it's Jesus, so that we'll be consistent with the title of our course, the statement is made, *"he whom God hath sent."* There is a definition right there, *"God hath sent."*

"Speaketh the words of God." Does that remind us of anything that we read, for instance in Deuteronomy? The prophet who was to come would open his mouth and what? God said, *"I will put my words in his mouth"* [Deuteronomy 18:18]. *"He whom God hath sent speaketh the words of God"* [John 3:34]. He has no time for his own personal views. "*For God giveth not,*" and here is that key word, *"the Spirit by measure [unto him]."* It isn't tentative then what we are seeing at the Jordan river baptism place. We are seeing the Spirit not being given in any limited way, according to what John is saying here. It's an overwhelming investment as far as Jesus' career and mission are concerned.

What's the point made again in John 8, Verse 29? But first, *"He that sent me."* Again, we find on Jesus' lips the statement that God sent him. There's a defined and divine purpose behind Jesus being here at all. Who is comprehending that divine purpose? Only God knows what a divine purpose is: *"The Father hath not left me alone,"* and Jesus adds, "*I do always those things that please him.*" What a summary description that would be of our life and career, *"I do always those things that please him."*

Mark 1:11.We're going to see this pleasure of Deity emphasized again. *"There came a voice from heaven [saying],"* What? *"Thou art my beloved Son, in whom I am well pleased." "Thou art my beloved Son."* There is information. Jesus told us that the Father bore witness to him directly. Here is one of those cases, *"Thou art my beloved Son."* Can we get another witness to that?

Psalm 2:7, an Old Testament chapter that is used over and over again in the New Testament as a prophecy of the Messiah. The words are almost identical, aren't they? *"Thou art my Son;"* Mark had reported, *"Thou art my beloved Son."* Also is added [in Psalm 2:7], *"this day have I begotten thee."* So we have a role in prophecy of a Son of the Father, a representative Son of the Father, because there are many sons of God also mentioned even in the Old Testament [Genesis 6:2,4; Job 1:6; 2:1; 38:7]. This is something special: This Son of God who knows his relationship to the Father.

END TAPE 1, SIDE B.

BEGIN TAPE 2, SIDE A

Obviously based on the rule, *"only the Father knoweth the Son and only the Son knoweth the Father"* [Matthew 11:27; Luke 10:22].

On the ringing of that prophecy, *"this day have I begotten thee"* [Psalm 2:7; Acts 13:33], and it has to do with sonship with God.

[In] Luke 1:35 the angel announces the coming nativity of Jesus. It says, first of all, *"The Holy Ghost shall come upon thee."* That's the spirit moving again.*"The Highest shall overshadow thee: [and] that Holy thing which shall be born of thee shall be called the Son of God."* Again fulfillment now harking back to what prophecy has pointed with a divinely-directed arrow, pointing human attention to the time of fulfillment.

[Luke] Chapter 4, Verse 3. Here is the question we alluded to in our opening remarks that the divine fact has been stated, *"Thou art the son of God"* [i.e. Matthew 3:17 at Jesus' baptism, and Matthew 17:5 at the transfiguration; also, Matthew 14:33; Mark 3:11; John 1:49]. It agrees squarely with prophecy, that one would have to come to identify himself so closely to God that he would be as son to father, and in his father's business, occupied solely by that commitment to the father.

The "if" comes in Verse 3, the qualification, *"If thou be the Son of God."* That is definitely sowing the seeds of doubt that you are, as if there were two points of view, not only God's point of view. Here is that wide diversion between that straight and narrow way Jesus talks about and that wide broad way that he also talks about. *"If thou be the Son of God."* These are tests which is another meaning of the word temptation.

Jesus responds to these questions in the test by quoting Scripture [in Verse 4], *"It is written."* Let's get the Father's word on the subject. No one can tempt me to put down my own word on the subject. My word is my Father's word. Prophecy says that one would come who would open his mouth and it would be filled only with God's word. No wonder, *"It is written"* is said by Jesus so often. Unfortunately, how little it is said by you and me. Before we make any move, do we ever think, "Well, is it written, does it have a thus-saith-the-Lord behind it?" Jesus says, *"It is written,"* the statement he finds in the Bible.

Notice that all of these *"It-is-writtens,"* Verse 4, Verse 8, and Verse 12, where Luke changes it to *"It is said."* They all relate to God. Man lives by the word of God; so life is flowing out of God to man. Therefore, how-could-you-be-tempted-to-look-for-life-elsewhere is implicit in that, right? In Verse 8, *"It is written, Thou,"* your whole attention, your whole loyalty, your whole devotion, your whole love, is to God. Love is flowing out from God. It's a total commitment. Man's focus is there. If all the love there is is flowing from God to man, how could you be tempted? There's no basis for any temptation, to look for love elsewhere, or life elsewhere. In Verse 12, *"It is said, Thou shalt not tempt the Lord thy God."* There is no possibility for an option other than God, an alternate to God. There are no facts elsewhere that could form the basis of a temptation to look for any truth or reality other than God. So, all truth is flowing from God as well. No wonder Satan has nothing left in Jesus' thought. *"Then the devil leaveth him and angels came and ministered unto him"* [Matthew 4:11].

Remember, too, what these temptations represent. They're power struggles. That's exactly what was the problem with his disciples often, the power struggles, "who shall be greatest?" [Mark 9:34; Luke 9:46; 22:24]. This is squarely on this, which is the most assertive thing in the human mind that would enthrone it somewhere in opposition to Deity or in collaboration with Deity. Oneness is oneness; it's not negotiable. That's the theology of Jesus.

[In Verse 3 of Luke 4] the first [temptation] is *"command this stone be made bread,"* have personal power, exercise a personal power other than through God [Verse 6].

Verse 5, *"all the kingdoms of the world in a moment of time"* and [Verse 6] *"all this power will I give you, and the glory."* Just simply worship me and all will be thine, political power, ruling over mankind. Comes all the way down to our domestic relationships, who makes the decision in the household, going all the way up to who makes the decisions for the world.

[Voice: "He said that he was a servant."] Of course, we will come into that as part of the divine definition of Jesus. He is a servant. He could not be anything other than a servant. That is his relationship to God; the Son is a servant. The desire to serve; it's not the element of serfdom that you get. Jesus is also talking about freedom, isn't he; that the truth makes you free? Being a servant to God must be your ticket to freedom.

Again, the radical use of terms here. We must get back to the divine intent, and not what we choose to read from the text or to accept from what ecclesiastical majorities or hierarchies have given out to be the facts over centuries.

The next one is priestly power in Verse 9, because *"he brought him to Jerusalem, set him on a pinnacle of the temple, and said, If thou be the Son of God."* The test is on that divine revelation. This is the first test for anyone and everyone then, **if** Jesus represents the human race in its finest, highest possible attainment. That doubting, nagging question is still there in the thoughts of every one of us, "**if** we are the sons of God," even though John said [In 1 John 3:2], *"Behold, now are we the sons of God."* The "if" we're still listening to. Jesus dismissed it because the "if" was not authorized divinely. It was not written, therefore it was not divinely authorized. He removed that challenge from his sense of identity. He needed to do that to be unequivocally the servant of God, the adherent to the truth of God, and the love of God, and the life of God.

The priestly power is shown also in Verses 9 and 10, in the attempt of Satan, hiding behind ecclesiasticism. *"It is written, He shall give his angels charge over thee, to keep thee:"* attempting to use the Bible to manipulate Jesus in a humanly oriented direction rather than divine. But Jesus sees through completely all of this.

Why this is a power struggle, I am indebted to my Dad particularly for this. He pointed out that Luke was the only gospel writer to indicate his clear understanding that this was a power struggle. God either has all power or He shares it with us or with Satan, that it's a dualism. Because, after rejecting personal, political, priestly power, temptations as being opposed to God in Verse 14, Jesus *"returns in the power of the Spirit,"* a power rarely tapped before or since, *"the power of the Spirit into Galilee."*

That's better than a Concorde [French supersonic jet plane], isn't it? That's how Jesus travels, *"the power of the Spirit."* It's the Spirit that was identified with his baptism, with his name, even with his ability to move from one place to the other on earth.

[Voice: "In the first verse it says he *'was led into the wilderness by the Spirit'* "] I know. That's right. He needed not just simply to take the revelation of the Spirit, that he was the Son of God, blandly or for granted.

We find that everything Jesus hears from God is tested in his life. If he's going to be a representative for us, what more relevant Messiah could one have than one who has faced every single obstacle you and I face, and overcame that obstacle? And from that other side of attainment invites all the rest of us to follow him. These temptations came to him; they were not entertained.

Let me ask you, is it a sin to be tempted? [Voice "No, as a rule."] Only if it's a sin to be tested. You could interview a few high school and college students on that point. Is it a sin to be tested? Paul says later on [in Hebrews 4:15] that Jesus was tempted in all points but without sin.

He was tested in all points but he didn't flunk, if we use that modern term. [Voice inaudible] You have just pinpointed a parallel between Moses and Jesus which the prophecy in Deuteronomy [18:18-22] said we were to look for. Recall that statement of total reliance on God in the wilderness for forty days without any proximity of food represents the environment out of which both the Commandments and the Beatitudes come. That one statement of God is in Moses' statement and it is in Jesus' statement. It's God's revelation to both of them, and both of them are utilizing it, with the effect that they could survive the effects of what would otherwise be starvation at the end of forty days without anything to eat or drink.

[Verse 14 of Luke 4] says, *"Jesus returned in the power of the Spirit into Galilee."* That's going to put us right in the middle of a controversy again about who Jesus is. This is one other aspect of that question. Where is the Messiah to come from?

Matthew 4:13. Why are we at Matthew 4:13? We're talking about Galilee, *"Jesus went in the power of the Spirit to Galilee"* [Luke 4:14]. What is Galilee as far as its relationship to the mission of the prophesied one? We discover [in Matthew 4:13,14] *"leaving Nazareth, he came and dwelt in Capernaum, which is upon the sea coast, in the borders,"* tribal territories, *"of Zabulon and Naphthali: That it might be fulfilled."*

Here it is. *"Search the Scripture,"* Jesus had said [John 5:39]. *"They are they which testify of him"* Notice in Verses 15 and 16 [of Matthew 4] are quotations from Isaiah 9:1 and 2 which state that Galilee would be the center of an awakening where *"the people which sat in darkness,"* in density, *"would see great light: and them which sat in the region and shadow of death light has sprung up."*

Do you see what a beautiful statement that is because the psalmist also uses it [in Psalm 107:10,14]? Death is referred to as a shadow and the only remedy for a shadow is what? [Voice: "Light."] There we have it. Imagine how easily death can be winked out with the presence of more light. It was right here in the light of prophecy that we see even death itself would be extinguished as a power over the life and health of humanity.

In John 7:41 the debate continues: *"Others said, This is the Christ. But some said, Shall Christ come out of Galilee?"* Verse 42: *"Hath not the scripture said, That Christ cometh of the seed of David, and out of the town of Bethlehem, where David was?"* That [precursor] Scripture is Micah 5, Verse 2. Are those two prophecies mutually exclusive? Can it also be Galilee as well as Bethlehem?

Nicodemus has a real problem. He's the one who came to Jesus by night. He tries to defend Jesus in front of his colleagues of the Sanhedrin, the governing body of ecclesiastical Judaism. This is their answer to him in Verse 52 [of John 7], *"Art thou also of Galilee? Search, and look: for out of Galilee ariseth no prophet."*

We've just searched and looked and found, [haven't] we? Here are the biblical authorities of the period declaring that there is no reference to anything that would happen in Galilee of any significance in prophecy. We have just read [in Isaiah 9:1,2], *"And out of Galilee will come that great light that would shine in the darkness."* Where then do these so-called Scriptural authorities come off in saying that there is no Scriptural reference to this? Jesus knew his Scripture better than those who were trained to know the literate Scripture.

We are now going to enter into what is perhaps the biggest controversy of all. It's the main obstacle [about] Jews being interested in Christianity. It is also the main dividing point, perhaps, between the denominations of Christendom.

John 5: 17.*"Jesus answered them, My Father worketh hitherto, and I work."* Immediately the Jews jumped to the conclusion that Jesus is indicating he's the equivalent of God in the next verse [18]," *The Jews sought the more to kill him, because he not only had broken the Sabbath, but said also that God was his Father, making himself equal with God."*

Let's follow that and see from Jesus' own lips, remembering that he has to get his own information from God Himself, from the Father, on every topic; remembering that if Jesus is God, that would be one of the most important facts to know in all of the New Testament. Rather than left equivocal, it would be stated emphatically and clearly. But let's see how the almost torrents of human opinion try to carry the day even contemporaneously with Jesus on this issue.

John 10, Verse 30. Jesus famous statement, *"I and my Father are one."* What happens next?" [Verse 31,] again, *"the Jews took up stones again to stone him."* Of course, this was a violent thing to the Jews: Monotheism, no such thing as a personal God. Here is how Jesus chooses to respond, using the Scripture itself as the answer. He says in Verse 32, When Jesus asked, *"for which of these works do you stone me?"* [In Verse 33,] *"The Jews explained, it's not for your works; it's for blasphemy; because you, being a man, makest yourself God."*

Here's the issue this early. Jesus answers. This may seem obtuse; but, again, when Jesus said to search the Scriptures, he didn't mean to scan them. *"Jesus answered them"* in Verse 34, *"Is it not written in your law, I said, Ye are Gods?"* That's in Psalms 82, Verse 6, a cross-reference that continues, *"and all of you [are] children of the Highest."*

Notice in [John 10] Verses 35 [and 36], Jesus says, *"If he called them gods, unto whom the word of God came, and the scripture cannot be broken; Say ye of him, whom the Father hath sanctified, and sent into the world, Thou blasphemest; because I said, I am the Son of God?"* Any problems with that? That's a *peshere,* what the rabbis called a *peshere,* or an interpretation of an earlier biblical passage. It's the rabbinical method.

[Voice inaudible] The word is *elohim* in the original. Could it mean that we are discussing many gods in the context of a monotheistic book? We couldn't be turning personalities on earth into gods. That's why we have to search the Scriptures. There's a meaning that's deeper. What makes any of us look like God? When we are God-like; when we are what Genesis 1 says we are, *"the image of God."* Then everywhere we are, whatever we think, whatever we do is simply the likeness of God. So, it is God-like.

Leaving that point aside, and going into Jesus' admission here that he isn't saying he is God: "Why are you blaming me if the Scripture appears to call those-who-are-the-children-of-the-highest gods," implying because of their image-relationship to God, "why are you saying I am blaspheming because all I've said is that I am the Son of God?"

[In] John 12:49 this [controversy] continues. As we said earlier, this "who-is-Jesus?" is at the crux of virtually every controversy. Crux meaning cross, it's right there at the cross as well. *"I have not spoken of myself; but the Father which sent me, he gave me a commandment, what I should say, and what I should speak."* So when Jesus is calling himself the Son of God, he is, therefore, saying, to be consistent, that God has revealed this nature of Jesus to him, because *"only the Father knoweth the Son"* [Matthew 11:27; Luke 10:22].

[John] Chapter 14:28, the last two lines, starting with *"For," "For my Father is greater than I." How can you say "I and my Father are one"* [John 10:30] and also say, *My Father is greater than I"?* They are contradictions on the surface but not at the depth of searching-the-Scripture that we have been invited to do by Jesus himself. One could be at-one, or as the Aramaic translation is, *"I and my Father are in accord."* One can be in accord with the Father, but the Father, Jesus says, is greater than he, greater than the Son.

[John] Chapter 5, Verse 19. Jesus is going further along this topic. What about the nature of the Son which only the Father knows? The Son can do how much? *"Nothing of himself."* There is no initiative, no ability to originate. *"The Son [simply] can do nothing of himself but what he seeth the Father do."*

Again, Jesus' theology, the One that he's inviting mankind's attention to. Everything goes to God, total commitment, total life, total truth, total love, total health, everything must be sought in God; including our identity must be sought in God. That seems like a sore limitation on our ability on earth or in heaven. Let's recognize that, as far as I can see, there is only one theology that this is compatible with. That is the one in Genesis 1 where the Father and son and Mother and daughter, by implication, are related to one another as original to image.

Here's how we can test this out. If this is what Jesus has in mind, if this is what the Father is revealing about relationship, then substitute the word image, and original, in this statement and see if it works,*"The image can do nothing of itself but what the image sees the original do."* Does it work? Fits exactly, doesn't it? Let's see if this is the point Jesus is making.

END OF TAPE 2, SIDE A

BEGIN TAPE 2, SIDE B

Look in [John 5], Verse 21, keeping that in mind, original and likeness. *"As the Father raiseth up the dead,"* guess what? *"so the Son quickeneth,"* raiseth the dead. As the original, so the image. In Verse 23, *"that all [men] should honour the Son."* If they honour the original, they must honor the image. In Verse 26, *"As the Father hath life in himself; so hath he given the Son to have life in himself."*

Then, as to underscore this for all time, how Christ Jesus saw himself, recognizing that he had to go to God for the information. Verse 30, *"I can of mine own self do nothing."* The image can of its own self do nothing.

You and I know that's not a description of total inadequacy, total helplessness, is it? Because after he says, *"I can of mine own self do nothing."* He went out and did everything. The only reason he could go out and do everything is based on the same theology. The image can only do as much as the original is capable of doing. If the original does all and is capable of being infinite and doing all and nothing is impossible to the original, guess what the image looks like? [Voice: "Just like the original."]

That, we find, is how Jesus applies that theology. Through his works, he finds it in the Father. He finds this great breakthrough of news, that you and I are not limited by biology, by statistics, by heredity, by IQ tests. We are inheritors of a dominion that is unlimited because [of] who we really are, and only the Father knows us, to declare this. We are image, and we are image of a full, complete allness which is known as God. The access to allness then is implicit in the image's relationship to that original.

Still in this controversy, whether Jesus is God, whether this is a man-made imposition on theology, or whether it is God's revelation and how Christ Jesus saw it, you find again a subordinate role in Mark 13, Verse 32,"*Of that day and [that] hour knoweth no man, no, not the angels which are in heaven, neither the Son, but the Father.*" If the precision of theology is that the Son is always and only the image of the Father, or of God, could the image ever masquerade as the original? [Voice: "No."] There is a decided difference then, and Jesus, if he is the Son, if that's what's been revealed by God, and the Son can do nothing but what he seeth the Father do, then Son is image, and image is not original.

Careful to observe tendencies of the human mind to exalt, and idolize and deify him, in Luke 18, Verse 19, Jesus said, "*Why do you call me good? There [is] none good, save one, and [that's] God.*" Again, the commitment to oneness. You cannot divide out that oneness. It's oneness that belongs to God as original. One can relate to that oneness and have all the glory, and all the unity, and all the harmony that belongs to that oneness, but the relationship is due to what Genesis 1 tells us exists between God and man. It's the original and the likeness of the image.

The Jews, having charged Jesus with being equal with God, have apparently not been able to sustain that very long, due to his own teachings, and due to what you and I have discovered. Since they are thrashing about for a charge anyway, in Luke 22, Verse 70, comes the next inquiry: "*Art thou then the Son of God? And he said unto them, Ye say that I am.*"

Notice, Jesus is not in the business of what he later says [in Matthew 7:6], "*casting pearls before swine,*" where they would "*turn and rend him*" with it. They are not seriously interested in the spiritual facts. He knows that. They're looking for an excuse to execute him, and he knows that.

John 19, Verse 7 shows that the whole accusation against Jesus has changed for the Jews from the one, that said he made himself God, to he makes himself the Son of God. "*The Jews answered him, We have a law, and by our law he ought to die, because he made himself the Son of God.*"

[Voice inaudible] They would quote what they feel they are finding in the Torah. They know, although sometimes the word is used loosely, when Jesus himself said, *"You will read in your law,"* he's quoting from the Psalms [e.g., 82:6], which isn't really the law. In general, the Samaritans were much more precise about what law meant. They only accepted the Torah. The Jews went beyond and took in the prophets and the writings.

The only one entitled to this designation would be the Messiah. The Mes-siah would have been linked, probably, by Jewish thinkers and writers with the Son of God. This was the relationship. It made Jesus a claimant to a very important expected Savior. This is blasphemy. You could be charged with that.

In fact, that was the investigation with John [the Baptist]. When John was getting his great popular following, down come the authorities from Jerusalem who said, "Who are you?" You had to be very careful how you answered that. Are you that prophet that is to come, from Deuteronomy [18:22]? Are you the Christ? Just what are you? He denied all of them, very safely, too. You could be excommunicated, and even worse than that, if you claimed to be something or someone that you weren't in prophecy. In a sense that's probably what they're revoking here.

They charged Jesus with breaking the law because he was the Son of God. Here is Jesus' position on this topic, Matthew 5:17, "*Think not that I am come to destroy the law, or the prophets: I am not come to destroy, but to fulfil.*" There's the Father's purpose that he's supposed to fulfill what has gone before him.

All the prophets and the whole substance of the law are pointing to him as the one who is capable of living all of those things, that these are not impossible ideals. They can be exemplified on earth. When humanity has a role model that we can now follow, other than Adam, which is the opposite role model, as Paul tells us [1 Corinthians 15:22], *"For as in Adam all die, even so in Christ shall all be made alive,"* then the human race will begin to uplift itself and be restored into the native sense of that genesis of man as related in the first chapter of The Bible.

Jesus had said he was there to fulfill the law and the prophets. What is he doing in [Matthew] 8, Verse 16, but *"casting out the spirits with [his] word and healing all that were sick"?* It is stated afterwards that this is actually what? A fulfillment which was spoken by Isaiah. This is taken from the 53rd Chapter, Verse 4, where it states [in Matthew 8:17] *"Himself took our infirmities, and bare [our] sicknesses."*

So, one of the Scriptural responses to fulfillment is healing, that healing is a fulfillment, and therefore, it must be in prophecy. So, Jesus is not defining himself as healer. He is fulfilling the deifically-defined role that man in his native state is already at-one with the healing power in being in accord with God.

In Luke 4, Verse 16, he comes to Nazareth. There in the synagogue he is handed the book of Isaiah [61:1,2] and what does he read? We talk again about fulfillment. In [Luke 4,] Verse 18 here is the Spirit of the Lord upon Jesus. We've seen that right from the baptism.

Here is the job. Once you use "*anointed*" in the Scriptures, it means Messiah, or Christ. This is a verse that was definitely regarded as a prediction of the Messiah. Look at the verbs to see what the prophetic mission of the Messiah would be: "*To preach, to heal, to deliver, to recover, and to set at liberty.*" Again, in Verse 19, "*To preach the acceptable year of the Lord.*" In Verse 21, he announces to his hometown congregation, *The Scripture is fulfilled in your ears.*

Jesus doesn't have problems solely with the ecclesiastical authorities of his nation. He also has to wrestle with the doubts of those often closest to him, including John the Baptist, who, in prison [Matthew 11:2,3], sends two of his disciples to ask Jesus, "*Art thou he that should come, or do we look for another?*"

What a crushing blow that would have been for John, who had committed his all to Jesus' being the one, the Messiah. Here he has such doubts, in prison, awaiting his own execution, he wonders. So, again, this underlying unrest about who Jesus is. How does Jesus respond to John's question? As if the fulfillment, as well as the answer to this question, is in the very works [Verses 4 and 5]. What did Jesus say bore witness to him, one of the seven that we listed? The works. He is letting the works, the deeds, answer that question for John. Then he says in Verse 6, "*blessed is [he], whosoever shall not be offended in me.*"

About that offense. One of you mentioned this before when we were listing the various opinions, running too high or too low, about Jesus. In Matthew 13, Verse 55 is the question, "*Is not this the carpenter's son?*" What does Verse 57 say in its opening sentence? "*They were offended in him.*"

It continues with Jesus identifying himself as a prophet. Is he endorsed in that designation of himself and his role as a prophet? Did anything in the earlier scriptures indicate that a prophet would come? Yes [Isaiah 61:1,2]. We have Scripture behind it. In other words, Jesus is not opening his mouth unless it's God's word that is filling it. It's consistent with what God has revealed before, either that, or God is susceptible of changing His mind. James [1:17] tells us that is not part of His nature, that he is *"without variableness."* This is why we can rely on the revelation of prophecy.

We can even rely on symbolism in the Bible. If *Revelation* throws us into a quandary, for example, that last book of the Bible, because it's filled with symbols, remember that the consistency of the Bible up to that point has been that every symbol, every word, has two or three witnesses to it. We see a candlestick in the Bible, in many cases, even explained as symbolic of something? When we run into the candlesticks that represent the churches, shouldn't we, in order to let that revelation pour into us from the source, from the Father, search the Scriptures and become students of those symbols? One symbol is worth a thousand words, to paraphrase the other statement.

One of Jesus' definitions of error is what? Matthew 22, Verse 29, *"Not knowing the scriptures, or the power of God."* Are we guilty of that error? Over, and over, and over again, until we can exemplify in our own lives the model which Jesus set for us, and no move is made or thought taken before *"It is written"* precedes it. [At least 80 *"It-is-writtens"* in Bible: 17 in Old Testament and 63 in New Testament]

Let's watch this confidence in who-Jesus-is break down under pressure for the disciples. You know what the first thing that goes, as far as an underpinning is concerned, when Jesus is crucified? His place in prophecy as the Messiah is invalidated in the disciples' thinking.

In Verse 21 of Chapter 24 [of Luke] the disciples on the road to Emmaus say: *"We trusted that it had been he which should have redeemed Israel."* Look at all the heavy freight on that statement. Notice that the speakers come out with A-plus and guess what grade Jesus gets? *"We trusted."* We did exactly what we were supposed to. *"That it had been he which should have redeemed Israel."* Who's that? That's the Messiah.

So when persecution begins to build up its pressure on the church at any moment in its history, we should look for the same kind of thing, this same kind of apostasy, this same kind of cooling off. Is it true really that this church and its founder are protected in the divine word of prophecy? That's the first thing that seems to go even among disciples who counted themselves faithful.

In fact, in Verse 25, Jesus rebuke to this state of thought, *"O fools, and slow of heart to believe all that the prophets have spoken."* What is Jesus again using as the basis for knowing him? [Voice: "The prophets."] That's right. In Verse 26 he discovers, where the disciples had not, nor had the Jews as a nation discovered it, that the Messiah was to suffer, but not just terminate there, but to enter into his glory, also overcome, to face the entire problem that faces humanity as a whole and overcometh.

In Verse 27 these disciples do not even know it's Jesus. He's a stranger. It's only the Bible teaching them this point. Isn't that what Jesus said [in John 6:45], *"They shall all be taught of God"?*

Suppose this were Jesus saying, "Hey, I'm your Master. I just came out of the tomb. I'm back. I'm resurrected. Now look, let me tell you about the Bible." Can you imagine the bewilderment? They wouldn't even listen to the Bible. They'd believe anything Jesus had to say. Jesus is a stranger to them. He lets the Bible carry the message. The impersonal strength of this is evident because it states [in Luke 24:27] that he went through *"Moses, all the prophets, and expounded unto them in all the scriptures the things concerning himself."* That's some scriptural lesson. It's hardly ever done. We're going to try to do part of that today. See what he had in thought.

What was the result? Verse 31, *"Their eyes were opened, and they knew him."* They finally knew him! They knew him now because of what the Father had revealed through the Scriptures. Exactly what Jesus had said [in John 5:39] was necessary, *"Search the scriptures; they are they which testify of me."*

"Don't let your ideas be colored by my personality, or anything that might look like my opinion. You go to the Bible and see if that persuades you, if that convinces you, if the logic and the revelation coincide there. Then you'll know who I am because that's the only way I discovered who I am, is from the Father. He's the only one who knows the Son. So there's no easier route for you to take than the one I had to take." In essence, Jesus is saying, "Go to the Bible and have the Scriptures opened."

Look what happened. This is such an exciting discovery that to wonder if the Bible has an immediate effect on us, or whether it's just simply an ancient collection of literature, you and I should be able to feel our hearts burning within us, as those disciples did, when they went through the Scriptures and the Scriptures were opened. Without that, the Scriptures are locked. Why are we saying it took this kind of trip through the Scriptures to open them? They had been closed or we would never have had to mention the fact that they needed to be opened.

Just for a cross reference, 2 Peter, Chapter 1, Verses 20 and 21, tells us about the importance of prophecy. There the author says, *"no prophecy of the scripture is of any private interpretation."* What a relief! That's what has caused denominational factions. But no prophecy of the Scriptures is of any private interpretation. Even Jesus could not privately interpret the Scriptures. *"For the prophecy came not in old time by the will of man: but holy men of God spake [as they were] moved by the Holy Ghost."*

Recall again the subject of who Jesus was, was so important that he brought it up at Caesarea Philippi. He said [in Matthew 16:13; Mark 8:27], *"Whom do men say I the son of man am?"* Remember Peter's response and the relationship that would have to the church, that the church also would have to be built on this kind of recognition of the relationship between the founder of the church and God's own appointment of his mission. If the founder is in prophecy, what about the church that he founded? It also has that protection of prophecy. It's God's idea on earth, already stated as God's idea, and stamped with God's authority and approval in prophecy.

That seems to be the method that we discover, that nothing that appears that is important or major to mankind's spiritual progress can be claimed to be important or major if it is not in prophecy. When Peter said that he [Jesus] was the Messiah, he [Jesus] charged his disciples they should tell no man [Matthew 16:20; Luke 9:21]. It was not something that was to be a popularized dogma. It was revelation from God to each searcher of the Scriptures.

In Luke 22, Verse 67, there is constant hammering on the part of Jesus' examiners among the ecclesiastical hierarchy. They want to know if he is the Christ. *"Art thou the Christ? tell us. And he said, If I tell you, you won't believe:"* It is not a matter of telling, is it? That would be dogma anyway. You don't just say, "Tell God's revelation." Because, then in effect, you are standing in place of God. God does the revealing.

In Verse 68 he [Jesus] says, *"If I also ask you, ye will not answer me, nor let me go."* He even saw the practical thing. Even if he told them, it would not affect his status in any way.

John 4:25. To one of the rare times when Jesus actually assented to his role as the Messiah. This is to a woman with a rather checkered past in history but showing the honor which Jesus bestowed upon womanhood in an age which left her secondary and quite subordinate. The woman says, *"I know that the Messiah is coming, which is called Christ: when he is come, he will tell us all things."* What does Jesus say to her in Verse 26? *"I that speak unto thee am [he]."* The "he" is not in the original, *"I am."* Many times Jesus keeps saying nothing but *"I am,"* and the translator throws in *"he."*

END TAPE 2, SIDE B

BEGIN TAPE 3, SIDE A

That's rather interesting, too, because God reveals His nature as *"I AM"* in Exodus [3:14]. For the image of that kind of original to say, *"I AM,"* is perfectly proper, isn't it? The image would have to be *"I AM"* unless somewhere in the original there's a little corner that is reserved for "I WAS," or "I WILL BE." It's either all "I AM," and, therefore, the image can say that, or it's a division, a contradiction in nature.

In John 10, Verse 24 the Jews again say, *"How long doest thou make us to doubt? If thou be the Christ, tell us plainly."* How often this has come up. In Verse 25, Jesus said, *"I told you, and ye believed not,"* and then turns them to what? To identifying the works; again the works. Just as he had done to John the Baptist, he turned the scribes and Pharisees.

Let's explore another title given to Jesus, which is the Son of man. Back in Job 25, Verse 6, we find Bildad, one of the shortest men in the Bible, Shuhite. [Chuckles] Bildad's spiritual stature seems to be about that size as well, because his last words are *"the son of man is a worm."* That's quite a revelation, *"The son of man is a worm."*

Is that the way Jesus regards this term? You should know that among all the terms Jesus applies to himself, this is the most used. It is his favorite. His favorite perhaps because to him it may be more relevant to his listeners, his students, his audience, and us.

Can we relate to the Son of man more quickly than we relate to the Son of God? As a matter of fact, we're living the Son of man regularly, aren't we? It is a term that deals in humanhood which, according to Bildad, can be at the worm level, or Psalm 8, Verse 6, it can be at the dominion level. So the Son of man yields either up or down. Psalm 8, Verse 4, talks about *"What is man, that thou art mindful of him? and the son of man, that thou visitest him?"* The answer is Verse 6, *"dominion."* That's far and away different from the worm that was discussed by Bildad.

Ecclesiastes may be an aid to our own examination and reasoning on the point of the Son of man. It's a term used throughout the *Bible*. To many commentators they simply think it means the representative man. That Jesus is the representative of an entirely different human race than Adam. That the entire human race would look completely different and still be a human race if it followed Jesus. By following Jesus, all of the problems, all of the headlines and tragedies that we read about today would have been overcome. There would be a state on earth where heaven was not a distant promise but a living reality, as it was for Jesus.

Ecclesiastes Chapter 3, Verse 21 raises this point, *"Who knoweth the spirit of man?"* The literal is *"the sons of man."* That literally in Hebrew *"is ascending and the spirit of the beast that is descending to the earth."* What could more graphically explain what seems to us to be twin pressures, one leading up and one leading down?

This ascending, do you remember that Jesus says [in John 6:62] *[What] and if you see the Son of man ascend up to where he was before? He says* [in John 20:17] to Mary Magdalene, *"Go and call my brethren that I ascend to my Father and your Father, and my God and your God."* The same origin, the same original, and therefore, we must be capable of imaging forth this same ascension. Even human experience is an ascension. Resurrection means in Greek a step upwards.

How many steps are there, upwards? There may be many steps. In fact, Paul said [in 1 Corinthians 15:31], *"I die daily."* That sounds very ominous unless you suddenly search the Scriptures and don't just skate over that point. If he died daily, and he's still around to tell about it, he must have been resurrected daily. Something must have dropped away from him that never did belong, atrophied from no longer honoring it as part of being or identify, and it leaves. It departs. We're freer because of it.

Remember when he was visited by Nicodemus and that statement [in John 3:7] he gives to Nicodemus which now has been so popularized, *"You must be born again."* But the real Greek behind it means, *"You must be born from above,"* showing that it's a question of origin, where did we come from?

Then Jesus takes this son of man, that Bildad says is a worm, and you know what he does with it? He says [John 3:13], *"No man ascended up to heaven."* That's what we are all supposed to be doing according to definition of mostly every religion in the globe: Improving, progress, moving ahead spiritually. But Jesus said forget it. *"No man ascendeth up to heaven save,"* here's the qualification, *"he that came down from heaven,"* namely, *"the Son of man which is in heaven."* Notice, there really is no commuting at all. The Son of man is in heaven.

But if we're going to discuss about arriving in heaven, there is no way you and I can even remotely hope for a destination of heaven unless that was our origin. Why? Because the logic of the Bible hits us again. The fountain rises no higher than its source. If you and I did not have a heavenly origin, there's no hope that we can have a heavenly destination, unless we started there. That whole radical definition of our nativity comes into play here in his discussion with Nicodemus and elevates Son of man to the possibility of on earth being in the heavenly state, the Son of man which is in heaven.

Was Jesus the Son of man in heaven even when he was on earth? Did he dwell at the level only of heavenly solutions and therefore resolved all earthly problems? That is possible for humanhood on earth, Jesus is saying. Not only possible, it's the native state of man ultimately, even humanly, to live with heaven here, which is the Lord's Prayer, *"as in heaven, so on earth"* [Luke 11:2]. There's not meant to be a distance between the two. When that Lord's Prayer is fulfilled, and after all, why do we pray it, and daily, and perhaps even more, if we really don't mean that the heavenly solution can be realized right here and now on earth? So that every earthly problem has its heavenly solution as Jesus proves.

Despite this heavenly standard of a new humanhood on earth set by Jesus, human nature yielding to the beast influence, the animal connection, that we all came from animalism, so what's the use anyway, everybody's doing it? To follow that wide and broad way to destruction, the Adam route that leads to death, is fighting any possible saving of humanity, [is] a built-in resistance. That's why the Son of man, who is capable of manifesting his heavenly origin right here on earth, therefore [has] freedom from all links to the animally-oriented problems.

Nevertheless, that Son of man is about to be delivered into the hands of men in Verse 44 of Luke 9. *"Let these sayings sink down into your ears."* Jesus must have really wanted us to listen to this, *"The Son of man shall be delivered into the hands of men."*

If you read the next verse, you'll find that they don't even understand what he's talking about, the dullness of thought. In receiving the simplicity of directing all of its focus and energy to God, and to nothing else, and let God's work be revealed in us as image, it's absolutely no effort for an image to be an image. All through the gospel accounts we find that Jesus is pointing back to the writing of the prophets, and they [his listeners] don't understand. Let's look at some of those.

John 12, Verse 14. There are homely details in this account that you would think would have absolutely no relevance or significance to us or to Jesus, except that it relates back to prophecy. We see the divine hand in these human events being fulfilled through Jesus' willingness to be the Messiah, the anointed one, going to God for what he needed to think and do.

In Verse 14, *"Jesus, when he had found a young ass, sat thereon; as it is written,"* Here is the quote, Verse 15, *"Fear not, daughter of Sion: behold, thy King cometh, sitting on an ass's colt."* That's Zechariah 9, Verse 9, [the] cross-reference. Look at Verse 16 [of John 12]. Were they understood? Not at the first, John admits himself. *"But when Jesus was glorified, then remembered they that these things were written of him, and they had done these things unto him."*

Can you imagine how their hearts must have burned when they began to see that all of this Old Testament, which many of them knew vast portions of, perhaps literally, suddenly came alive because it pointed to current events to them, and that Jesus was the one that prophets had predicted would come, and God had moved the prophets to so record?

When Jesus was on the back of that donkey heading to the gates of Jerusalem, you remember what the people did? Matthew 21, Verse 9 says, *"Multitudes followed, cried, Hosanna to the Son of David:" "Hosanna,"* Hebrew for "O, save," or "Save now." Notice the line, *"Blessed [is] he that cometh in the name of the Lord;"* remember that.

Notice also in Verse 15 that what bothered the chief priests and scribes the most was that children were crying, where? In the temple. That's the first Sunday School. In effect, the children are crying *"Hosanna to the son of David."* They're recognizing the Messiah before the hierarchy.

When they come to Jesus to silence the children doing this, Jesus doesn't silence them. As a matter of fact, finds a Scripture that prophesied that they would in Verse 16 [of Matthew 21], *"Have ye never read* [Psalm 8:2]," he said to those Scriptural authorities, *"Out of the mouth of babes and sucklings thou hast perfected praise?"*

You will note that, first of all, Verse 22 of Psalm 118 is one of the verses that your own research will show Jesus mentions: *"The stone [which] the builders refused is become the head [stone] of the corner."* He refers to that Psalm himself as being indicative of his mission [Matthew 21:42; Mark 12:10; Luke 20:17].

In Verse 25 [of Psalm 118], what does it say? *"Save now."* That's almost identical with *Hosanna.*

In Verse 26 up to the colon, *"Blessed be he that cometh in the name of the Lord."* That was what the multitudes were saying to Jesus as he was riding on the donkey, as Zechariah [9:9] said would happen. The people are saying what prophecy said they would say. Children were in the temple. In Verse 26, although it doesn't mention children in this place, it says, *"We have blessed you out of the house of the Lord."*

[Voice unclear] That's right, this is, in fact, part of the hymn that Jesus would have sung before he went out to meet the Gethsemane challenge. They sang a hymn and then went out to the Mount of Olives. It was Passover. The Passover hymn would have included Psalm 118.

If you want to really be about as close to Jesus as it is possible to become, read Psalm 116 when you're alone and Psalm 118. Remind yourself if you go through, although you probably won't have to, at the moment in Jesus' career when he resorted to these psalms for the remedy for what was about to follow.

It includes things [Psalm 118:6] as *"The Lord is on my side; what can man do unto me?"* [Verse 9,] *"It is better to trust in the Lord than put confidence in princes,"* and Pilate was coming up. [Verse 16,] *"The right hand of the Lord is exalted: and doeth valiantly."* Remember the right hand of the Lord is a prophetic synonym for the Christ. The Messiah is at the right hand of God. It also includes in Verse 17 of Psalm 118, *"I shall not die, but live, and declare the works of the Lord."* One of the most moving possible things, because Jesus said, *to be with him where he is* [John 17:24], you had to *"search the scriptures"* [John 5:39]. There he is. He's right there. We're with him in his preparatory prayer, prior to going out to Gethsemane.

In Matthew 26, Verse 23, *"He answered and said, He that dippeth [his] hand with me in the dish, the same shall betray me."* How does he know? The next line [Verse 24], *"The Son of man goeth."* How? *"As it is written of him:"* Do we credit that when we read it? That every aspect that Jesus was facing, he found in the Bible? His Father had forewarned him of what the cruelty of the animal nature in man would do, had also protected him in advance. [In] the Bible the solution preceded the problem and was there to be applied. *"The Son of man goeth as it is written of him."*

Imagine the boldness of Judas in Verse 25, *"Master, is it I? He said unto him, Thou has said."* No pointing of accusation. Here's the Master that could meet Judas in Gethsemane and call him friend and mean it. If we ever want to, consider reaching the concept of love which he manifested on earth.

You find in John 13:18, *"I speak not of you all."* Jesus had a Southern accent. [Chuckles] *"I know whom I have chosen: but that the scripture may be fulfilled,"* and there it is. *"He that eateth bread with me hath lifted up [his] heel against me."* That's Psalm 41:9.

I may no longer give you these references. Why? Because it's like John in the *Book of Revelation* [Chapter 10]. He was told by the angel [in Verse 8] to *"take the little book."* As marvelous a character as [he is], John is like us. [In Verse 9] he went up to the angel and said, *"Give me the little book."* The angel had to tell him again, *"Take [it] and eat it up."* There's really no way to revelation without taking it. It's never a hand out. That's the precision of Scriptural revelation on that point. It cannot be handed out. It must be taken.

To build up the real incentive within to take it, is what you find that Jesus does. When Jesus left the two in Emmaus, he left them and went off to meet others that resurrection eve [Luke 24:31]. What happened to them? They were so turned on, their hearts were burning. They didn't want to stay at Emmaus, even though they were hungry and sleepy and everything. They turned right around and went to Jerusalem. Jesus knew that would happen.

You can't rest when you're on the level of biblical inspiration. Time disappears. You move with it. It's at the speed of thought. It's at the speed of divine thought. No wonder Jesus could be from one place to another so rapidly because he understood the power of the Spirit and where it takes us.

Verse 19 of John 13, why did Jesus even go into that Bible verse? *"I tell you before it come, that, when it is come to pass, you may believe that I am,"* and then the translator adds, *"[he]."*

Matthew 26, Verse 14. *"Judas Iscariot,"* now we follow what happens, *"went unto the chief priests."* He made a contract with them [Verse 15], *"What will you give me if I deliver him to you?"* What was the covenant? *"Thirty pieces of silver."*

In Matthew 27, Verse 3 [we] find out what happened to them. *"Then Judas, which had betrayed him, when he saw that he was condemned, brings again the thirty pieces of silver to the chief priests and elders."* You know what they do with them, Verse 7? They *"buy the potter's field to bury strangers in."* You've got those points, thirty pieces and the potter's field?

Are we ready for this? Zechariah 11, Verse 12, *"And I said unto them, If ye think good, give [me] my price; and if not, forbear. So they weighed for my price thirty [pieces] of silver."* [Verse 13,] *"And the Lord said unto me, Cast it unto the potter: a goodly price that I was prised at of them. And I took the thirty [pieces] of silver, and cast them to the potter in the house of the Lord."*

Chapter 13, Verse 6, *"And [one] shall say unto him, What [are] these wounds in thine hands? Then he shall answer, [Those] with which I was wounded [in] the house of my friends."* Call Jesus friend.

Verse 7, *"Awake, O sword, against my shepherd, smite the shepherd, and the sheep shall be scattered."* Jesus himself refers to that verse [Matthew 26:31; Mark 14:27]. Does it happen as prophecy had predicted? Did Jesus say he was the shepherd? *"I am the good shepherd,"* he said [John 10:11]. Do you know what he says about the good shepherd? *"The good shepherd giveth his life for the sheep."* He knew prophecy. He didn't just assume the shepherd's role. It was prophetically his. He had to fulfill that role. He had to lay down his life for the sheep.

Matthew 26, Verse 53, *"Don't you think,"* Jesus said, *"I could not pray my Father,"* and what would happen? *"Twelve legions of angels would be here to lift me out of this event."*

In Verse 54 never would he do anything contrary to what is written. The scriptures had to be fulfilled.

Verse 56 repeats the point. It also tells us that the sheep scattered, *"All the disciples forsook him, and fled,"* and they had been told. They could have spared themselves that ignominy, that indignity of abandoning the one who had given them all they really had and who would later be the reason why they could take this message of divine freedom, via divine appointment, around the known globe.

Verse 67. What did they do to him? *"They spit in his face, they buffeted him, they smote him with the palms of their hands,"* and he was blindfolded as well, as another gospel [Luke 22:64] tells us.

[Verse 68] says, *"Prophesy unto us, thou Christ, Who is he that smote thee?"*

END TAPE 3, SIDE A

BEGIN TAPE 3, SIDE B

Jesus had gone through these details, didn't he, with his disciples after the resurrection? And that's when they understood. They must have gone through these verses just like we're doing because he went through Moses and the prophets.

[Isaiah] Chapter 50, Verse 6, *"I gave my back to the smiters, and my cheeks to them that plucked off the hair: I hid not my face from shame and spitting."* Isaiah 52:13 describes *"my servant shall gather you up,"* literally, *"prudently, he shall be exalted and extolled, and be very high."* But his human appearance during this trial would be a matter of astonishment [Verse 14], *"his visage was so marred more than any man, and his form more than the sons of men."*

Isaiah 53, Verse 12, about two-thirds of the way down into the verse, note it states, *"and he was numbered with the transgressors."* Does that suggest anything to you? The two thieves, perhaps, on either side of him. This can be a cross reference to that Isaiah verse, Luke 22, Verse 37. It is Jesus speaking, so it is consistent with our course title again, **How Christ Jesus Saw Himself.** In Isaiah, let me read to you the Luke verse It says,*"I say unto you, that this that is written must yet be accomplished in me, And he was reckoned among the transgressors:" "Reckoned among the transgressors."* Where does he get that quotation? From Isaiah 53 [Verse 12].

Let's study Isaiah 53. We're talking in Verse 2 of Isaiah 53 about a man, the masculine gender is here. I mention that only because that is particularly important. We want to have the specifics of the prophecy. The very next chapter the gender changes to the female. Here we are specifically referring to a man. *"He shall grow up."* It indicates there is an infant stage to maturity.

Verse 3, *"He's despised; he's rejected of men; he's a man of sorrows."* Who is this describing? *"We hid as it were [our] faces from him."*

In Verse 5, *"He [was] pierced,"* according to *The New English Bible,* rather than wounded, *"for our transgressions, [he was] bruised for our iniquities: and with his stripes we are healed."* Stripes, marks of lashes. Was Jesus scourged? Who does this fit? This is what we need to ask.

Because in that lonely desert of Gaza, where the man of Ethiopia, who was in charge of the queen's treasure, was sitting in a chariot reading Isaiah and Philip suddenly appears. He's reading this chapter. He says to Philip, who the Spirit tells to run up and talk to the man [Acts 8:29]. He says [in Acts 8:34], *"Of whom is the prophet speaking of himself or some other man?"* Philip immediately talks to him about Jesus.

That early, this chapter is important. But Jesus himself pointed to it. Why is he telling us in that this-that-is-written [Isaiah 53:12] *"he was numbered among the transgressors?"* Isn't he telling us to go search out what the Father has revealed of his mission? He is not presuming on any of these details. He is simply following God's directions.

In [Isaiah 53,] Verse 7, *"He was oppressed, afflicted; he didn't open his mouth."* Do you remember anything about that? *"He is brought as a lamb to the slaughter."* What was the festival being celebrated at that time? Passover. [In Verse 8,] *"He was taken from prison, from judgment. He was cut off out of the land of the living."* In Verse 9, *"He made his grave with the wicked, and with the rich in his death."*

Only Matthew [27:57] tells us Joseph of Aramathea was a rich man and the tomb belongs to him. Is this coincidence? Or is this the rock that

Jesus himself relied on to see him through all of these events in his mission, to know that he was right on the way?

[Isaiah 53,] Verse 9, Is it true *"he did no violence,"* and there was *"no deceit in his mouth?"*

John 19, Verse 28, Why could Jesus say something like this? *"After this, Jesus knowing that all things were now accomplished."* Jesus is not saying it but it's being said about him, that Jesus knew that all things were now accomplished. How did he know that? The very next line tells us, *"That the scripture might be fulfilled."* Notice he says, *"I thirst."*

[Verse 29.] They give him vinegar on a hyssop *"and put it to his mouth."* [The Old Testament cross reference is] Exodus 12, Verse 21 and 22. That's part of the Passover celebration. The remarkable coincidence, if that's what it is, between the details of the crucifixion and the Passover, the sacrifice of the Lamb at Passover.

When Jesus says in Verse 30, *"It is finished."* What does he mean? I'm wiped out! No, it's in Greek, *"It is fulfilled, it's completed."*

In Verse 32 the soldiers break the legs of the two thieves. That's to hasten the death. The Jews wanted that because they didn't want bodies marring the landscape during Passover, but Jesus was already dead. It says in Verse 33, *"they don't break his legs."* John says there is a Scripture behind Verse 36, *"A bone of him shall not be broken."* That's true of the Passover lamb. Here is the lamb, the real Lamb.

In Verse 34 *"the soldiers pierce his side and blood and water pour out."*

Verse 37, *"Another scripture said, They shall look on him whom they pierced."* That's Zechariah as well, [Chapter] 12, Verse 10.

One cannot really discuss the events of Jesus' career, especially those final days, without reference to the Old Testament. Jesus couldn't live through them without reference to the Old Testament, so we cannot comprehend them without that. To have the fulfillment shorn of its prophecy, or to have the prophecy shorn of its fulfillment, would mean it's not God's Word involved at either end. God's Word must be fulfilled. If God's Word at any point could be invalidated, there would be some power greater than God. It's all coming from the Father. Jesus' focus and commitment at this time to be sure, *"It is written."*

In [Matthew 27] Verse 34 we get another gospel account of some of these last events, *"They gave him vinegar to drink mingled with gall: and when he had tasted [thereof], he would not drink."*[Voice:"What was it?"] Supposedly an opiate. He tasted it and he rejected it. It was an attempt to tranquilize the victim so that the pain would not be that severe. When we think, in our drug-oriented age, that how many of those naming the name of Christ are on opiates, and have forgotten that their Master tasted it and rejected it.

[Voice: Inaudible question] No, he's on the cross. There was a vinegar on the hyssop. Symbolically it might relate to that but literally it wasn't part of the Passover service. Jesus was the Lamb itself on that cross. In fact, in those verses I gave you, the vinegar on the hyssop was sprinkled on the side posts and the lintel, almost a description of a cruciform.

Psalm 69, Verse 21, is a cross-reference to Verse 34, *"They gave me also gall for my meat; and in my thirst they gave me vinegar to drink."*

That's one of the crucial symptoms, if I can use one of the words based on cross. I don't want to go into those symptoms. You were just drained of everything. That was one of the first things that was felt. But he did not accept the drug. He took the vinegar without the drug later. It's clear that he rejected the drug only. He had been forewarned in Scripture. He was not deluded into taking it.

[Matthew 27,] Verse 35, *"They crucified him, parted his garments, casting lots."* *Why?* *"That it might be fulfilled that which was spoken of by the prophet."* Verse 36, *"sitting down,"* they did what? *"They watched him,"* just watched him. Verse 38, *"the thieves."* Verse 39, *"they wagged their heads and reviled him."*

Verse 40, can you believe that Jesus hears at the foot of his cross exactly what he had heard three years before [Matthew 4:3; Luke 4:3,9] in the temptation in the wilderness,*"If thou be the Son of God?"* Imagine, testing him at what would seem to be the weakest point of his career! Coming back at him, "Alright, I hit you when you were strong. Now I'm going to hit when you're down." The same question, *"If you be the Son of God?"* Is he going to waver?

[In Verse 41,] *"The chief priests mock him."* In Verse 43, they say, *"He trusted in God; let him deliver him now, if he will have him: he said, I am the Son of God."*
Look at the haunting nature of who is he? all the way to the end. Not, what is he teaching? Look at these marvelous works he's doing! Look how he's changing the whole aspect of the human race! None of that! But who is he claiming to be, *"if you are the Son of God?"* *"He said I am the son of God!"*

Then, Verse 46, Jesus has this famous outburst. Many Christians wish their Master had never said it, or it had been expurgated from the *Bible,* but there he says it, *"My God, my God, why hast thou forsaken me?"*

If our respect for the Master was already high, when one goes through an exercise like this, one begins really to know and comprehend what it means to be a disciple of a man who counted nothing more important than his loyalty and obedience to God. God's intent was to raise us up out of our delusions, and that was Jesus' job.

Psalm 22 begins [Verse 1] with that statement, *"My God, My God, why hast thou forsaken me?"* We already know how Jesus works. We already know he says *"It is written"* all the time. The reason he says it is to point our attention to it, as well. From the cross the Master is saying to you and me, "Please, consult Psalm 22. Search the Scriptures." The opening verse of a psalm identified the psalm to Hebrew students, and thus to us, and we are asked to look into it, search it.

Verse 6, where even perhaps a thought might have occurred to him, *"I am a worm: and despised of the people."* That would be giving into what definition of the son of man? Bildad. [Job 25:6,*"How much less man, that is a worm? And the son of man, which is worm?"*].

Verse 7, *"All they that see me" do what? "Laugh, shoot out the lip, and shake the head."* Wagging heads were reported at the scene.

What about Verse 8, because they're shaking the head saying this? Does this sound familiar? *"He trusted on the Lord that he would deliver him: let him deliver him, seeing he delighted in him."* It's all here. It was all being fulfilled. The chief priests and scribes that uttered that he-trusted-in-the-Lord remark, they were supposed to know the Bible literally. They didn't realize they were fulfilling the Bible in uttering this. Probably had absolutely no sense that it came from Psalm 22, but Jesus did. Because right after they said it, the next thing Jesus said is Verse 1 of Psalm 22 in which what the chief priests and scribes had uttered had been printed centuries before.

Verse 10, a reference even to, perhaps, the miraculous nature of Jesus' entry into the world, *"Thou art my God from my mother's belly."*
In Verse 13, *"They gaped upon me with their mouths."*
Verse 14, *"I'm poured out like water."* Any reference there? *"And all my bones are out of joint,"* exactly what the anatomical situation is.

One asked why he asked for the vinegar? Verse 15, *"My strength is dried up like a potsherd; and my tongue cleaveth to my jaws;"* Isn't it interesting when you asked the question why Jesus said, *"I thirst,"* you go through a document a thousand years before the event for your answer?

What about Verse 16, the last two lines? *"They pierced my hands and my feet."*

Verse 17, *"I may tell all my bones: they look and stare upon me."*

Verse 18, *"They part my garments among them, and cast lots upon my vesture."*

Do you think every hair was standing up on the disciples' heads, when Jesus went through the Scriptures with them? He was reading documents hundreds of years old. In reading them, describing the events that the disciples themselves had witnessed and had been part of.

In going over this great 53rd Chapter of Isaiah, I purposely skipped Verse 10 because it went into a later event. *"When thou shalt make his soul an offering for sin,"* to the Hebrew reader that meant when you did what? You sacrificed the animal. It's all over right? That should be the termination point? Look at the next few words, *"He shall see his seed."* After death, he shall see his seed? Or, is there a resurrection implied here? *"He shall see his seed,"* he shall what? [Voice:*"Prolong his days."*] How many days? [Voice:"Forty."] There were forty days between the resurrection and the ascension. Do you think that would have been meaningful? Is this partly why hearts would burn within them, as Jesus went over these events?

It was in that forty-day period, that forty-day period was vouchsafed in prophecy. It was there. It was vital then for the human race and its salvation. Nothing's in prophecy that isn't vital for the progress of humanity, out of the Adam lockstep to self-destruction, into the Christ-way of eternal life.

That radical turnaround requires prophecy. It cannot be human opinion that turns us anywhere, but prophecy that has been there for centuries, that hasn't moved, that hasn't budged. It simply needs our focus in order to be with Jesus where he is. Suddenly the whole history of the world is transformed, transfigured, if you will, into higher spiritual reasons and motives for accomplishing things on earth as in heaven, following the Master and his way. His way is marked by the Bible: IT-IS-WRITTEN signs all over, so that there are no detours.

Hosea 6, Verse 2, *"After two days will he revive us: in the third day he will raise us up, and we shall live in his sight."*

After Jesus had met with the two disciples on the road to Emmaus, he had a second meeting that night with his entire church. He set the order of service for all time for Christian church services.

Luke 24, Verse 44. As they all assembled, even the ones that had been on the road, what had that great shepherd been doing, that had laid down his life for the sheep? He was still doing it. After the resurrection, he did not take a few moments off. He was on the road bringing back the scattered sheep. What a responsibility he felt to fulfilling Scripture. It would have been dangerous if he hadn't, and he knew it.

He didn't swerve from the rock, always making sure that the rock of Scriptural revelation was beneath his feet before he took any venturesome move forward. He removed the venture from it. It was sure asGod had said in Proverbs [22:21] that he gives man *"the certainty of the words of truth."* Why? That we may turn around and *"answer those words of truth to them that send unto us."* The apodictical [uncontestable because of having been demonstrated] rocklike revelation of God, the only resource that man needs, only recourse. Jesus never ran into a problem that hadn't already an it-is-written solution in the Bible.

In [Luke 24,] Verse 44 he talks about, again *"the law of Moses, prophets, and the Psalms."* He shows us that, very definitely, part of the church service he ordains is reading the Bible.

The second part in Verse 45 is applying the key to the Bible because it says, *"Then opened he their understanding, that they might understand the scriptures."*

Verse 46 is his resolution, *"Thus it is written, and thus it behoved the Messiah to suffer, and to rise from the dead the third day."*

How did Christ Jesus see himself? Where did he look? To whom did he go? Was he convinced of his own words, that only the Father knoweth the Son? One of the beauties of the Son's character as image, is to take the Father's Word on the subject, and so must we.

Thank you.

[Applause]

END TAPE 3, SIDE B

***

CITATION INDEX TO VOLUME 23
How Christ Jesus Saw Himelf

Citation Index compiled by tranScriptures of Columbia, S.C.

(Books listed in alphabetical order)

ACTS
(8:29) Then the Spirit said unto Philip, Go near, and join thyself to this chariot. **(8:34)** And the eunuch answered Philip, and said, I pray thee, of whom speaketh the prophet this? of himself, or of some other man?

COLOSSIANS
(3:1) If ye then be risen with Christ, seek those things which are above, where Christ sitteth on the right hand of God.

(13:33) God hath fulfilled the same unto us their children, in that he hath raised up Jesus again; as it is also written in the second psalm.

1 CORINTHIANS
(15:22) For as in Adam all die, even so in Christ shall all be made alive.

(15:31) I protest by your rejoicing which I have in Christ Jesus our Lord, I die daily.

DEUTERONOMY
(17:6) At the mouth of two witnesses, or three witnesses, shall he that is worthy of death be put to death; [but] at the mouth of one witness he shall not be put to death.

(18:18) I will raise them up a Prophet from among their brethren, like unto thee, and will put my words in his mouth; and he shall speak unto them all that I shall command him. **(18:19)** And it shall come to pass, [that] whosoever will not hearken unto my words which he shall speak in my name, I will require [it] of him. **(18:20)** But the prophet, which shall presume to speak a word in my name, which I have not commanded him to speak, or that shall speak in the name of other gods, even that prophet shall die. **(18:21)** And if thou say in thine heart, How shall we know the word which the Lord hath not spoken? **(18:22)** When a prophet speaketh in the name of the Lord, if the thing follow not, nor come to pass, that [is] the thing which the Lord hath not spoken, [but] the prophet hath spoken it presumptuously: thou shalt not be afraid of him.

ECCLESIASTES
(3:21) Who knoweth the spirit of man that goeth upward, and the spirit of the beast that goeth downward to the earth?

EXODUS
(3:14) And God said unto Moses, I AM THAT I AM: and he said, Thus shalt thou say unto the children of Israel, I AM hath sent me unto you.

(12:21) Then Moses called for all the elders of Israel, and said unto them, Draw out and take you a lamb according to your families, and kill the passover. **(12:22)** And ye shall take a bunch of hyssop, and dip [it] in the blood that [is] in the bason, and strike the lintel and the two side posts with the blood that [is] in the bason; and none of you shall go out at the door of his house until the morning.

GENESIS
(1:2) And the earth was without form, and void; and darkness [was] upon the face of the deep. And the Spirit of God moved upon the face of the waters.

(6:2) That the sons of God saw the daughters of men that they [were] fair; and they took them wives of all which they chose. **(6:4)** There were giants in the earth in those days; and also after that, when the sons of God came in unto the daughters of men, and they bare [children] to them, the same [became] mighty men which [were] of old, men of renown.

HEBREWS
(4:15) For we have not an high priest which cannot be touched with the feeling of our infirmities; but was in all points tempted like as [we are, yet] without sin.

HOSEA
(6:2) After two days will he revive us: in the third day he will raise us up, and we shall live in his sight.

(12:13) And by a prophet the LORD brought Israel out of Egypt, and by a prophet was he preserved.

ISAIAH
(9:1) Nevertheless the dimness [shall] not [be] such as [was] in her

vexation, when at the first he lightly afflicted the land of Zebulun and the land of Naphtali, and afterward did more grievously afflict [her by] the way of the sea, beyond Jordan, in Galilee of the nations. **(9:2)** The people that walked in darkness have seen a great light: they that dwell in the land of the shadow of death, upon them hath the light shined.

(50:6) I gave my back to the smiters, and my cheeks to them that plucked off the hair: I hid not my face from shame and spitting.

(52:13) Behold, my servant shall deal prudently, he shall be exalted and extolled, and be very high. **(52:14)** As many were astonied at thee; his visage was so marred more than any man, and his form more than the sons of men:

(53:2) For he shall grow up before him as a tender plant, and as a root out of a dry ground: he hath no form nor comeliness; and when we shall see him, [there is] no beauty that we should desire him. **(53:3)** He is despised and rejected of men; a man of sorrows, and acquainted with grief: and we hid as it were [our] faces from him; he was despised, and we esteemed him not. **(53:4)** Surely he hath borne our griefs, and carried our sorrows: yet we did esteem him stricken, smitten of God, and afflicted. **(53:5)** But he [was] wounded for our transgressions, [he was] bruised for our iniquities: the chastisement of our peace [was] upon him; and with his stripes we are healed. **(53:7)** He was oppressed, and he was afflicted, yet he opened not his mouth: he is brought as a lamb to the slaughter, and as a sheep before her shearers is dumb, so he openeth not his mouth. **(53:8)** He was taken from prison and from judgment: and who shall declare his generation? for he was cut off out of the land of the living: for the transgression of my people was he stricken. **(53:9)** And he made his grave with the wicked, and with the rich in his death; because he had done no violence, neither [was any] deceit in his mouth. **(53:10)** Yet it pleased the LORD to bruise him; he hath put [him] to grief: when thou shalt make his soul an offering for sin, he shall see [his] seed, he shall prolong [his] days, and the pleasure of the LORD shall prosper in his hand. **(53:12)** Therefore will I divide him [a portion] with the great, and he shall divide the spoil with the strong; because he hath poured out his soul unto death: and he was numbered with the transgressors; and he bare the sin of many, and made intercession for the transgressors. **(54:13)** And all thy children [shall be] taught of the Lord; and great [shall be] the peace of thy children.

(61:1) The Spirit of the Lord God [is] upon me; because the Lord hath anointed me to preach good tidings unto the meek; he hath sent me to bind up the brokenhearted, to proclaim liberty to the captives, and the opening of the prison to [them that are] bound; **(61:2)** To proclaim the acceptable year of the Lord, and the day of vengeance of our God; to comfort all that mourn;

JAMES
(1:17) Every good gift and every perfect gift is from above, and cometh down from the Father of lights, with whom is no variableness, neither shadow of turning.

JOB
(1:6) Now there was a day when the sons of God came to present themselves before the Lord, and Satan came also among them.

(2:1) Again there was a day when the sons of God came to present themselves before the Lord, and Satan came also among them to present himself before the Lord.

(25:6) How much less man, [that is] a worm? and the son of man, [which is] a worm?

(38:7) When the morning stars sang together, and all the sons of God shouted for joy?

JOHN
(1:46) And Nathanael said unto him, Can there any good thing come out of Nazareth? Philip saith unto him, Come and see. **(1:49)** Nathanael answered and saith unto him, Rabbi, thou art the Son of God; thou art the King of Israel.

(3:7) Marvel not that I said unto thee, Ye must be born again. **(3:13)** And no man hath ascended up to heaven, but he that came down from heaven, [even] the Son of man which is in heaven. **(3:34)** For he whom God hath sent speaketh the words of God: for God giveth not the Spirit by measure [unto him].

(4:25) The woman saith unto him, I know that Messias cometh, which is called Christ: when he is come, he will tell us all things. **(4:26)** Jesus saith unto her, I that speak unto thee am [he].

(5:17) But Jesus answered them, My Father worketh hitherto, and I **(5:18)** Therefore the Jews sought the more to kill him, because he not only had broken the sabbath, but said also that God was his Father, making himself equal with God. **(5:19)** Then answered Jesus and said unto them, Verily, verily, I say unto you, The Son can do nothing of himself, but what he seeth the Father do: for what things soever he doeth, these also doeth the Son likewise. **(5:21)** For as the Father raiseth up the dead, and quickeneth [them]; even so the Son quickeneth whom he will. **(5:23)** That all [men] should honour the Son, even as they honour the Father. He that honoureth not the Son honoureth not the Father which hath sent him. **(5:26)** For as the Father hath life in himself; so hath he given to the Son to have life in himself; **(5:30)** I can of mine own self do nothing: as I hear, I judge: and my judgment is just; because I seek not mine own will, but the will of the Father which hath sent me. **(5:31)** If I bear witness of myself, my witness is not true. **(5:32)** There is another that beareth witness of me; and I know that the witness which he witnesseth of me is true. **(5:33)** Ye sent unto John, and he bare witness unto the truth. **(5:34)** But I receive not testimony from man: but these things I say, that ye might be saved. **(5:35)** He was a burning and a shining light: and ye were willing for a season to rejoice in his light. **(5:36)** But I have greater witness than [that] of John: for the works which the Father hath given me to finish, the same works that I do, bear witness of me, that the Father hath sent me. **(5:37)** And the Father himself, which hath sent me, hath borne witness of me. Ye have neither heard his voice at any time, nor seen his shape. **(5:38)** And ye have not his word abiding in you: for whom he hath sent, him ye believe not. **(5:39)** Search the scriptures; for in them ye think ye have eternal life: and they are they which testify of me. **(5:46)** For had ye believed Moses, ye would have believed me: for he wrote of me. **(5:47)** But if ye believe not his writings, how shall ye believe my words?

(6:45) It is written in the prophets, And they shall be all taught of God. Every man therefore that hath heard, and hath learned of the Father, cometh unto me. **(6:62)** [What] and if ye shall see the Son of man ascend up where he was before?

(7:41) Others said, This is the Christ. But some said, Shall Christ come out of Galilee? **(7:42)** Hath not the scripture said, That Christ cometh of the seed of David, and out of the town of Bethlehem, where David was? **(7:52)** They answered and said unto him, Art thou also of Galilee? Search, and look: for out of Galilee ariseth no prophet.

(8:13) The Pharisees therefore said unto him, Thou bearest record of thyself; thy record is not true. **(8:14)** Jesus answered and said unto them, Though I bear record of myself, [yet] my record is true: for I know whence I came, and whither I go; but ye cannot tell whence I come, and whither I go. **(8:17)** It is also written in your law, that the testimony of two men is true. **(8:18)** I am one that bear witness of myself, and the Father that sent me beareth witness of me. **(8:29)** And he that sent me is with me: the Father hath not left me alone; for I do always those things that please him.

(10:8) John 10:8 All that ever came before me are thieves and robbers: but the sheep did not hear them. **(10:11)** I am the good shepherd: the good shepherd giveth his life for the sheep. **(10:24)** Then came the Jews round about him, and said unto him, How long dost thou make us to doubt? If thou be the Christ, tell us plainly. **(10:25)** Jesus answered them, I told you, and ye believed not: the works that I do in my Father's name, they bear witness of me. **(10:30)** I and [my] Father are one. **(10:31)** Then the Jews took up stones again to stone him. **(10:32)** Jesus answered them, Many good works have I shewed you from my Father; for which of those works do ye stone me? **(10:33)** The Jews answered him, saying, For a good work we stone thee not; but for blasphemy; and because that thou, being a man, makest thyself God. **(10:34)** Jesus answered them, Is it not written in your law, I said, Ye are gods? **(10:35)** If he called them gods, unto whom the word of God came, and the scripture cannot be broken; **(10:36)** Say ye of him, whom the Father hath sanctified, and sent into the world, Thou blasphemest; because I said, I am the Son of God?

(12:3) Then took Mary a pound of ointment of spikenard, very costly, and anointed the feet of Jesus, and wiped his feet with her hair: and the house was filled with the odour of the ointment. **(12:4)** Then saith one of his disciples, Judas Iscariot, Simon's [son], which should betray him, **(12:5)** Why was not this ointment sold for three hundred pence, and given to the poor? **(12:6)** This he said, not that he cared for the poor; but because he was a thief, and had the bag, and bare what was put therein. **(12:7)** Then said Jesus, Let her alone: against the day of my burying hath she kept this. **(12:14)** And Jesus, when he had found a young ass, sat thereon; as it is written, **(12:15)** Fear not, daughter of Sion: behold, thy King cometh, sitting on an ass's colt **(12:16)** These things understood not his disciples at the first: but when Jesus was glorified, then remembered they that these things were written of him, and [that] they had done these things unto him. **(12:27)** Now is my soul troubled; and what shall I say? Father, save me from this hour: but for this cause came I unto this hour. **(12:28)** Father, glorify thy name. Then came there a voice from heaven, [saying], I have both glorified [it], and will glorify [it] again. **(12:29)** The people therefore, that stood by, and heard [it], said that it thundered: others said, An angel spake to him. **(12:30)** Jesus answered and said, This voice came not because of me, but for your sakes. **(12:49)** For I have not spoken of myself; but the Father which sent me, he gave me a commandment, what I should say, and what I should speak.

(13:18) I speak not of you all: I know whom I have chosen: but that the scripture may be fulfilled, He that eateth bread with me hath lifted up his heel against me. **(13:19)** Now I tell you before it come, that, when it is come to pass, ye may believe that I am [he].

(14:28) Ye have heard how I said unto you, I go away, and come [again] unto you. If ye loved me, ye would rejoice, because I said, I go unto the Father: for my Father is greater than I.

(15:26) But when the Comforter is come, whom I will send unto you from the Father, [even] the Spirit of truth, which proceedeth from the Father, he shall testify of me: **(15:27)** And ye also shall bear witness, because ye have been with me from the beginning.

(17:24) Father, I will that they also, whom thou hast given me, be with me where I am; that they may behold my glory, which thou hast given me: for thou lovedst me before the foundation of the world.

(19:7) The Jews answered him, We have a law, and by our law he ought to die, because he made himself the Son of God. **(19:19)** And Pilate wrote a title, and put [it] on the cross. And the writing was, JESUS OF NAZARETH THE KING OF THE JEWS. **(19:28)** After this, Jesus knowing that all things were now accomplished, that the scripture might be fulfilled, saith, I thirst. **(19:29)** Now there was set a vessel full of vinegar: and they filled a spunge with vinegar, and put [it] upon hyssop, and put [it] to his mouth. **(19:30)** When Jesus therefore had received the vinegar, he said, It is finished: and he bowed his head, and gave up the ghost. **(19:32)** Then came the soldiers, and brake the legs of the first, and of the other which was crucified with him. **(19:33)** But when they came to Jesus, and saw that he was dead already, they brake not his legs: **(19:34)** But one of the soldiers with a spear pierced his side, and forthwith came there out blood and water. **(19:36)** For these things were done, that the scripture should be fulfilled, A bone of him shall not be broken. **(19:37)** And again another scripture saith, They shall look on him whom they pierced.

(20:17) Jesus saith unto her, Touch me not; for I am not yet ascended to my Father: but go to my brethren, and say unto them, I ascend unto my Father, and your Father; and [to] my God, and your God. **(20:27)** Then saith he to Thomas, Reach hither thy finger, and behold my hands; and reach hither thy hand, and thrust [it] into my side: and be not faithless, but believing. **(20:28)** And Thomas answered and said unto him, My Lord and my God.

1 JOHN

(3:2) Beloved, now are we the sons of God, and it doth not yet appear what we shall be: but we know that, when he shall appear, we shall be like him; for we shall see him as he is.

LUKE

(1:35) And the angel answered and said unto her, The Holy Ghost shall come upon thee, and the power of the Highest shall overshadow thee: therefore also that holy thing which shall be born of thee shall be called the Son of God.

(2:49) And he said them, How is it that ye sought me? wist ye not that I must be about my Father's business?

(4:1) And Jesus being full of the Holy Ghost returned from Jordan, and was led by the Spirit into the wilderness, **(4:3)** And the devil said unto him, If thou be the Son of God, command this stone that it be made bread. **(4:4)** And Jesus answered him, saying, It is written, That man shall not live by bread alone, but by every word of God. **(4:5)** And the devil, taking him up into an high mountain, shewed unto him all the kingdoms of the world in a moment of time. **(4:6)** And the devil said unto him, All this power will I give thee, and the glory of them: for that is delivered unto me; and to whomsoever I will I give it. **(4:8)** And Jesus answered and said unto him, Get thee behind me, Satan: for it is written, Thou shalt worship the Lord thy God, and him only shalt thou serve. **(4:9)** And he brought him to Jerusalem, and set him on a pinnacle of the temple, and said unto him, If thou be the Son of God, cast thyself down from hence: **(4:10)** For it is written, He shall give his angels charge over thee, to keep thee: **(4:12)** And Jesus answering said unto him, It is said, thou shalt not tempt the Lord thy God. **(4:14)** And Jesus returned in the power of the Spirit into Galilee: and there went out a fame of him through all the region round about. **(4:16)** And he came to Nazareth, where he had been brought up: and, as his custom was, he went into the synagogue on the sabbath day, and stood up for to read. **(4:18)** The Spirit of the Lord [is] upon me, because he hath anointed me to preach the gospel to the poor; he hath sent me to heal the brokenhearted, to preach deliverance to the captives, and recovering of sight to the blind, to set at liberty them that are bruised, **(4:19)** To preach the acceptable year of the Lord. **(4:21)** And he began to say unto them, This day is this scripture fulfilled in your ears.

(5:21) And the scribes and the Pharisees began to reason, saying, Who is this which speaketh blasphemies? Who can forgive sins, but God alone? **(5:30)** But their scribes and Pharisees murmured against his disciples, saying, Why do ye eat and drink with publicans and sinners?

(7:34) The Son of man is come eating and drinking; and ye say, Behold a gluttonous man, and a winebibber, a friend of publicans and sinners!

(9:19) They answering said, John the Baptist; but some [say], Elias; and others [say], that one of the old prophets is risen again. **(9:21)** And he straitly charged them, and commanded [them] to tell no man that thing; **(9:35)** And there came a voice out of the cloud, saying, This is my beloved Son: hear him. **(9:46)** Then there arose a reasoning among them, which of them should be greatest. **(9:44)** Let these sayings sink down into your ears: for the Son of man shall be delivered into the hands of men.

(9:45) But they understood not this saying, and it was hid from them, that they perceived it not: and they feared to ask him of that saying.

(10:22) All things are delivered to me of my Father: and no man knoweth who the Son is, but the Father; and who the Father is, but the Son, and [he] to whom the Son will reveal [him].

(11:2) And he said unto them, When ye pray, say, Our Father which art in heaven, Hallowed be thy name. Thy kingdom come. Thy will be done, as in heaven, so in earth. **(11:15)** But some of them said, He casteth out devils through Beelzebub the chief of the devils.

(15:2) And the Pharisees and scribes murmured, saying, This man receiveth sinners, and eateth with them.

(16:31) And he said unto him, If they hear not Moses and the prophets, neither will they be persuaded, though one rose from the dead.

(18:19) And Jesus said unto him, Why callest thou me good? none [is] good, save one, [that is], God.

(20:17) And he beheld them, and said, What is this then that is written, The stone which the builders rejected, the same is become the head of the corner?

(22:24) And there was also a strife among them, which of them should be accounted the greatest **(22:37)** For I say unto you, that this that is written must yet be accomplished in me, And he was reckoned among the transgressors: for the things concerning me have an end. **(22:64)** And when they had blindfolded him, they struck him on the face, and asked him, saying, Prophesy, who is it that smote thee? **(22:67)** Art thou the Christ? tell us. And he said unto them, If I tell you, ye will not believe: **(22:68)** And if I also ask [you], ye will not answer me, nor let [me] go. **(22:70)** Then said they all, Art thou then the Son of God? And he said unto them, Ye say that I am.

(24:21) But we trusted that it had been he which should have redeemed Israel: and beside all this, to day is the third day since these things were done. **(24:25)** Then he said unto them, O fools, and slow of heart to believe all that the prophets have spoken:

(24:26) Ought not Christ to have suffered these things, and to enter into glory? **(24:27)** And beginning at Moses and all the prophets, he expounded unto them in all the scriptures the things concerning himself. **(24:31)** And their eyes were opened, and they knew him; and he vanished out of their sight. **(24:44)** And he said unto them, These [are] the words which I spake unto you, while I was yet with you, that all things must be fulfilled, which were written in the law of Moses, and [in] the prophets, and [in] the psalms, concerning me. **(24:45)** Then opened he their understanding, that they might understand the scriptures, **(24:46)** And said unto them, Thus it is written, and thus it behoved Christ to suffer, and to rise from the dead the third day:

MARK

(1:11) And there came a voice from heaven, [saying], Thou art my beloved Son, in whom I am well pleased.

(2:6) But there were certain of the scribes sitting there, and reasoning in their hearts, **(2:7)** Why doth this [man] thus speak blasphemies? who can forgive sins but God only? **(2:16)** And when the scribes and Pharisees saw him eat with publicans and sinners, they said unto his disciples, How is it that he eateth and drinketh with publicans and sinners?

(3:11) And unclean spirits, when they saw him, fell down before him, and cried, saying, Thou art the Son of God. **(3:22)** And the scribes which came down from Jerusalem said, He hath Beelzebub, and by the prince of the devils casteth he out devils.

(6:3) Is not this the carpenter, the son of Mary, the brother of James, and Joses, and of Juda, and Simon? and are not his sisters here with us? And they were offended at him.

(8:27) And Jesus went out, and his disciples, into the towns of Caesarea Philippi: and by the way he asked his disciples, saying unto them, Whom do men say that I am? **(8:28)** And they answered, John the Baptist: but some [say], Elias; and others, One of the prophets.

(9:7) And there was a cloud that overshadowed them: and a voice came out of the cloud, saying, This is my beloved Son: hear him. **(9:34)** But they held their peace: for by the way they had disputed among themselves, who [should be] the greatest.

12:10) And have ye not read this scripture; The stone which the builders rejected is become the head of the corner:

(13:32) But of that day and [that] hour knoweth no man, no, not the angels which are in heaven, neither the Son, but the Father.

(14:27) And Jesus saith unto them, All ye shall be offended because of me this night: for it is written, I will smite the shepherd, and the sheep shall be scattered.

(15:29) And they that passed by railed on him, wagging their heads, and saying, Ah, thou that destroyest the temple, and buildest [it] in three days, **(15:30)** Save thyself, and come down from the cross. **(15:31)** Likewise also the chief priests mocking said among themselves with the scribes, He saved others; himself he cannot save. **(15:32)** Let Christ the King of Israel descend now from the cross, that we may see and believe. And they that were crucified with him reviled him.

MATTHEW
(3:16) And Jesus, when he was baptized, went up straightway out of the water: and, lo, the heavens were opened unto him, and he saw the Spirit of God descending like a dove, and lighting upon him: **(3:17)** And lo a voice from heaven, saying, This is my beloved Son, in whom I am well pleased.

(4:3) And when the tempter came to him, he said, If thou be the Son of God, command that these stones be made bread. **(4:11)** Then the devil leaveth him, and, behold, angels came and ministered unto him. **(4:13)** And leaving Nazareth, he came and dwelt in Capernaum, which is upon the sea coast, in the borders of Zabulon and Nephthalim: **(4:14)** That it might be fulfilled which was spoken by Esaias the prophet, saying, **(4:15)** the land of Zabulon, and the land of Nephthalim, [by] the way of the sea, beyond Jordan, Galilee of the Gentiles; **(4:16)** The people which sat in darkness saw great light; and to them which sat in the region and shadow of death light is sprung up.

(5:17) Think not that I am come to destroy the law, or the prophets: I am not come to destroy, but to fulfil.

(7:6) Give not that which is holy unto the dogs, neither cast ye your pearls before swine, lest they trample them under their feet, and turn again and rend you.
(8:16) When the even was come, they brought unto him many that

were possessed with devils: and he cast out the spirits with [his] word, and healed all that were sick: **(8:17)** That it might be fulfilled which was spoken by Esaias the prophet, saying, Himself took our infirmities, and bare [our] sicknesses.

(9:11) And when the Pharisees saw [it], they said unto his disciples, Why eateth your Master with publicans and sinners?

(11:2) Now when John had heard in the prison the works of Christ, he sent two of his disciples, **(11:3)** And said unto him, Art thou he that should come, or do we look for another? **(11:4)** Jesus answered and said unto them, Go and shew John again those things which ye do hear and see: **(11:5)** The blind receive their sight, and the lame walk, the lepers are cleansed, and the deaf hear, the dead are raised up, and the poor have the gospel preached to them. **(11:6)** And blessed is [he], whosoever shall not be offended in me. **(11:19)** The Son of man came eating and drinking, and they say, Behold a man gluttonous, and a winebibber, a friend of publicans and sinners. But wisdom is justified of her children. **(11:27)** All things are delivered unto me of my Father: and no man knoweth the Son, but the Father; neither knoweth any man the Father, save the Son, and [he] to whomsoever the Son will reveal [him].

(12:24) But when the Pharisees heard [it], they said, This [fellow] doth not cast out devils, but by Beelzebub the prince of the devils.

(13:55) Is not this the carpenter's son? is not his mother called Mary? and his brethren, James, and Joses, and Simon, and Judas? **(13:57)** And they were offended in him. But Jesus said unto them, A prophet is not without honour, save in his own country, and in his own house.

(14:2) And said unto his servants, This is John the Baptist; he is risen from the dead; and therefore mighty works do shew forth themselves in him. **(14:33)** Then they that were in the ship came and worshipped him, saying, Of a truth thou art the Son of God.

(16:7) And Jesus answered and said unto him, Blessed art thou, Simon Barjona: for flesh and blood hath not revealed [it] unto thee, but my Father which is in heaven. **(16:13)** When Jesus came into the coasts of Caesarea Philippi, he asked his disciples, saying, Whom do men say that I the Son of man am? **(16:14)** And they said, Some [say that thou art] John the Baptist: some, Elias; and others, Jeremias, or one of the prophets. **(16:20)** Then charged he his disciples that they should tell no man that he was Jesus the Christ.

(17:5) While he yet spake, behold, a bright cloud overshadowed them: and behold a voice out of the cloud, which said, This is my beloved Son, in whom I am well pleased; hear ye him.

(21:9) And the multitudes that went before, and that followed, cried, saying, Hosanna to the Son of David: Blessed [is] he that cometh in the name of the Lord; Hosanna in the highest. **(21:15)** And when the chief priests and scribes saw the wonderful things that he did, and the children crying in the temple, and saying, Hosanna to the Son of David; they were sore displeased, **(21:16)** And said unto him, Hearest thou what these say? And Jesus saith unto them, Yea; have ye never read, Out of the mouth of babes and sucklings {thou hast perfected praise}? **(21:42)** Jesus saith unto them, Did ye never read in the scriptures, The stone which the builders rejected, the same is become the head of the corner: this is the Lord's doing, and it is marvellous in our eyes?

(22:29) Jesus answered and said unto them, Ye do err, not knowing the scriptures, nor the power of God.

(26:14) Then one of the twelve, called Judas Iscariot, went unto the chief priests, **(26:15)** And said [unto them], What will ye give me, and I will deliver him unto you? And they covenanted with him for thirty pieces of silver. **(26:23)** And he answered and said, He that dippeth [his] hand with me in the dish, the same shall betray me. **(26:24)** The Son of man goeth as it is written of him: but woe unto that man by whom the Son of man is betrayed! it had been good for that man if he had not been born. **(26:25)** Then Judas, which betrayed him, answered and said, Master, is it I? He said unto him, Thou hast said. **(26:31)** Then saith Jesus unto them, All ye shall be offended because of me this night: for it is written, I will smite the shepherd, and the sheep of the flock shall be scattered abroad. **(26:53)** Thinkest thou that I cannot now pray to my Father, and he shall presently give me more than twelve legions of angels?

(26:54) But how then shall the scriptures be fulfilled, that thus it must be? **(26:56)** But all this was done, that the scriptures of the prophets might be fulfilled. Then all the disciples forsook him, and fled. **(26:67)** Then did they spit in his face, and buffeted him; and others smote [him] with the palms of their hands, **(26:68)** Saying, Prophesy unto us, thou Christ, Who is he that smote thee?

(27:3) Then Judas, which had betrayed him, when he saw that he was condemned, repented himself, and brought again the thirty pieces of silver to the chief priests and elders, **(27:7)** And they took counsel, and bought with them the potter's field, to bury strangers in. **(27:34)** They gave him vinegar to drink mingled with gall: and when he had tasted [thereof], he would not drink. **(27:35)** And they crucified him, and parted his garments, casting lots:{that it might be fulfilled} which was spoken by the prophet, They parted my garments among them, and upon my vesture did they cast lots. **(27:36)** And sitting down they watched him there; **(27:37)** And set up over his head his accusation written, THIS IS JESUS THE KING OF THE JEWS. **(27:38)** Then were there two thieves crucified with him, one on the right hand, and another on the left **(27:39)** And they that passed by reviled him, wagging their heads, **(27:40)** And saying, Thou that destroyest the temple, and buildest [it] in three days, save thyself. If thou be the Son of God, come down from the cross. **(27:41)** Likewise also the chief priests mocking [him], with the scribes and elders, said, **(27:42)** He saved others; himself he cannot save. If he be the King of Israel, let him now come down from the cross, and we will believe him. **(27:43)** He trusted in God; let him deliver him now, if he will have him: for he said, I am the Son of God. **(27:46)** And about the ninth hour Jesus cried with a loud voice, saying, Eli, Eli, lama sabachthani? that is to say, My God, my God, why hast thou forsaken me? **(27:57)** When the even was come, there came a rich man of Arimathaea, named Joseph, who also himself was Jesus' disciple:

MICAH

(5:2) But thou, Bethlehem Ephratah, [though] thou be little among the thousands of Judah, [yet] out of thee shall he come forth unto me [that is] to be ruler in Israel; whose goings forth [have been] from of old, from everlasting.

2 PETER

(1:17) For he received from God the Father honour and glory, when there came such a voice to him from the excellent glory, This is my beloved Son, in whom I am well pleased. **(1:20)** Knowing this first, that no prophecy of the scripture is of any private interpretation. **(1:21)** For the prophecy came not in old time by the will of man: but holy men of God spake [as they were] moved by the Holy Ghost.

PROVERBS

(22:21) That I might make thee know the certainty of the words of truth; that thou mightest answer the words of truth to them that send unto thee?

PSALMS

(2:7) I will declare the decree: the Lord hath said unto me, Thou [art] my Son; this day have I begotten thee.
(8:2) Out of the mouth of babes and sucklings hast thou ordained strength because of thine enemies, that thou mightest still the enemy

and the avenger. **(8:4)** What is man, that thou art mindful of him? and the son of man, that thou visitest him? **(8:6)** Thou madest him to have dominion over the works of thy hands; thou hast put all [things] under his feet:

(22:1) My God, my God, why hast thou forsaken me? [why art thou so] far from helping me, [and from] the words of my roaring? **(22:6)** But I [am] a worm, and no man; a reproach of men, and despised of the people. **(22:7)** All they that see me laugh me to scorn: they shoot out the lip, they shake the head, [saying], **(22:8)** He trusted on the LORD [that] he would deliver him: let him deliver him, seeing he delighted in him. **(22:10)** I was cast upon thee from the womb: thou [art] my God from my mother's belly. **(22:13)** They gaped upon me [with] their mouths, [as] a ravening and a roaring lion.

(22:14) I am poured out like water, and all my bones are out of joint: my heart is like wax; it is melted in the midst of my bowels. **(22:15)** My strength is dried up like a potsherd; and my tongue cleaveth to my jaws; and thou hast brought me into the dust of death. **(22:16)** For dogs have compassed me: the assembly of the wicked have inclosed me: they pierced my hands and my feet. **(22:17)** I may tell all my bones: they look [and] stare upon me. **(22:18)** They part my garments among them, and cast lots upon my vesture.

(41:9) Yea, mine own familiar friend, in whom I trusted, which did eat of my bread, hath lifted up [his] heel against me.

(69:21) They gave me also gall for my meat; and in my thirst they gave me vinegar to drink.

(82:6) I have said, Ye [are] gods; and all of you [are] children of the most High.

(107:10) Such as sit in darkness and in the shadow of death, [being] bound in affliction and iron; **(107:14)** He brought them out of darkness and the shadow of death, and brake their bands in sunder.

116 & 118
[If the reader wishes to be "about as close to Jesus as it is possible to become," Mr. Crisler recommends study of both of these chapters in their entirety.]`

(118:6) The Lord [is] on my side; I will not fear: what can man do unto me? **(118:9)** [It is] better to trust in the Lord than to put confidence in princes. **(118:16)** The right hand of the Lord is exalted: the right hand of the Lord doeth valiantly. **(118:17)** I shall not die, but live, and declare the works of the Lord. **(118:22)** The stone [which] the builders refused is become the head [stone] of the corner. **(118:25)** Save now, I beseech thee, O Lord: O Lord, I beseech thee, send now prosperity. **(118:26)** Blessed [be] he that cometh in the name of the Lord: we have blessed you out of the house of the Lord.

REVELATION

(10:8) And the voice which I heard from heaven spake unto me again, and said, Go [and] take the little book which is open in the hand of the angel which standeth upon the sea and upon the earth. **(10:9)** And I went unto the angel, and said unto him, Give me the little book. And he said unto me, Take [it], and eat it up; and it shall make thy belly bitter, but it shall be in thy mouth sweet as honey.

(11:3) And I will give [power] unto my two witnesses, and they shall prophesy a thousand two hundred [and] threescore days, clothed in sackcloth.

ZECHARIAH

(9:9) Rejoice greatly, O daughter of Zion; shout, O daughter of Jerusalem: behold, thy King cometh unto thee: he [is] just, and having salvation; lowly, and riding upon an ass, and upon a colt the foal of an ass.

(11:12) And I said unto them, If ye think good, give [me] my price; and if not, forbear. So they weighed for my price thirty [pieces] of silver. **(11:13)** And the LORD said unto me, Cast it unto the potter: a goodly price that I was prised at of them. And I took the thirty [pieces] of silver, and cast them to the potter in the house of the LORD

(12:10) And I will pour upon the house of David, and upon the inhabitants of Jerusalem, the spirit of grace and of supplications: and they shall look upon me whom they have pierced, and they shall mourn for him, as one mourneth for [his] only [son], and shall be in bitterness for him, as one that is in bitterness for [his] firstborn.

(13:6) And [one] shall say unto him, What [are] these wounds in thine hands? Then he shall answer, [Those] with which I was wounded [in] the house of my friends **(13:7)** Awake, O sword, against my shepherd, and against the man [that is] my fellow, saith the LORD of hosts: smite the shepherd, and the sheep shall be scattered: and I will turn mine hand upon the little ones.

***

by B. Cobbey Crisler

WORD INDEX TO VOLUME 23
How Christ Jesus Saw Himself

Word Index compiled by tranScriptures of Columbia, S.C.

Bold font - Volume number; Normal font - Page number
A.D. - *anno domini;* C.E..- Common Era
B.C. - Before Christ; B.C.E. - Before Common Era;
NT - New Testament; OT - Old Testament
c. about; e.g. - for example; i.e. - that is

---

in the image's relationship to the Original. The Son is image, and image is not Original. "Why do you call me good? There is none good, save One, and that's God." The commitment is to Oneness. That Oneness belongs to God as Original. One can relate to that Oneness and have all the glory, and all the unity, and all the harmony that belongs to that Oneness. The relationship is due to what Genesis 1 tells us exists between God and man. It's the Original and the likeness of the image. **23:**150-153; For the image to say, "I AM" is perfectly proper **23:**157,158; the Son of man goeth as it is written of him."**23:**162;

Jesus' witnesses to his identity and mission: 5 Ws **23:**137,138; J's self-W **23:**140; J's 2 Ws **23:**141; J's 6th W; J's 7th possible witness **23:**142;

SYMBOLS

Anointed - in Scripture it means Messiah or Christ, i.e., Christ Jesus, with the prophetic mission "to preach, to heal, to deliver, to recover, and to set at liberty, and to preach the acceptable year of the Lord." **23:**154;

Apostasy - a state of thought, a kind of cooling off which Jesus' disciples experienced when their confidence in who-Jesus-is broke down under pressure of persecution, the first thing that seems to go, even among disciples who counted themselves faithful; Jesus' rebuke to that state of thought, "O fools, and slow of heart to believe all the prophets have spoken." **23:**155; On the walk to Emmaus after his resurrection Jesus went through "Moses, all the prophets, and expounded unto them in all the scriptures the things concerning himself," i.e., "Search the Scriptures; and they are they which testify of me." **23:**156;

Beelzebub - prince of the devils **23:**134;

Born again - means "born from above" in Greek **23:**159

Comforter - 6th witness to Jesus' identity and mission **23:**142;

Dove - symbol of the Holy Ghost/Spirit **23:**143,144;

Emmaus - the road on which Jesus met two disciples on res-

it and eat it up." **23:**162; R of God is rocklike and uncontestable because of having been demonstrated **23:**170;

Sacrifice - an offering for sin, i.e., Jesus **23:**169
Shepherd, the good = Jesus' prophesied role **23:**164;
Son of God - **23:**156 (Also) see Jesus' theology above)
Son of man - humanhood which can be at the dominion-level or at the worm-level; thus, the SoM yields either up ("What is man, that thou art mindful of him? And the son of man, that thou visitest him?") or down ("the SoM is a worm.") **23:**158; i.e., the twin pressures, one leading up, the spirit of the sons of man ascending, and the spirit of the beast that is descending to the earth; human experience is an ascension. Resurrection means in Greek a step upwards. **23:**159; *"No man ascendeth up to heaven save he that came down from heaven, even the SoM which is in heaven."* Every earthly problem has its heavenly solution as Jesus proved. Jesus freed himself from all links to animally-oriented problems. **23:**160; Jesus was willing to be the Messiah, the anointed one, going to God for what he needed to think and to do **23:**160;
Symbols - the real native tongue of the Bible. Every symbol, every word, in the Bible up to *Revelation* has two or three witnesses to it. Search the Scriptures and become a student of those symbols **23:**143,155;

Temptations - Satan's 3 tests of Jesus: personal, political, and priestly power struggles in collaboration with Deity or in opposition to Deity **23:**146;
Transfiguration - voice in a cloud's witness to Jesus' identity **23:**144;
The Way - the Christ way of eternal life *versus* the Adam-lockstep to self-desruction **23:**169;

Who is Jesus? - Who is Jesus of Nazareth/Jesus the Christ/Christ Jesus? **23:**134-137,170;

SYMBOLS END

***

by B. Cobbey Crisler

Bibliography

W.D. Davies, *The Setting of the Sermon on the Mount,* Univerisity Press, Cambridge 1977.

C.H. Dodd, *According to the Scriptures,* James Nisbet & Co., Ltd. 1961.

Leona Glidden Running, David Noel Freedman, *William Foxwell Albright, A Twentieth Century Genius,* The Two Continents Publishing Group, Lt. Morgan Press, 1975.

Joseph H. Thayer, *Thayer's Greek-English Lexicon of the New Testament,* Baker Book House, Grand Rapids, MI 1997.

Gerhare Kitle, Editor, Geoffrey W. Bromley Translator & Editor, Gerhard Friedrich, Editor *Theological Dictionary of the New Testament;* 9 Volumes, William B. Erdmans Publishing Co., Grand Rapids, MI 1974.

And he led them out as far as Bethany, and he lifted up his hands, and blessed them. And it came to pass, while he blessed them, he was parted from them, and carried up into heaven. And they worshipped him, and returned to Jerusalem with great joy...

(Luke 24: 50-52)

Photograph by Gordon N. Converse

To Dr. B. Cobbey Crisler

Bible Lecturer Emeritus

Ah, what memories I have of this fine young man
As virile, vigorous, hale and hearty,
Working for God—I was always his fan;
I knew the Christ was in this one so hardy;
I followed his progress through lectures many;
I would not have missed a single "any."

A widespread traveler and speaker he,
Teaching and imparting his messages great
To receptive listeners so attentively,
In many a town, in many a state,
Who heard the truth from his sainted lips:
Bible stories and characters, mingled with quips.

How much we enjoyed his good laughs, too,
Of the "dwarf" Bildad the "Shoe-height"
And seeming power of Nehemiah's Gashmu,
Of algebraic equations which now just might
Translate the beatitudes into wholesome math
For all to recall as a memory path.

Never will I forget this calm, quiet prophet
Who worked so hard to bring forth
And reflect the truth for us to profit
By his inspiration, so full of worth;
He shared his knowledge with all mankind;
His words live on, the whole world to bind.

Henry G. Rutledge, Jr.
Penned May 10, 1998

Audio Tapes

Vol. 1	Walk to Emmaus	19.00
Vol. 2	Case of JOB	48.00
Vol. 3	After the Master, What! (Book of ActS)	48.00
Vol. 4	Heal the Sick: A Scriptural Record	48.00
Vol. 5	A Visit with the Beloved Disciple (Gospel of John)	48.00
Vol. 6	Jesus & the Equality of Woman	24.00
Vol. 6	Jesus & the Equality of Woman Video	24.00
Vol. 7	Auditing the Master: A Tax Collector's Report (Gospel of Matthew)	48.00
Vol. 8	What Mark Recorded	32.00
Vol. 9	Song of the Lamb	9.00
Vol. 10	Light in the Bible from Opacity to Transparency	48.00
Vol. 11	As Researched by Like	48.00
Vol. 12	The Church Its Scriptural Continuity	48.00
Vol. 13	The Holy City: Its Biblical Basis & Development	48.00
Vol. 14	The Holy Ghost: Its Scriptural Role	17.00
Vol. 15	The Gethsemane Decision	24.00
Vol. 16	God's Word as Communication	42.00
Vol. 17	God and Man: Their Biblical Relationship	24.00
Vol. 18	War in Heaven: The Conquest of Inner Space	18.00
Vol. 19	Deity and devil in the Scriptures	24.00
Vol. 20	The Remnant	20.00
Vol. 21	Secret of His Tabernacle	20.00
Vol. 22	Simon Peter: The Character of a Disciple	24.00
Vol. 23	How Christ Jesus Saw Himself	24.00
Vol. 24	Leaves of the Tree: Prescriptions from Psalms	24.00
Vol. 25	Freedom: A Biblical Definition	24.00
Vol. 26	Apocalyptic Picture: Prophecy and Parody	40.00
Vol. 27	Glory: Divine Nature in the Bible	24.00

Send orders to: Logos Productions, P.O. Box 222951, Carmel, CA 93922 • email: janetc@redshift.com
California residents add 7.25% sales tax. Please add $5.00 for shipping and handling.